THE IRISH TIMES

BOOK

of the

YEAR

2010

EDITED BY

PETER MURTAGH

Gill & Macmillan

Gill & Macmillan Ltd
Hume Avenue
Park West
Dublin 12
with associated companies throughout the world
www.gillmacmillan.ie

© 2010 *The Irish Times*
978 07171 4788 5
Design by Identikit Design Consultants, Dublin
Print origination by Carole Lynch
Index compiled by Helen Litton
Printed and bound in Italy by LEGO SpA

*The paper used in this book is made from the wood pulp
of managed forests. For every tree felled, at least one tree
is planted, thereby renewing natural resources.*

A CIP catalogue record is available for this book
from the British Library.

5 4 3 2 1

Contents

Introduction

The *Irish Times Book of the Year 2010* is an eclectic collection of some of the serious and not so serious material that graced the pages of the newspaper between October 2009 and September 2010. Unfortunately, for those of us living in Ireland, the times in which we live remain grim for many. The effects of the recession and of a banking crisis caused by a regulatory system that was asleep, together with an absence of common sense and proper ethical standards inside the banks, continue to be felt by everyone.

The outstanding political figure of the period covered by this book is Finance Minister Brian Lenihan. In his professional life he has been obliged to take decisions regarding the banks and public finances that for good or ill have affected everyone and dominated the political scene. At a personal level he has had to cope with a crisis in his health. He appears to be handling both challenges with remarkable fortitude and good humour. The incomparable Miriam Lord and Political Editor Stephen Collins have observed and written about him, though in very different ways. The antics of other politicians, from George Lee to Ivor Callely, have also been the subject of much reporting, not least by Lord – also reflected here.

John McManus's Monday morning Business Opinion column remains required reading for anyone trying to understand government policy on the banks. The same can be said for Simon Carswell's unrivalled reporting and analyses. During the year, they were joined by our new Economics Editor, Dan O'Brien, a sample of whose clear-headed thinking on Anglo Irish Bank appears here.

Two major official reports devoured newspaper space during the year. The Ryan Report into how the Roman Catholic Archdiocese of Dublin handled allegations of clerical sex abuse of children convulsed the church, and continues to do so. Powerful analysis by Mary Raftery of the church's actions, as revealed by the report, kept readers well informed as to the issues at stake, as did reporting and analysing throughout the year by Religious Affairs Correspondent Patsy McGarry. The publication of the long-awaited Bloody Sunday Report and the reaction to it – both in Derry and in the House of Commons in London – resulted in some fine reporting by veteran reporter Dick Grogan, who witnessed the 1972 tragedy, and by Róisín Ingle who was four months old when it happened but was with the people of the Bogside when the innocence of those who died was finally acknowledged.

Irish Times foreign correspondents had a characteristically busy year. Mary Fitzgerald got behind the kidnap and release of Goal aid worker Sharon Commins; Derek Scally reported on the tragic death of the president of Poland; Clifford Coonan patrolled the dangerous streets of Bangkok as anti-government protesters and the Thai army squared up to each other; Foreign Editor Denis Staunton was insightful on the whys and wherefores of Israeli government actions that sometimes mystify and anger the rest of the world; Paddy Agnew showed that when it comes to José Mourinho, he is as perceptive on football as he is on Vatican politics; Lara Marlowe got up close and uncomfortable with Sheriff Joe Arpaio of Phoenix, Arizona; and Mark Hennessy and Arthur Beesley both hit the ground running after their appointments to, respectively, London and Brussels.

Closer to home, Kathy Sheridan's fine writing was evident in her reporting on the funeral of broadcaster Gerry Ryan, among many other subjects she covered during a busy year. Frank McNally's Irishman's Diary continues to amuse and delight readers, as does the writing of Róisín Ingle in her resumed Saturday Magazine column, along with Ann Marie Hourihane, Michael Harding, Newton Emerson, Maurice Neligan and others. In a memorable opinion column, Roscommon man John Waters wrote of the agonies of liking his life in Dalkey, Co. Dublin.

The Irish Times would be nothing without its sports writers, and Tom Humphries, Gerry Thornley, Philip Reid and Seán Moran were kept busy all the way up to this year's All-Ireland finals, which traditionally close this anthology.

My thanks to all concerned. The selection is entirely unscientific and based on nothing more than my taste for excellent writing, drawing and photography by the colleagues with whom I am privileged to work. My problem, as always, is choosing what *not* to include – this book could be twice the length with all the excellent material for which there is simply not enough room. Special thanks to Linda O'Keeffe and Emma Allen in the Editor's office; to Faisal Mansoor in the systems department; and to Aoife O'Kelly and all at Gill and Macmillan who make everything happen smoothly and without fuss.

Peter Murtagh
September 2010

Journalists and Photographers

Paddy Agnew is Rome Correspondent.

Eileen Battersby is Literary Correspondent.

Arthur Beesley is Brussels Correspondent.

Rosita Boland is a features writer.

Brian Boyd is a freelance journalist specialising in the pop music industry and comedy.

Eoin Burke-Kennedy is an online *Irish Times* journalist.

Eoin Butler is a freelance writer whose work often appears in the Saturday Magazine.

Sarah Carey is an *Irish Times* columnist.

Simon Carswell is Finance Correspondent.

Donald Clarke is *Irish Times* film critic.

Stephen Collins is Political Editor.

Clifford Coonan is Beijing Correspondent.

Kevin Courtney is an *Irish Times* music journalist.

Paul Cullen is Consumer Affairs Correspondent.

Pamela Duncan is an *Irish Times* reporter.

Aidan Dunne is *Irish Times* art critic.

Editorials are unsigned but are published in the name of the Editor.

Newton Emerson is a satirical writer whose column, Newton's Optic, appears weekly.

Hilary Fannin is a freelance journalist and former *Irish Times* TV critic.

Mary Fitzgerald is Foreign Affairs Correspondent.

Dick Grogan is a retired *Irish Times* journalist. He reported from Derry in January 1972 on the events and aftermath of Bloody Sunday.

Michael Harding is a freelance writer based in Mullingar, where he surveys his life and the world about him.

Shane Hegarty is Arts Editor and also writes a column in Saturday's Weekend Review.

Mark Hennessy is London Correspondent.

Mary Hennigan is a sports writer.

Ann Marie Hourihane is an *Irish Times* columnist.

Tom Humphries is a sports journalist and author of LockerRoom, a weekly sideways glance at the world of sports.

Róisín Ingle is a reporter, feature writer and columnist in the *Irish Times* Magazine.

Lorna Kernan was *Irish Times* TV editor prior to her retirement.

Terence Killeen is a former *Irish Times* subeditor, and expert on the life and writings of James Joyce.

George Kimball is a sports writer based in the United States of America.

Conor Lally is Crime Correspondent.

Karlin Lillington writes about new technology.

Hugh Linehan is editor of *irishtimes.com* and an occasional columnist.

Miriam Lord is a political sketch writer.

Fiona McCann is a freelance journalist, living with her husband in the United States after working for many years in Dublin.

Patsy McGarry is Religious Affairs Correspondent.

Harry McGee is a member of the political staff.

John McManus is Business Editor.

Frank McNally writes An Irishman's Diary.

Emmet Malone is Soccer Correspondent.

Lara Marlowe is Washington Correspondent.

Fionola Meredith is a freelance journalist based in Belfast.

Seán Moran is GAA Correspondent.

Orna Mulcahy is Property Editor and an occasional columnist.

Maurice Neligan is a former cardiac surgeon who writes a weekly column in HEALTHplus, a supplement published on Tuesdays.

Pamela Newenham is an *Irish Times* reporter.

Carl O'Brien is Chief Reporter.

Dan O'Brien is Economics Editor.

Ross O'Carroll Kelly is the *nom de guerre* of Paul Howard.

Fintan O'Toole is an Assistant Editor and an *Irish Times* columnist.

Michael Parsons is a local correspondent based in Kilkenny.

Conor Pope works on *The Irish Times* website and writes PriceWatch, a weekly probing of the cost of consumer durables.

Mary Raftery is a freelance writer and former *Irish Times* columnist specialising in the issue of clerical sex abuse of children.

Philip Reid is Golf Correspondent.

Derek Scally is Berlin Correspondent.

Kathy Sheridan is an *Irish Times* journalist.

Gerry Smyth is a managing editor specialising in arts and features at the *Irish Times*, and also a poet.

Denis Staunton is Foreign Editor.

Gerry Thornley is Rugby Correspondent.

Michael Viney writes Another Life, a column about the natural world, from his home overlooking the Atlantic in west Mayo.

Arminta Wallace is an arts and features writer.

John Waters is an *Irish Times* columnist.

Photographers and illustrators whose work features in this year's edition include *Irish Times* staff members and external contributors Alan Betson, Cyril Byrne, Brenda Fitzsimons, Matt Kavanagh, Eric Luke, Dara Mac Dónaill, Frank Miller, Bryan O'Brien, David Sleator, Martyn Turner and Michael Viney.

The Irish Times Book of the Year 2010 also features the work of freelance photographers and illustrators, together with photographers attached to Irish and international photo agencies, who are identified and credited in the captions.

Jacket cover photographs were taken by Arthur Ellis/Press22, Eric Luke, Daragh McSweeney/Provision, David Sleator, Shaun Best/Reuters, Joe Keogh, Alan Betson, Hans Deryk/Reuters, Arthur Carron/Collins, Reuters/Benoit Tessier, Julien Behal/PA, Brenda Fitzsimons, Matt Kavanagh and Yvette Monaghan/Studio77.

FRIDAY, 2 OCTOBER 2009

Is it All Over for Roman Polanski?

Donald Clarke

We have neither the space (nor the moral confidence) to deliver a definitive judgment on whether the Swiss coppers were right to bang up Roman Polanski last week. You've heard the arguments already.

Nobody contests the assertion that, 32 years ago, the director had sex with a 13-year-old girl in Jack Nicholson's Hollywood home. After his arrest, when his lawyer realised the authorities seemed unlikely to honour a plea bargain, Polanski fled the US for life as a celebrated émigré in France.

Does it matter that the victim no longer wishes the case to be pursued? What do we make of the queasy suggestion – particularly prevalent in French circles – that the ability to produce masterpieces absolves an artist of any moral responsibility? Is it fair to regard Polanski's tragic personal history as a mitigating factor in the original offence? There's too much to be discussed on each of those unanswerable questions.

We are on somewhat more secure ground when we move to ponder what effect the original arrest and subsequent exile have had on Polanski's career. Accept, first, that Roman Polanski is a film-maker of genius. A graduate of the Polish National

Electoral officer Hugh O'Donnell takes a break with Garda Brendan McCann before carrying the ballot box to another cottage on Inishfree Island off the coast of Co. Donegal, where just seven people are registered to vote in the Lisbon Treaty referendum. Photograph: Paul Faith/Press Association.

Film School in Lódz, he began his career – first at home, later in Hollywood – by delivering a run of masterpieces which, in quality and resonance, have been equalled only by the likes of Ingmar Bergman or Alfred Hitchcock.

Knife in the Water, Repulsion, Cul-de-Sac, Rosemary's Baby, Macbeth, Chinatown: any of those films could have assured the director's place at the top table. Even his supposed early failures (the peculiar comedy *The Fearless Vampire Killers* and the existential farce *What?*) are imbued with a sense of casual unease and steadfast pessimism which are entirely Polanksi's own.

Yet, right from the beginning of his career, the director's awful life story loomed over critical assessments of his work. Born in Paris, Roman Polanski, a Polish Jew, moved back to Krakow with his family three years before the Nazis crossed the border. He somehow managed to escape the ghetto, but his mother and sister were murdered in Auschwitz and his father barely survived the Mauthausen-Gusen concentration camp.

The compulsion to look at key films such as *Repulsion* (Catherine Deneuve goes crazy in South Kensington) and *Rosemary's Baby* (Mia Farrow is raped by the devil in New York) and discover traces of the director's grim early life may seem facile and reductive. On the other hand, it would take an odd fellow – odder even than Roman Polanski – to get through a career without allowing those experiences to leak into the work.

Amateur psychologists were given even more to work with when, in 1969, Charles Manson, the rotting zombie who prowled the mass grave of hippiedom, and his gang of hopped-up idiots broke into Polanski's house and murdered his pregnant wife, the actress Sharon Tate, and four other guests.

His first film after the murders, a version of *Macbeth*, is just about the most gory, hopeless version of a Shakespeare play ever put on celluloid. Where can that have come from? When Polanski made *Chinatown*, an imperishable slab of late noir,

he stomped his foot until Robert Towne's happy ending was darkened up to his grim satisfaction.

By 1977, when the grisly crime happened, Polanski, though barely in middle age, could be regarded as a walking repository of the West's recent great miseries. An escapee of the Holocaust, he had been raised in the Soviet Bloc during the Cold War, before drifting to the US and experiencing the sourest, most poisonous effusions of the over-romanticised hippie era. Now, he was among (though surely not quite of) the chemically enhanced hedonists who occupied the wealthier parts of California during the vulgar 1970s.

Then, truth be told, Polanski and the Zeitgeist parted ways. When he moved to France, he somehow failed to turn himself back into a European director. Instead, working in countries that had not got around to arranging extradition treaties with the United States, he became the maker of superior but always slightly uncomfortable Europuddings. The term was coined to describe co-productions between various nations, which, as a result of their mongrel financing, never seem quite sure of their identities.

Polanski has, to be sure, made good films since fleeing Los Angeles, and those works have continued to mine his gruesome past. *Tess*, his adaptation of Thomas Hardy's *Tess of the d'Urbervilles*, dealt with a young girl who is led astray by an older cad (ahem?). *The Pianist*, for which he won an Oscar in 2003, engaged directly with his experiences during the war. These are prestige, worthy projects, but they have none of the evil energy that clogged up masterpieces such as *Repulsion* and *Chinatown*.

Maybe, as his near contemporary Francis Ford Coppola would eventually do, Polanski simply ran out of creative steam. After all, there aren't many directors who manage to stay both innovative and dangerous – Sam Fuller? Werner Herzog? – into their Werther's Original years. It is, however, hard to escape the conclusion that living cosily in Europe, away from the cut, thrust and backstabbing,

Ciara Fox wears a head piece entitled The Race *by artist Michael Burton, at the WHAT IF . . . exhibition in the Science Gallery at Trinity College, Dublin. Photograph: Julien Behal/Press Association.*

softened Polanski and deprived him of a useful amount of malign vigour.

What next? If he does end up serving time in the US, Polanski – now 76 – is unlikely to shoot another film. If the great survivor somehow bounds free once more then, granted an umpteenth life, he may undergo some sort of psychic reupholstery.

Either way, we will get to see at least one more Roman Polanski film. At the time of his arrest, he was engaged in post-production on an adaptation of Robert Harris's *The Ghost*, a *roman à clef* concerning someone very like Tony Blair, starring Pierce Brosnan and Ewan McGregor.

If Terry Gilliam can shake off the death of his lead actor, Heath Ledger, and finish *The Imaginarium of Doctor Parnassus*, then the folk behind *The Ghost* can knock their footage into a

serviceable print. After all, they've just got themselves a million dollars' worth of free publicity. Nobody ever suggested the movie industry wasn't run by cynics.

MONDAY, 5 OCTOBER 2009

Leinster Enjoy this Demolition Derby

Gerry Thornley

Magners League: Leinster 30 Munster 0

As Derbies go, this was some demolition. In practically every facet, and virtually every position, the European champions bossed the Magners League holders off the park and, just to add the gloss, it was the old firm, so to speak, of Gordon D'Arcy, Brian O'Driscoll and Shane Horgan who varnished the win with the tries. Save for a bonus point, they could hardly have scripted it better.

The only time Munster threatened the scoreboard was when Ronan O'Gara attempted a 40-metre penalty into the wind at the end of the first quarter, and he duffed it so horribly that the ball scarcely rose above crossbar height.

Kurt McQuilkin, who must be one of the candidates to take over from Michael Cheika when the Australian completes his five-year reign at the end of this season, has overseen some compelling defensive performances by Leinster in the last three seasons. But few have been more conclusive than this.

The trust each and every player has in each other and their defensive system has become the European champions' bedrock. And as much as anything, it was the thunderous hits put in by the likes of Kevin McLoughlin (one tackle on Donncha O'Callaghan early on setting the tone), Shane Jennings and Jamie Heaslip – a three-man, backrow wrecking team – which drew the lines in the sand.

All across the park, though, whether carrying or tackling, Leinster dominated the collisions. Indeed, it's hard to recall any team inflicting such physical carnage on Munster in quite some time. The memory of Denis Leamy driving Cian Healy back and of pumping his legs to work himself free of Jennings stand out because they were such rare examples of Munster-winning collisions.

Otherwise the abiding image of the game was of Munster players running into blue walls or being driven backwards. From there Leinster counter-rucked to win a dozen or more turnovers at the breakdown.

McLoughlin, Leo Cullen and co. also wreaked damage on the Munster throw. The bare statistic of five lost lineouts barely tells the tale, given the contrasting quality in this source of possession, and

Munster didn't help themselves or the nervy Denis Fogarty with the long delays in communicating their calls.

The Munster scrum also suffered the indignity of being shunted back and penalised at one scrum. By the time John Hayes had been red-carded and their seven-man scrum lost one feed against the head, their pack had long since been beaten up anyhow.

As seismic a moment as any in the match was the purpose with which the Leinster pack marched downfield after Jonathan Sexton had drilled a penalty up the touchline. You could have thrown a rug over them then and again, from Cullen's ensuing take, as they rumbled remorselessly infield toward the Munster posts. The three points that followed courtesy of Sexton's second penalty was almost secondary to the statement of intent.

By then, too, Sexton – who ran the show beautifully, oozing confidence throughout – had carved through the thin red line and Horgan had taken Denis Hurley on the outside. The presence and impact of Brian O'Driscoll, bearing in mind it was his first game back after three months, was staggering. With him back, Leinster were full of inventive running and ideas, and it was no surprise when the great one engineered the breakthrough.

One more good lineout ball 35 metres out – curiously uncontested by Munster – McLoughlin's carry put Leinster on the front foot, from where O'Driscoll took Sexton's pacey pass to brilliantly fix Marcus Horan and Denis Leamy and put Horgan through the ensuing gap. Horgan, once again revelling against the Munster red, had the presence of mind to pass across his body inside for D'Arcy to score.

When Jean de Villiers has bad dreams one ventures O'Driscoll now features in them. The Springbok won't enjoy watching the video of the Irish captain making him look as if he was jogging on the spot as he accelerated around him; nor will Keith Earls as O'Driscoll eluded his despairing tackle for the 45th-minute killer try.

Munster had briefly flickered into life either side of the break, but Hines pilfered a loose ball near the Leinster line when, perhaps, he might have been offside. Tellingly, nine of the first 10 players into the dressingrooms at the end of the half were wearing blue, and once Healy – in the high point of another fine game – drifted Leamy back from a close-range indirect penalty, Munster wilted.

Save for further evidence of Tomás O'Leary's remarkably swift return to fitness and form, there were few Munster crumbs of comfort. Their running game utterly lacked their normal depth against Leinster's impressive line speed. This left O'Gara obliged to take the ball into contact more than he would have liked. Even Paul Warwick's cameo was undone by the infield pass which Horgan, who had covered huge ground from the opposite wing, picked off for the *coup de grace*.

MONDAY, 5 OCTOBER 2009

Recession Focused Minds on how Vital EU is to our Fortunes

Stephen Collins

The decision of the Irish people to ratify the Lisbon Treaty by such an overwhelming majority is a clear signal that most of the country's citizens want to live in an outward-looking country at the heart of the European project, rather than retreat back to an isolated position on the periphery.

The endorsement of the treaty at the second attempt could, to adapt Séamus Mallon's famous phrase, be regarded as Lisbon for slow learners, given that the legal guarantees merely specified what was not in the treaty and did nothing to change the actual text.

However, that misses the point that second time around the electorate really engaged with the issue, as the turnout showed. The political parties woke up to their responsibilities and, in tandem with a range of civic society groups, brought home to voters the importance of a Yes vote for the country on every level.

The way in which voters were able to put aside their feelings about the Government and vote on the merits of the issue, in terms of our future relationship with the EU, demonstrated that people can be persuaded to act in the national interest if the political class does its job properly and explains the issues and campaigns with conviction.

The reasons for the big change of heart from the first referendum last year are many, but it is hard to escape the conclusion that the economic crisis focused the minds of many voters on the importance of good relations with our EU neighbours in order to restore the country's prosperity.

The emphasis by all those campaigning for a Yes vote on the economy and jobs, rather than the intricate details of the Lisbon Treaty, was crucial in keeping the minds of voters on the big picture rather than having them distracted by the legal niceties of the treaty.

An allied issue was whether the people of Ireland wanted their country to be perceived as a vibrant member of the biggest trading bloc in the world or a disgruntled small nation standing in the way of progress at EU level.

An added dimension was whether Ireland wanted to ally itself with the most anti-EU elements in British politics and ultimately crawl back into a subservient relationship with our closest neighbour.

The involvement of UKIP with the No campaign came as manna from heaven for the Yes side, as it showed the kind of allies that Ireland would have if the treaty was rejected again.

The outcome of the referendum has cleared the way for normal politics to resume in Ireland and for the European Union as a whole to get down to real business, after so many years of tortuous negotiations about institutional reform.

Brigid Laffan of the Ireland For Europe campaign photographed held high in Dublin Castle after the results of the Lisbon Treaty referendum were announced. Also in the photograph are former MEP Pat Cox and Brendan Halligan of Ireland for Europe. Photograph: Brenda Fitzsimons.

On the narrow domestic political front, the Yes vote came as an enormous relief to Taoiseach Brian Cowen and his Government. His tenure in office was marred almost from the start by the defeat of Lisbon I. He had to attend his first European Council meeting in June last year and explain to his prime ministerial colleagues why Ireland had voted No to a treaty which had been agreed under its presidency.

Cowen's confidence never seemed to recover from that disastrous start. A second defeat would almost inevitably have forced him out of office and possibly resulted in an immediate general election.

While the referendum victory is unlikely to result in any reversal of his party's current political standing, it will at least buy him some time. It should also give him the confidence to do what needs to be done in the national interest on the issue of the public finances.

Minister for Foreign Affairs Micheál Martin has come out of the campaign with his reputation enhanced. He spoke with passion and authority throughout the campaign and handled himself effectively in media jousts with difficult opponents like Declan Ganley and Joe Higgins. In the longer term that will boost his chances of succeeding Brian Cowen when the Fianna Fáil leadership becomes vacant.

The major Opposition parties can take an equal amount of encouragement from the referendum result. Fine Gael and Labour put the national interest first by campaigning for a Yes vote. This was particularly important given the collapse of the Fianna Fáil vote in the recent local and European elections. The Opposition parties had to persuade their voters to back Lisbon if it was to have any chance of being ratified.

Fine Gael leader Enda Kenny toured the country canvassing for a Yes vote and addressing public meetings in nearly every constituency. The commitment to putting the national interest ahead of an understandable desire to finish off a wounded government by a half-hearted campaign shows that Kenny has the credentials to lead the country after the next election.

Labour leader Eamon Gilmore also put the national interest first by campaigning hard for a Yes, particularly given the fact that so many working-class voters who should be his party's natural support base were in the No camp.

The Yes campaign of a variety of civic society groups was of at least equal importance. Pat Cox played an important role and Ryanair chief Michael O'Leary put his money where his mouth was and, despite the misgivings of some on the Yes side about his flamboyant style, he clearly had an impact.

The No side probably missed the presence of Declan Ganley for most of the campaign although his return in the final two weeks didn't make all that much difference.

Ganley's cynical 'tribute' to Brian Cowen on Saturday morning was typical of the way he behaved in both referendum campaigns but, second time around, the voters were less susceptible to his smoothly presented anti-European message.

The posters put up by Ganley's Libertas organisation and the right-wing group Cóir were clever and eye-catching but, ultimately, the voters had more important things on their mind when they went to the polling stations.

Cóir spokesman Richard Greene has spoken about setting up a new political party to represent the No voters. That would be no bad thing and it would be a real test of how many support the organisation's message.

Sinn Féin, the only political party on the No side, probably made a tactical blunder by not claiming ownership of the commissioner issue as an excuse to get off the No hook. The party had made it a key part of its No campaign last year and could have claimed the decision to retain a commissioner as a tangible victory and taken a different stance second time around.

Instead the party campaigned for a No, as it has done in every European referendum since 1972, which is unlikely to have done anything to enhance the party's long-term prospects, following a series of disappointing election results.

The victory of the No side last year did inestimable damage both to Ireland's reputation and its interests. The scale of the victory by the Yes side has already done a lot to restore both. Politics at EU and domestic level can now move on to other issues.

WEDNESDAY, 7 OCTOBER 2009

Straight Talking Gilmore Dispenses with the Bull

Dáil Sketch, by Miriam Lord

Hallelujah! Finally, an Irish political leader has found a backbone, climbed off the fence and said it like it is. Yesterday in the Dáil, Eamon Gilmore stood up and told John O'Donoghue to resign or be removed from office. At that moment, the look of shock on the faces of his fellow TDs showed just how disconnected some have become from the real world.

The Labour leader was just doing his job. But when he got to his feet and began, 'On Sunday, when I read the report of the expenses claimed by the Ceann Comhairle over the last two years . . .'

Jill Kerr, from the Ulster Museum, puts the finishing touches to Peter the Polar Bear after the bear was reinstated as part of the Window on Our World exhibition, in advance of the reopening of the museum. Photograph: Paul Faith/Press Association.

a chilly hush descended on the chamber, like he was informing them of a sudden death among one of their number. 'I felt that the pattern of extravagance was unacceptable,' said Eamon in regretful tones, as the temperature plunged further.

What he was doing was unprecedented. Where the general public is concerned – and in terms of thinking the public is miles ahead of the people who represent them in Leinster House – Eamon Gilmore was simply stating the obvious, and not before time. But they were stunned in the Dáil.

Since the details of the Ceann Comhairle's five-star skites around the racecourses of the world came to light, politicians from all sides have been drowning in a sea of fudge.

The saga of his lavish jaunts, conducted under the cover of important State business, has enraged the public. It's made a laughing stock of John O'Donoghue and added to an overwhelming sense of cynicism and distrust in the political process. But his colleagues have been turning cartwheels – in the interest of due process, of course, and maybe it's best not to cast stones if you're not free of sin yourself.

Who in the last few days hadn't wanted to fling a shoe at the radio, or put a boot through the TV as yet another senior TD was wheeled out to pussy-foot around the question of the Ceann Comhairle – and his wife – living the high life at the taxpayers' expense?

The question of whether O'Donoghue should or should not resign was met with hemming and hawing, dithering and double-speak and enough hedging to keep them beating around the bush until the public interest waned.

Cartoon by Martyn Turner.

In Leinster House, they can dish it out but they can't take it. When one of their own dirties his bib, the instinctive reaction is to whip it off, put it through the washing machine and then commission a report to see what measures can be put in place to curb dribbling in the future.

All eyes were on John O'Donoghue when he ascended the chair to preside over Leaders' Questions. He has had a torrid few weeks, mostly trying to avoid explaining away the growing evidence concerning his penchant for first-class air travel, limousines, wildly expensive hotels and classic horse races.

The Opposition had expressed itself most concerned. The Government hadn't expressed itself one way or the other. The nation vigorously expressed itself on Liveline yesterday afternoon, leaving Leinster House in no doubt as to their view of the matter.

Anywhere else and the Bull would have been taken by the horns a long time ago and put out of his misery. (He's not very happy about the way he is being treated in the media and has made his views known in this regard.) Anywhere else – across the water, for example – and he would have become an ex-ceann comhairle a long time ago.

But this is Leinster House, and these are Irish politicians, and they're too nice to say what has to be said, when it has to be said, to whom it has to be said.

For them, there is always an easier way. This time, where O'Donoghue was concerned, it was decided his case would be put to the Houses of the Oireachtas Commission. John O'Donoghue is chairman of the commission. It meets in private.

Just the job for Brian Cowen. 'I want to see full transparency, in respect of what we do here. We have nothing to hide.' Shut the Bull into a meeting of the commission so, because 'it's important that the confidence of the House in the Ceann Comhairle can be confirmed on the basis of a discussion and a decision to be taken at that committee meeting . . .' And so on.

As he said yesterday, you won't find Biffo impugning any man's integrity. He gave another poor performance in the Dáil, totally misreading the public mood. A mood bolstered by a slew of damning receipts from the Ceann Comhairle's office.

When the time came, it didn't come as a surprise to John O'Donoghue. He wasn't ambushed. Eamon Gilmore told him he had run out of road, and if the Taoiseach did not accede to a meeting on his future, he would be taking a certain course during Leaders' Questions.

Those Fianna Fáil backbenchers who were later muttering about 'nasty politics' didn't know that Deputy Gilmore had signalled his intentions.

In the chair, the Ceann Comhairle waited for what he must have known was going to happen. He twiddled a paper clip in his fingers; his foot tapped nervously on the floor. Then it was time. He put both elbows on the arm rests and clasped his hands together, fingers entwined, staring straight ahead. Eamon Gilmore seemed a little nervous, but he ploughed ahead, convention be damned.

'A Cheann Comhairle,' he said, addressing him directly. 'I regret to say this, but I consider that your position is no longer tenable.' In the chamber, the low hum of conversation stopped.

John O'Donoghue nodded his head slightly. That was all.

'I think you will either have to resign, or I think you will have to be removed from office.'

Deputy Gilmore said his party would be tabling a motion of no confidence in him.

'Thank you, Deputy Gilmore,' said O'Donoghue in a very soft voice. He paused, then looked to his left. 'Em . . . Taoiseach.'

Brian Cowen rose in reply. He sounded shaken and repeated his view that the commission was the proper place to air the matter.

The place was so quiet. It was that hush you hear when a deputy is in grave trouble. Ministers looked thoughtful. It was almost as if TDs were embarrassed – for the Ceann Comhairle, whom they like, and perhaps, for themselves, and the things they have to do sometimes.

'This was something that I found very difficult to do. It's a sad day,' said Eamon Gilmore afterwards. But somebody had to do it. As Enda Kenny realised when he took to the plinth an hour later, calling on O'Donoghue to resign. Stable doors and horses came to mind.

Gilmore acted decisively and it will stand to him. As for John O'Donoghue – the Bull, the Bill, Johnny Junkets, Johnny Cash – there'll be no stewards' inquiry to throw him a lifeline. He's finished. Why did it take so long?

WEDNESDAY, 7 OCTOBER 2009

Ruling Signals the End of Carroll's Property Empire

Simon Carswell

The epic 11-week quest for court protection for Liam Carroll's Zoe group, his heavily insolvent property development business, ended in just a matter of minutes in the Supreme Court yesterday.

The case began life as a rushed application late on Friday, July 17th, and a pre-emptive strike to prevent the Dutch-owned ACCBank collapsing the group as it aggressively sought the repayment of €136 million in unpaid debts.

The battle ended with little more than a whimper concerning procedural matters from the group and its significant legal team comprising two senior counsel, two barristers, law firm Eversheds O'Donnell Sweeney and a team from accountants KPMG.

The liquidation of two companies at the apex of the group appears little more than a formality leading to the collapse of one of the largest property development groups in the country.

The Chief Justice John Murray extinguished any hope of the group securing the appointment of an examiner who could have put in place its survival plan, saying that the group should not have been allowed to proceed with a second bid for court protection after a first attempt was rejected.

The first application had been shot down by both the High Court and the Supreme Court, but Mr Justice John Cooke allowed the group to apply to appoint an examiner for a second time on August 21st.

Yesterday the Chief Justice ruled that the second bid for examinership and court approval for a rescue was an abuse of process and the administration of justice. The Supreme Court found that Zoe companies had in their first application for protection 'consciously and deliberately' withheld from the court information that was available to them and could have been obtained by them.

The court was referring to a key business plan drafted last December by KPMG for the Zoe group and Mr Carroll's two other groups, Dunloe and Orthanc, which set out how they proposed to survive the collapse of the property market. The group had also failed to submit letters of support from seven lenders to the group in the first application. (ACC was the only bank opposed to the plan.)

These letters would have backed up the group's claim that the banks would provide further loans to keep the group afloat over the course of the three-year plan and show they were willing to accept a two-year moratorium on interest payments due on loans.

The Chief Justice said that although no bad faith was involved in the Zoe group's decision not to submit this evidence, the second petition for protection nonetheless amounted to an abuse of process. The Supreme Court will give its reasons in full next Wednesday.

Cartoon by Martyn Turner.

Carroll and his wellbeing played a crucial part in the ultimate failure of the group's attempts to secure protection. The High Court was told by Zoe group's finance director John Pope last August that Carroll had been suffering from stress when he chose not to submit the crucial business plan in the first application and that his judgment had been impaired. Pope said that he had underestimated the stress that his boss was suffering.

This proved fatal for the group's survival plan when the High Court and Supreme Court rejected the first bid for protection saying that insufficient evidence had been offered to show that the group had a reasonable chance of survival given the current and likely future state of the property market.

Carroll was hospitalised between the first and second applications for examinership and unable to direct the second bid.

The costs of the case are significant and likely to be added to the Zoe group's massive debt pile of €1.3 billion, almost all of which is owed to the group's eight lenders.

The two petitions for protection were before the courts on 18 days − 13 days in the High Court and five days in the Supreme Court. Eight senior judges heard submissions by the group over the 11 weeks.

Mr Justice Murray said last month that Zoe's appeals were having 'a very heavy effect on important cases' and other parties were having to wait a significant time to have their cases heard.

Legal sources estimated that Zoe's own bill from the various actions stands at about €500,000.

ACC, which is owned by Dutch financial giant Rabobank, is not expected to be able to recover its costs as the court is likely to award costs against Vantive Holdings, the Zoe group company that led the two failed petitions, given that the bank's appeal was successful and that the company is heavily insolvent.

Then there are the costs faced by the Zoe group's employees, contractors, suppliers, creditors and six other lenders who made appearances in court supporting the second bid for protection.

The group now faces the prospect of an array of receivers being appointed by its banks over the group's companies to protect the lenders' interests in assets supporting loans of €1.3 billion.

A stay remains until next Wednesday over two High Court orders liquidating Vantive and Morston Investments, two companies at the apex of Zoe which channelled bank loans down to property companies across the group.

An appeal by Zoe against the appointment of the liquidator seems little more than a moot issue given that the group is facing a shortfall of more than €1 billion and the door has been slammed shut on examinership/protection.

The group could argue that the court has discretion not to appoint liquidators to the firms, but the prospect of the companies' avoiding being wound up is slim.

A receiver appointed by ACC in August can now take control of four of the seven Zoe companies that sought protection following the Supreme Court's decision.

These companies own prime sites in the north Dublin docklands. The receiver is likely to adopt the same position to be taken by the National Asset Management Agency, the State's 'bad bank', if and when the legislation setting up Nama is passed and it takes over loans with a face value of €77 billion from the banks for a discounted price of €54 billion.

There is still the possibility of ACC's €136 million debt being bought out by Zoe's two largest lenders − Allied Irish Banks (AIB) and Bank of Scotland (Ireland) (BoSI). But the chances of this happening are remote given that this would set a dangerous precedent in other cases of heavily indebted developers where smaller lenders seek repayment from big lenders.

While the banks examine the potential fallout from the Supreme Court's ruling, they will be preparing to issue demand letters seeking repayment of their loans on the back of which they can move to appoint receivers.

Members of Boyzone and other friends of Stephen Gately pay their respects as his coffin is placed inside the hearse after his funeral at St Laurence O'Toole's Church, Sheriff Street, Dublin. Photograph: Eric Luke.

If this proceeds as expected, the receivers are likely to adopt a sit-and-hold approach with the group's assets as they wait until life reappears in the property market and they can recover more of the money owing by the group.

The big unknown is how Zoe's foreign lenders – BoSI, KBC Bank Ireland and Ulster Bank – will react. They account for almost half of the group's debts and do not have the luxury of selling loans to the only buyer around (Nama).

ACC's owner, Rabobank, may seek to sell the properties backing its loans in an effort to recoup as much of its €136 million debt as possible to appease the market which is fearful that Rabo's small Irish subsidiary may cost the bank its treasured triple-A rating.

This is the big imponderable. However, one thing is certain: yesterday's ruling leaves the fate of Carroll's group in the hands of his banks. His reign over the Zoe property empire is coming to a close.

MONDAY, 12 OCTOBER 2009

The Boy who Came out of his Shell

Kevin Courtney

You don't expect boyband members to die young. You expect them to wither away on reality TV shows or become lost in panto-land, but you don't expect them to be found dead on a sofa at the tender age of 33 after a night out on the town. It's just not rock 'n' roll.

The untimely death is very much the preserve

of the hard-living rocker, whose passing can usually be attributed directly to a drink and drugs lifestyle. Boyband members aren't permitted to enter this pantheon – those elite places are usually reserved for those with a willingness to push things to the extreme.

You could hardly call Stephen Gately a hard-living rocker, but that doesn't make his death on Saturday any less significant. He may have just been a second-string singer in a boyband long past their prime, but let's not forget that this was Ireland's very first boyband, and in setting out into unknown territory with only their raffish charm, a few dance moves and the managerial skill of Louis Walsh to guide them, Boyzone were something akin to pioneers.

U2 may have shown the world that the Irish were a rock force to be reckoned with, but it was Boyzone who gained Ireland entry into the united nations of pop.

Walsh formed Boyzone in 1993 after seeing the success of Take That and reckoned he could replicate that success on home ground. There was no shortage of bright-eyed, fresh-faced youngsters willing to audition for the chance of a lifetime, and Walsh quickly had a line-up of presentable young Irish fellas ready to roll out.

Within a day of forming, Boyzone were on *The Late Late Show* 'freeform' dancing to a generic disco backing track, while a bemused Gay Byrne – and an equally bemused nation – looked on. They didn't have any songs, their singing ability was still an unknown factor, and their line-up would go through a few swift changes, but their youth, vigour and enthusiasm was not in question.

It didn't take long for the nation to become

Residents of Sheriff Street in central Dublin, the area where Stephen Gately grew up, watch his funeral. Photograph: Eric Luke.

intimately acquainted with the Boyz: Ronan Keating quickly emerged as the band's leader; Shane Lynch was the fly guy, Keith Duffy was the charmer, Mikey Graham was the boy next door – and Stephen Gately, well, he was the baby in the band. The diminutive singer, however, soon showed he had more than enough charisma to hold his own in this famous fivesome.

Although Ronan was the band's lead vocalist, Gately proved well able to take the lead when needed. In Boyzone's early career, the rest of the group were accused of merely miming behind Keating, but on the Andrew Lloyd Webber song 'No Matter What', Gately showed that he had a perfectly serviceable set of pipes – a bit reedy and slight, perhaps, but distinct enough to earn him co-lead vocalist status.

Boyzone's success made them the envy of every budding Irish rocker, and an easy target for every Irish critic – including this one. But they were an instant success with the people that mattered, the teenage girls who were crying out for something to fill up the empty spaces on their bedroom walls.

After Take That broke up in 1995, Boyzone were perfectly poised to take their place in the hearts and pillowcases of a generation of broken-hearted fans. Many girls who needed counselling after Take That broke up found solace in the smiling Irish eyes of Ronan, Keith, Shane, Mikey and Stephen.

During their short six years together, Boyzone enjoyed success beyond their wildest dreams, scoring 16 Top Ten hit singles, including six Number Ones, and selling more than 10 million albums. Boyzone's success signalled a change in the aspirations of Irish teenagers – across the nation, youngsters were putting aside the guitars and practising their dance moves instead. Bewitch'd, featuring two sisters of Shane Lynch, had a UK No. 1 with 'C'est La Vie', and Westlife took the baton from Boyzone and went on to even bigger success in the Noughties.

Meanwhile, tabloid newspaper the *Sun* was preparing to break a massive story – it was about to reveal details of Stephen Gately's relationship with Dutch singer Eloy De Jong of boyband Caught in the Act. Rather than be outed by the *Sun*, Gately chose to come out himself, and became another pop pioneer – the first boyband member to openly admit to being gay.

Pop music has long sought to cover up homosexuality, fearing it may scare away its target audience of teenage girls; Gately's coming-out was a bombshell that exploded the flimsy myth of manliness that many pop acts try and promulgate. In a genre that values tanned, toned physique, high-pitched vocals and effete dance moves, it's hardly a shocking revelation that some who work in this milieu might possibly be gay.

Gately never got a chance to find out if Boyzone's fanbase would remain loyal after learning the truth. The band broke up in 2000 after much internal bickering; this time there were few tears in teen-land – they were too busy mooning over Ireland's next big boyband, Westlife.

Gately was not quite left high and dry by Boyzone's break-up, however. Considered the nicest guy in the band, he had no shortage of famous friends, including Elton John and his partner David Furnish, who introduced him to businessman Andrew Cowles. Gately and Cowles were married in a civil ceremony in 2006.

While Keating embarked on a successful solo career, Gately gravitated towards his first love – stage musicals. He had appeared in many musicals as a teenager growing up in Dublin's Sheriff Street. Now, he fulfilled his childhood dream by starring in *Joseph and his Amazing Technicolour Dreamcoat* in London's West End; he counted Sir Andrew Lloyd Webber among his friends. He also starred as the Childcatcher in *Chitty Chitty Bang Bang* at the London Palladium, and had a short run in a touring production of *Godspell*.

And, yes, Gately did feature in panto-land in recent years, but at least he embraced it with gusto and that same boyish enthusiasm that prompted him to make a holy show of himself on that fateful *Late Late Show* all those years ago.

At the time of his death, Gately was enjoying a second crack at the charts with the reformed Boyzone; despite reports of sluggish ticket sales for their concerts, the band scored their 17th Top Five hit last year with 'Love You Anyway' and were planning to release a new album in 2010.

More poignantly, Gately had been putting the finishing touches to a children's fantasy book, *The Tree of Seasons*. His final Twitter post talked about focusing on finishing his book. For many, Stephen Gately will always be the little boy lost who finally learned to stand on his own two feet.

MONDAY, 19 OCTOBER 2009

It's Too Little Too late for me and Maradona

Tom Humphries

A number of years ago myself and young Mr Duggan of this parish found ourselves at large in the city of Sydney during the early hours of the morning. We had time to kill and a thirst to deal with. It was the era when the newspaper was disgustingly rich and we were living like a couple of Ceann Comhairles out on a jolly.

The Olympic Games were happening in the city just then and young Mr Duggan was such a prodigy at the scribbling that I was unsure as to whether he would even be served. In time, however, we repaired to a subterranean bar. I remember thinking that, if I could just set Duggan on the road to alcoholism and ruin, my job would be safe for a few years longer.

In that narrow little bar we passed a mildly bizarre night in the company of the proprietors, a group of young fellas whose twin passions were hookers and Mike Tyson. I remember the clammy,

squirmy discomfort as they proudly showed us the barstools upon which various styles of paid-for sexual congress had been achieved.

Just as discomfiting was their devotion to Iron Mike. I remember us walking back to our hotel as dawn was creeping up (I contemplated cleaving Duggan's skull with a large rock – just to keep the job safe when the recession came, you know) and debating the Tyson thing with Duggan.

He could see the almost nihilistic attraction of Tyson. I couldn't get past my political correctness. I was genuinely surprised Tyson, for whom one could feel disdain or sympathy (he being a victim in his own way) would be held in such affection. It seemed like an unlikely response to deep-set alienation.

And since then (realising that if I could artificially develop an intellect as broad as Duggan's the job might be safe) I have spent more time than is normal or healthy trying to develop an appreciation of Mike Tyson. To an extent it has worked, although he still wouldn't be among my top-10 rapist thugs to get stuck in a lift with. The pathos of his life, though, is compelling, and as his decline becomes a morality tale in itself, Tyson assumes a certain appeal. You could root for him.

The Germans must have a word for that distressing feeling when you just don't get that thing which people you admire and respect understand instantly. The great advantage about being so shallow is that you can do something about it.

I remember once being involved in a conversation with people who had funny but expensive haircuts and were very ironic. I realised to my horror that the band Wet Wet Wet – whom I considered not just progressive but winningly cheerful – might as well have been war criminals for all the respect they enjoyed among my friends. The next day I bought the entire back catalogue of Portishead and became broody and thoughtful for quite some time.

I have applied the same process to Diego Armando Maradona, but in his case I have gotten nowhere. I still find his lack of class, his inability to

John Archer with Tasha, a Singapore Cat, International Gold Champion at the Cork Cat Show in Cobh.
Photograph: Michael Mac Sweeney/Provision.

comport himself with any semblance of dignity, to be in absurd and depressing conflict with his genius as a footballer. How can the inspired beauty of his play co-exist with his crass boorishness?

Funny thing is that Maradona started at or near the top in my estimation. As with the rest of the world, I feel the rules of fairness should generally cease to apply when the victims are the English soccer team, and the Hand of God goal is one of those things I never tire of watching. That summer, in fact, to be living as a feckless young fella in London and watching that tournament unfold as Maradona's stage was one of the great pleasures of life.

Last week, though, with the most extraordinarily gifted panel of players at his disposal, Maradona watched his side slump over the line into next year's World Cup finals. He did so after a qualifying campaign which mixed the banal with the ridiculous, a campaign that included the distinctive low of a record 6-1 defeat to Bolivia.

It was all done and dusted when Maradona gave a press conference during which he told the media, 'You lot take it up the a★★★', before adding coyly, 'if the ladies will pardon the expression.' This, we can assume, is the same sad homophobia that surfaced in Maradona when he accused Pele of living 'a gay life' (a heinous insult in Maradona's view) after Pele withheld his seal of approval from Maradona on account of his past as a coke fiend.

Anyway, Maradona added a rider (sorry) by grabbing his genitals in a gesture of machismo disdain. 'But certain people who have not supported me, and you know who you are, can keep sucking,' he added.

And with that, a tipping point for me, I realised that for the first time I would not be rooting for Argentina to win next year's World Cup.

(Of course, Maradona's insult was less gratuitous and wounding than he imagined. In a figurative way, at least, we sports journalists do experience precisely that which Maradona said we experience. People like Diego have never grown up enough to realise that the media doesn't exist as some sort of corpulent fan club, and there is, Diego implied, a certain lack of dignity involved in the trade-off between objective comment and continued access.)

Again, I had been trying hard to cultivate an appreciation of Maradona.

Having supported Carlos Menem during the 1990s, and allegedly been friends with the Neapolitan mafia, the Camorra, while he was playing in that city, the little fella has come around to more progressive causes in recent times, getting tattoos of Fidel and Che in the precise places where I have my Portishead tats. We are a lot alike.

Sadly, it's too little too late for me and Diego. If you can't win with a bit of grace and class and dignity, can't comport yourself with a serenity and wisdom that age can bring, perhaps the adulation was misplaced and greatness is sometimes conferred on the irredeemably callow.

I have this discussion with people about my little Diego problem, and they say to me that I have to look at where he came from, as if a hard upbringing was a guarantor of a poor personality. Most of the great footballers, many of the greatest sports people we have known, grew up in poverty and found a way out through their talents.

That experience gave them a sense of perspective and an appreciation of the world at large which seems to be lacking in Maradona's self-centred universe.

Pity.

SATURDAY, 24 OCTOBER 2009

How Tribe Leader Brokered Ransom Deal to Free Kidnapped Aid Workers

Mary Fitzgerald

In Darfur they say little happens without Musa Hilal knowing about it. As chief of the region's largest Arab tribe, Hilal is a man who inspires awe and fear in equal measure. His allies speak of him in reverential tones, testament to the considerable clout he wields both in Darfur and Khartoum.

But for others in the troubled corner of western Sudan, whose name has become synonymous with one of the most devastating humanitarian crises this century, even the merest mention of Hilal summons up memories of some of the worst violence committed during a conflict that has cost the lives of some 300,000 people.

Human Rights Watch (HRW) says scores of victims and witnesses have named Hilal as the top commander of the Janjaweed, the name many in Darfur use to describe the marauding government-backed militias held responsible for numerous attacks between 2003 and 2004, in which civilians were massacred and raped in front of their families while their villages were razed.

Last year, HRW described Hilal as 'the poster child for Janjaweed atrocities' in Darfur. Five years ago, the US State Department named him as one of six militia leaders alleged to be responsible for

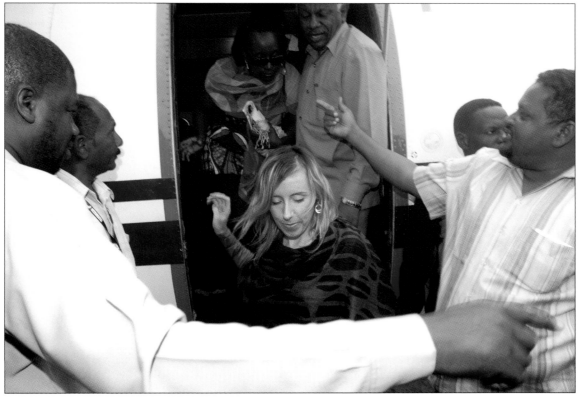

Released hostages, Dubliner Sharon Commins (front, centre) and Ugandan Hilda Kawuki (back, left), disembark from a plane on arrival at Khartoum airport, 19 October 2009. The two kidnapped aid workers from Irish Goal aid agency were released after a three-month ordeal in Sudan's Darfur region saying they could not wait to see their families. Photograph: Reuters/Mohamed Nureldin Abdallh.

serious crimes. In 2006, the UN imposed travel bans and asset freezes on Hilal and three others.

But given his stature as the leader of the Mahameed tribe, and his deep connections with the Khartoum government – last year it appointed him special advisor to Sudan's president, Omar al-Bashir – it is likely that Musa Hilal knows more than most about the circumstances surrounding the kidnapping and, more than 100 days later, the release of Goal aid worker Sharon Commins and her Ugandan colleague Hilda Kawuki.

He granted a rare interview to *The Irish Times* this week in Khartoum. Hilal (48) divides his time between a villa on the outskirts of the Sudanese capital and his home turf in Darfur. He has three

wives and more than a dozen children. At his surprisingly lightly-guarded home, one of several domestic staff proffered orange juice and glasses of sweet tea, along with bowls of sugared almonds, dates, cardamom-scented toffee and the contents from a tin of Quality Street. Some time later, Hilal swept into the room and offered his hand in greeting. A tall, imposing figure with an athletic build, he wore a pristine white robe with a white lace skullcap and brown loafers.

Abdul Bagi al-Jailani, Sudan's minister for humanitarian affairs and the man Minister for Foreign Affairs Micheál Martin last week described as the Irish Government's main point of contact in the case, had earlier told me that President al-Bashir himself had asked Hilal to assist in securing the release of the two women.

Settling down on a plush sofa, Hilal recounted his version of the abduction and release, one that at times contradicted that given by the Sudanese, Irish and Ugandan authorities, most dramatically when he revealed that, contrary to official assertions, the kidnappers were paid a ransom to free the women.

The core group involved in the abduction numbered eight men, Hilal said, five of whom were Arab and three he referred to as 'zurga', a derogatory term that can be translated as 'blacks'. The word is often used in Sudan to describe those of non-Arab lineage. Asked if any of the kidnappers were from his own Mahameed tribe, Hilal said yes, but added that he does not know them personally.

When I mentioned how strange it seems that, given the ethnic tensions that have convulsed Darfur in recent years, the gang was drawn from both Arab and African tribes, he replied: 'These people are simply bandits . . . they are gangs that just gather together.'

The way Hilal tells it, the kidnappers had two motives: they wanted money and also to highlight their belief that aid and development efforts by the international community in Darfur were concentrated on African tribes such as the Fur, the people who give the region its name, which means 'Land of the Fur'.

Sharon Commins, the Goal aid worker kidnapped in Sudan, meeting President Mary McAleese at Áras an Uachtaráin at a reception for her and her family and dignitaries involved in her rescue. Photograph: Alan Betson.

'There is no political dimension in what they do but they want some organisations to provide them with certain facilities and services. They feel that the organisations are focusing only on the Fur and others like them,' Hilal said.

Asked why the abduction of the Goal workers, which stretched to three months, two weeks and one day, lasted so long compared with previous cases, Hilal said it was because agreement could not be reached on the ransom. The gang appeared to receive conflicting signals over whether money would be handed over, and they demanded different sums at different stages, with an initial sum of 500 million Sudanese pounds (€150,000) mooted.

More trouble loomed when the Sudanese government relayed the explicit message that they would not allow the payment of a ransom, Hilal recalled. The kidnappers responded by threatening to take the women to neighbouring Chad.

Hilal claimed that he, working through his own mediators, persuaded the gang to drop the Chad plan. 'This is the truth. Had I not intervened through these mediators, this situation wouldn't have been sorted out like this. These guys would not have killed the girls but they would have taken them to Chad or any other place.'

Hilal says he also helped arrange the phone call that took place between Sharon and her mother shortly after Micheál Martin visited Khartoum last month to discuss the abduction with Sudanese officials. At no point did Hilal meet with any of the Irish team working on the case, he said.

In the last stages before the release, the Sudanese ministry for humanitarian affairs finalised everything, Hilal explained. 'I just [convinced] the kidnappers back to the 500 million pounds sum and the government paid that amount,' he said.

Jailani had also insisted that criminal charges would be brought against the kidnappers, claiming that the Sudanese authorities know them 'by name, clan and family'. But when I asked him if any moves had been made to arrest them, given that the Sudanese apparently know their identities and location, Jailani replied: 'This is not the time for that, but we are going to arrest them and bring them to justice sooner or later. Through the mediators we told them that at this moment we will not touch them so just release the ladies, but we didn't give any immunity or forgiveness.'

Hilal, however, claimed the government has no information about the gang's current whereabouts, and added that the kidnappers had forced the mediators to swear on the Koran that they would not reveal their identities. For his part, Hilal is in favour of prosecuting those responsible. 'If their identities become known and the government is serious about it, I would support their being brought to justice,' he said.

The circumstances surrounding the Goal kidnapping raise several questions about what has transpired in Darfur in recent years.

The region erupted into violence in 2003, when rebels complaining of marginalisation and discrimination in favour of Arab tribes took up arms against the Khartoum government. In the ensuing fighting, during which the Sudanese army bombed from the air and allied militias laid waste to what was left of the villages below, a new word – Janjaweed – burned itself into the consciousness of the world.

The term Janjaweed itself had long been used to refer to bandits from the area where Sudan's western border melts into Chad. The bandits roamed the vast plains of Darfur, robbing Arabs and non-Arabs, nomads and farmers. But the militias that became known as Janjaweed after the rebels first struck six years ago were used by Khartoum as something akin to a counter-insurgency proxy force in place of, and sometimes alongside, its regular army.

Similar militias had been deployed in the two decades long civil war in southern Sudan. Members of the militia in Darfur were paid a salary, and their notoriety grew not only because of their violence and brutality, but also because they were given free rein to loot and seize livestock and land from the non-Arab tribes whose men bolstered the rebels' ranks.

In August, the outgoing commander of the joint UN-African Union peacekeeping force in Darfur said the six-year war between rebels and government forces had effectively ended but the region remained unstable, with banditry proving a particular problem. Analysts say the continuing instability is very much linked to the question of what happened to all those fighters who answered Khartoum's call to arms only to now find themselves without jobs or money.

'The Janjaweed were paid by the government before, but now there is no payment so they are doing things like kidnapping for money,' a member of one of the constellation of rebel groups still operating in Darfur told me. 'The government doesn't have the same control over the Janjaweed that they once had. This creates a very dangerous situation.'

When I put this to Musa Hilal, he first complained that the word Janjaweed has been misused. 'There is no organised entity called the Janjaweed. . . . It is a local word that we use to refer to any person practising highway robbery or burgling houses. No one can claim he has control over unorganised criminals.'

But are those who once joined the militias disgruntled and desperate because their government stipends have dried up? 'Maybe,' he answers.

Jailani, whose predecessor as humanitarian affairs minister, along with President al-Bashir, has been charged by the International Criminal Court in relation to alleged war crimes committed in Darfur, insisted that banditry is an inevitable consequence of the conflict. 'These people are idle and illiterate and they have guns in their hands so what do you expect from them? We have to keep them busy by initiating projects for them so they can lead a quiet life and we can get rid of banditry in the area,' he said.

Asked if any of the Goal kidnappers had been involved in the fighting that has wracked the region since 2003, Jailani paused. 'That is a very interesting political question,' he replied. 'I cannot say yes or no. I'm not sure.'

Musa Hilal batted away questions regarding his role in Darfur with a well-practised ease. It is not true, he insists, that he gave orders for innocent people to be killed and villages to be destroyed. He dismissed accusations that ethnic cleansing was part of Khartoum's strategy in Darfur, insisting that Darfuris of all ethnicities have lived together and intermarried for some time.

Is he a war criminal as so many have charged? 'No, this is not true,' he replied. Does he fear being prosecuted in the future? 'No. Why should I be afraid? What evidence do they have?'

He argued that the tensions that have torn Darfur apart have been caused by external forces. 'The problem is we Darfuris of different backgrounds have become pawns in the hands of others. . . . We have become something like a commodity.

'The people of Darfur can accomplish peace themselves. If you get all the movements and the leaders, put them together for two weeks, they would reach peace. If the outsiders wash their hands of this issue we will be able to find a solution together.'

WEDNESDAY, 28 OCTOBER 2009

Protestants Surrendering their Sense of Superiority

Newton Emerson

There's not much of a Protestant ethos on display in the row over school funding. The sight of Protestants begging Minister for Education Batt O'Keeffe for money shows how far my Southern co-religionists have fallen.

The only financial transaction any self-respecting Protestant should have with someone of O'Keeffe's standing is to give him a euro with the words: 'Here's something for yourself, my good man.'

Archbishop of Dublin Most Rev. Dr John Neill delivering his Presidential Address to the Dublin and Glendalough Diocesan Synods in the Parish Centre of Christ Church, Taney, Dublin. Photograph: Dara Mac Dónaill.

Instead, we have the pathetic spectacle of Protestants acting as if O'Keeffe is not just their equal but their better. Acting as if he was their equal would be bad enough; surrendering the presumption of superiority is appalling.

Effortless superiority is the very definition of the Protestant ethos and what better sort over which to exude it than some Fianna Fáil bogman?

O'Keeffe's statements should provoke no reaction stronger than mild amusement. When he claims Protestants are wealthy and privileged, a modest nod of agreement should suffice. When he becomes flustered over legal and constitutional issues, it should be politely noted that a person of his limitations is bound to find these things confusing.

It is absurd of Protestants to imply that the funding cut was ordered by some secret Catholic professional organisation in O'Keeffe's department. Catholics are neither professional nor organised. Also, Protestants really ought not to be humouring made-up Irish names. O'Keeffe is correctly known as Barry Keith and should be referred to as such.

Under no circumstances should Protestants actually highlight the effect of Keith's decisions. People of Keith's type should not be seen to have any effect on respectable society whatsoever. If the withdrawal of funding causes hardship for certain Protestant institutions and individuals, they should conceal the fact behind a well-scrubbed façade of genteel self-reliance.

They should raise more money themselves through traditional Protestant activities such as working, saving or running a business that does not depend on corrupt links to the planning system.

They certainly should not cry poverty like some common whining Irishman.

The special pleading of the Protestant churches sounds almost Catholic. The Church of Ireland Archbishop of Dublin, the Most Rev. John Neill, calls the funding cut 'grossly unfair' and says 'a minority is as entitled to schools under their own patronage as much as the majority'. It is embarrassing to hear a Protestant clergyman use terms like 'unfair', 'entitled to' and 'minority'. Life is not fair, entitlements are for losers and the elite are always a minority.

The row has raised the question of whether Protestants need separate schools at all. Catholic schools are necessary because Catholicism is an arcane and inconsistent creed which requires years of indoctrination to have any hope of lodging in the human mind.

In Ireland, especially those areas currently under native control, Catholics are also required to learn a dead language and a false version of history. It is obvious that this necessitates a dedicated school system.

Protestantism, by contrast, is a straightforward and naturally ordered faith, allied to the default Anglo-Saxon culture of western civilisation. Armed only with a few words of warning, it should be perfectly possible for Protestant children to attend Catholic schools and emerge more or less completely unscathed by the experience.

For 90 years, Catholic schools have failed to teach anyone Irish. It seems a little far-fetched to fear that they could teach Protestants to be Catholic.

Cartoon by Martyn Turner.

TUESDAY, 3 NOVEMBER 2009

Jedward are Pure Essence of an Extinct Culture

Fintan O'Toole

Often, the most poignant and potent moment of a culture is its dying gasp. Before the end, as a world implodes, there is a last great gathering of its energies. A shaman has a vision in the forest and arrives back with a millennial vision of salvation in which the ancient spirits are revived. A writer emerges to chronicle a way of life with a steely clarity forged from the urgent knowledge that it must be recorded before it dies. A painter evokes its colours and essences with a feverish intensity imbued with the magical hope that, if only it can be captured, it will not fade. A singer sustains a plaintive dying fall on the air and, in that note, a whole world hovers on the edge of extinction.

And so we get the unbearably poignant last gasp of Celtic Tiger culture. The nation turns its lonely eyes to the last recesses of hope. Where is the shaman who can conjure up the spirits of our dying world that they may walk among us one more time? Where are the artists who can evoke the passing era with such divine intensity that we can believe, for a moment, that it will linger forever? Where are the voices that can sustain that last plangent note in which, when we close our eyes, we can imagine that the past will always be with us?

Step forward John and Edward Grimes, aka Jedward, aka the terrible twins of the *X Factor* TV show who have no discernible talent but who got enough public votes on Sunday night to stay in the competition yet again. Jedward are the pure essence of a culture we have inhabited for 15 years and that is now functionally extinct. As Simon Cowell, one of the talent show judges, puts it: 'They are completely deluded and they live in a fantasy world, but they're lovely.'

Who better to embody the nation we have been?

Admittedly, there is a certain falling off here. Traditionally, the standard of last gasps in Irish culture has been pretty high. One thinks, for example, of the great flowering of Gaelic poetry in the 18th century (exemplified by 'Caoineadh Airt Uí Laoghaire'). Or of the potent recollections of the Blasket Island writers of the 1920s and 1930s. Or of John McGahern's haunting hymns to the rhythms and speech of a rural way of life on the eve of its eclipse. There used to be a certain grandeur to these things.

Grandeur would be out of place for the Celtic Tiger, though. It wasn't big on stoicism, tragedy or nobility. It was as shallow and brazen as the reflection of a full moon in a puddle of spilt lager. It is entirely appropriate that the figures who should emerge from its twilight to sing its last lament should be ludicrous, deluded and disposable.

And Jedward do capture the essence of Tiger culture with stunning precision. Born and raised within its brassy ambit, they embody its ruling values to perfection. They have boundless ambition and no talent; phenomenal energy and no point; hyper-confidence and no substance. They are completely immune to useless emotions like embarrassment and shame. With their American accents and plastic appearance (they look like they're actually designed as models from which toy manufacturers will make Jedward dolls), they are supremely vacuous.

They are wrapped in the magical cloak of self-delusion that is woven by year after year of lavish assurance that you are utterly, unalterably wonderful.

And they are, indeed, lovely. Two years ago, they would have been worth hating, or at least holding up as examples of our folly. But now that reality, in all its relentless grimness, has overtaken the fantasies they embody, they have a deeply poignant charm. They are like indigenous peoples from tribes that have been safely conquered. While their culture was alive, and they were throwing spears, they were to be regarded with brutal disdain. Now that it's all but dead, they acquire the warm, nostalgic luminosity of the exotic.

There was, after all, something nice and cosy about self-delusion. It felt good to be released from self-awareness. It was fun to swagger. The drug of limitless self-confidence, even if (indeed especially if) it suppressed a continuing sense of failure, delivered a euphoric high. All that pointless energy made us glow.

It's not just that Jedward, by being so gloriously out of synch with the times, remind us of those boom years. Their graceless dancing does summon up the ancestral spirits of 2006, but they don't just bring us back there. They return us instead to a more innocent version of that recent past. They give us the madly disproportionate ambition, the impregnable self-regard, the supreme sense of entitlement, the shamelessness. But they do so without the harm.

What we get with Jedward is a detoxified version of the toxic cocktail of arrogance and ineptitude that has done so much harm. They allow us to relive the boom culture without its vicious consequences. Who wouldn't prefer to vote for that than for the real thing?

MONDAY, 9 NOVEMBER 2009

When Love Overcomes East-West Divisions

Derek Scally, in Berlin

While the rest of the world talks about German unity, couples like Katja and Hendrik live it. Both were born in Berlin, but Katja grew up in the western neighbourhood of Mariendorf while Hendrik spent his childhood on

Fireworks illuminate the Brandenburg Gate in Berlin, 9 November 2009, during celebrations to mark the 20th anniversary of the fall of the Berlin Wall. Photograph: Reuters/Wolfgang Rattay.

Hendrik and Katja. Photograph: Derek Scally.

the other side of the Berlin Wall in Treptow.

'We were about 5km apart as the crow flies,' says Hendrik. 'The same weather yet another world.' He had relations and penpals in West Germany but was never allowed travel there, while she had never been to East Berlin.

'I always saw the [East Berlin] television tower,' says Katja, 'but I couldn't understand the rest: I had no idea what was around it, what it looked like.' Today they live around the corner from the monumental tower, just off the pompous Soviet-style Karl Marx Allee, formerly Stalinallee.

The two are perplexed that anyone would find their relationship interesting. Yet Katja and Hendrik are a statistical rarity: two decades after 1989, just 4 per cent of German couples are of the east-west, or Ossi-Wessi variety. According to dating agency Elite Partners, four decades of

division have left different attitudes and priorities on family, work, holidays and each other.

Today some 70 per cent of 'Wessis' say they consider it important to know whether their partner is an Ossi or Wessi, while just 38 per cent of easterners said they cared.

For Katja and Hendrik their background wasn't an issue when they met at a party 11 years ago last week. 'The most important question for us was "your place or mine?"' laughs Katja. 'I don't even remember when it finally came up where we were from.' Though they didn't meet until 1998, the two experienced similar feelings of euphoria after the fall of the wall, followed by disappointment at meeting the 'other' Berliners.

'All the East Berlin girls had red hair, were studying childcare and were called Peggy and Mandy,' says Katja. 'We joked that the East Berlin men were better in bed. That research was never fully completed.' Hendrik remembers West Berlin women as an interchangeable bunch in identical clothes, all sporting pony tails.

'I remember, too, thinking how confident the West Berliners seemed, yet they were unable to talk to someone in a bar,' he says. 'The easterners lacked confidence in general but were raised to go up to people and introduce themselves.' That bit of East German nurturing is what brought Hendrik and Katja together in 1998.

Their compatible personalities have kept them together for 11 years, yet there are moments when their different pasts are present. 'Eastern men have many good sides. For instance they are generally less chauvinistic,' says Katja. 'They know how to do the dishes; you don't have to ask them.' Hendrik is pleased by the compliment, putting it down to the fact that eastern parents both worked and, out of necessity, shared the housework.

Warming to the theme, Katja says she 'can't keep her mouth shut', while Hendrik is more careful and cautious about speaking.

'I'm more likely to wait and see. Initiative was never encouraged in East German schools,' he says. 'It was always about collective thinking and never initiative.' That rings a bell with Katja. 'Today that means that Hendrik will say he'd like a new bed,' she says, 'while I'm the one who has to find and buy the new bed.' Their politics are different too: Katja has a positive view of socialism whereas Hendrik says his East Berlin childhood inoculated him against that for life.

Despite their political differences, both agree that Chancellor Merkel – born in the West, raised in the East – is a stroke of luck for Germany. 'She's not a beauty but she's charming,' says Katja. Adds Hendrik: 'She's not slick, she's slightly awkward but she has a very human air about her.' The two are philosophical about this evening's anniversary in their home town.

For them and thousands of other east-west couples here, the united German capital is an experiment in living, where their priorities and goals have changed over the years. In particular the fixation about reaching a 'West German' living standard has softened – on both sides. 'That "West standard" was only ever calculated in financial terms, salary and GDP, a big car and a home you never saw because you worked too much,' says Katja. 'What I've learned from Hendrik's eastern friends is that health, personal happiness and perhaps working a little less are all just as important.'

SATURDAY, 14 NOVEMBER 2009

Lenihan Brave to Risk Unpopularity for Country's Good

Stephen Collins

The concerted recent effort to soften up the public for swingeing budget cuts must mean that the Government has gone past the point of no return and decided to take whatever steps are necessary to begin restoring order to the public finances, regardless of the political consequences.

It seems that Brian Lenihan is willing to take the risk of going down in history as the Ernest Blythe of Fianna Fáil. The similarity of the choices faced by Blythe in 1924 and Lenihan in 2009 are uncanny. The core of the issue in both cases involved the preservation of Irish economic sovereignty at a time of deflation and rising public spending.

Blythe's solution was to cut the old age pension and public service pay by 10 per cent and it was never forgotten. To a large extent his reputation was destroyed because of the bad job he made of explaining what he had done. By contrast Lenihan is good at explaining himself. If he holds his nerve he may actually achieve the opposite reputation to Blythe and, in time, come to be

Pictured is Jack O'Connor, president of the Irish Congress of Trade Unions, at the launch of 'Congress 10 Point Plan for National Recovery' at Congress House, Parnell Square, Dublin. Photo: James Horan, Photocall Ireland.

recognised as the man who saved the country from economic disaster.

In the short term, though, it will not be easy for Lenihan or the Government. The depressing lesson of Irish politics is that the steady appeasement of powerful interest groups is much more likely to generate popular support than a genuine attempt to act in the broad national interest.

The scale of the problem now facing the country is a direct result of the way Bertie Ahern's governments pandered to two powerful lobbies: the construction industry and the public service unions. One led to the banking crisis and the other to an unsustainable increase in spending that has undermined the public finances' stability.

The world crisis certainly made matters worse but there is no escaping the fact that the underlying problem is stamped 'made in Ireland'.

The remedy will involve a lot of pain for everybody and the only thing at issue is whether it will be short and sharp or long, drawn out and possibly fatal.

It will take strong political nerves to ignore the howls of protest that will inevitably follow the budget cuts in the pay packets of public servants and welfare recipients. Some effort by Lenihan to tackle wealthy professionals, who have so far refused to lower their exorbitant fees, might make the cuts a little more palatable for ordinary citizens but it won't make the pain any easier to accept.

Both the Minister and Taoiseach have pointed out that deflation on a scale not seen since the early 1930s has actually resulted in a rise in living standards this year for those in receipt of welfare payments and has cushioned the impact on workers affected by pay cuts. Selling that message after the budget will not be easy, though.

The crucially important message that Lenihan is trying to get across is that if the pain is faced now, the country will be able to get back to growth and rising living standards in a relatively short time. Lenihan and Brian Cowen have stressed that tax revenues have fallen to 2003 levels but they are only proposing to trim spending back to 2006 levels.

If they can get spending back to the levels of three years ago and, over the course of the next four years, broaden the tax base so that it comes into balance with spending, the country will still be far better off than it has been for most of its history as an independent state.

While the public anger at the way the country was run for the past decade is justifiable, anger itself is not a solution, as Cowen pointed out. The irony is that most of the anger is being directed at those who are trying to find a solution to the country's problems rather than at those who created such a fool's paradise.

Labour Party leader Eamon Gilmore has made a habit in the Dáil of denouncing not only the Government but so-called 'hardline commentators who wish to inflict more pain on the poor' for pointing out the need to get spending under control if the country is to avoid another 1980s-style decade of depression.

While Gilmore has been strong on rhetoric, he has been very weak on realistic alternative solutions. While that tactic may buy Labour short-term popularity it will leave the party with big problems if it does manage to get into government in the next two years.

Over the past year Fine Gael has made much more of an effort to face up to reality, while still holding Fianna Fáil to account. Enda Kenny took the lead a year ago in pointing up the absurdity of the last national pay agreement, but in more recent times he has tended to give the impression that soft options are available. In the past week he strongly opposed any changes in child benefit, without specifying how savings can be made in the social welfare budget. He has promised that Fine Gael will produce detailed policies in the next few weeks and that may make the party's position more coherent.

While spending cuts remain the focus of the Government's budgetary strategy this year, it is puzzling that it appears to have put tax reform on the back burner. A significant broadening of the tax base will have to go hand in hand with controlling spending.

It is striking that Fianna Fáil again appears to be funking the task of bringing in a property tax. For 30 years experts have repeatedly pointed to the need for a property tax, on the grounds of equity and economic efficiency.

However, the party that irresponsibly abolished rates has stubbornly resisted common sense for fear of antagonising voters. Given that it is willing to risk the public anger at spending cuts there is no reason why it should not at least begin work on devising a rational, fair property tax.

THURSDAY, 19 NOVEMBER 2009

Heartbreak of Henry's Hand of God, Part II

Emmet Malone, in the Stade de France

A heroic Irish performance counted for nothing last night at the Stade de France in Paris where the referee's failure to spot Thierry Henry's use of his hand when setting up the night's decisive goal for William Gallas ended the visitors' hopes of making it to South Africa next summer.

It was, as they might say on the television, shameful stuff from the Barcelona striker whose carefully constructed public image is largely based on a projected sense of fairness and decency, but that will be forgotten by June 11th next year when

France rather than Ireland will be limbering up for their first game of the World Cup finals.

Thanks to towering performances by Irish players in almost every area, Giovanni Trapattoni's men came within a whisker of defeating their hosts by the two-goal margin required during the initial 90 minutes.

Chances missed by Damien Duff and Robbie Keane will come to feature in another chapter in Ireland's book of historical World Cup woes. Henry, though, is sure to go down as the real villain of the piece.

Had Ireland fought and then faded as they had on Saturday none of it would have mattered. But this time, they were actually the better side, their energetic assault on their hosts paying dividends from the start as they created a steady stream of scoring chances while the French struggled to find any sort of rhythm.

After all the talk of the threat Ireland might pose from set-pieces, it was from a ball won in open play by John O'Shea that the Irish goal came, the Manchester United defender feeding Kevin Kilbane to send an unmarked Duff beyond the French back four to the line from where he pulled it back low for Keane to slot home from a yard or two outside the six yard box.

Trapattoni's men must have felt they'd earned their lead several times over with the way they had taken the game to their opponents, but the French will wonder quite how they defended the move so poorly with Bacary Sagna losing Duff entirely while three defenders were stranded as Keane arrived to stroke the ball in.

Even prior to that it had been the Irish who had been the game's dominant force, even if they never quite found their range in or around the danger area.

Ireland's Robbie Keane (2nd right) scores a goal against France's Hugo Lloris (centre), as William Gallas (right) and Patrice Evra (left) react in their World Cup qualifying playoff return leg match at the Stade de France stadium, in Saint Denis near Paris, 18 November 2009. Photograph: Reuters/Benoit Tessier.

France's William Gallas (2nd left) scores a goal against Ireland's Shay Given (centre) in their World Cup qualifying playoff return leg match at the Stade de France stadium, in Saint Denis near Paris, 18 November 2009. Photograph: Reuters/Charles Platiau.

Liam Lawrence, one of a string of outstanding performers over the course of the night, and Duff both had good chances to pick out one or other of the Irish strikers but neither quite judged the weight of their cross correctly and the locals successfully cleared their lines.

When the visitors got their first corner after 11 minutes, it actually was the French who nearly scored. Duff's ball from the left sailed over a crowded area to Andre-Pierre Gignac who broke at speed towards the left wing with Lawrence scurrying after him. The Toulouse striker shook off his man and fed Anelka who in turn pushed it between a couple of white shirts for Henry, whose shot was blocked by Whelan's lunging dive.

The Irish, on the other hand, created a succession of half chances while Duff engineered another one for his captain 25 minutes in. Keane swiped at it as it bounced in front of him but Hugo Lloris, as he did again and again over the course of the night, dealt with it rather coolly under pressure.

In short, Ireland had the best of the opening period and as the players made their way towards the dressingrooms, the crowd made it clear they were less than pleased. Their boos must have sounded sweet to the tired Irish players.

The home side's nerves, though, were to be further strained immediately after the break with first O'Shea missing the target from close range, but a tight angle, and then Duff failing to convert when put clean through on Lloris, who saved well but really shouldn't have had the opportunity.

It was perhaps Ireland's best spell of the game and they were aided by the succession of sloppy French errors. In midfield, Lassana Diarra never seemed to get a moment to direct his side's play in the way he had on Saturday. Anelka and Henry were subject to constant attention too, as when the latter broke quickly after Duff's scoring chance only to have his shot smothered by O'Shea and Given together.

O'Shea limped off shortly afterwards and the

balance of the game swung back in the home side's favour. Just when it might have looked to the Irish supporters, however, that their team might have passed up their best chances, the visitors came agonisingly close to scoring, with Lawrence playing a terrific low through ball for Keane, who then pushed the ball fractionally too far past Lloris with the result that he couldn't quite turn it home.

It was Ireland's last chance of normal time and a miss, the travelling supporters might well have sensed even then, they would rue as the night wore on. Sure enough, Henry stepped up to steal the show for the hosts eight minutes into extra time.

Gallas bundled the ball into the net from a couple of yards and, though they fought valiantly to save themselves, the Irish players were, in due course, bundled out of the World Cup.

SATURDAY, 21 NOVEMBER 2009

Hit and Myth

Brian Boyd

In July of this year, President Obama was to speak to the American people on prime-time television to announce details of important changes to the healthcare system in the US. He requested the usual 9 p.m. slot from the NBC network. NBC replied by saying that they would be delighted to offer the president the 8 p.m. slot. The president said thanks but 9 p.m. is the traditional time for addressing the nation. NBC said the 8 p.m. slot is great – you'll love it, Mr President. Obama asked whether there was a problem. NBC said there was indeed a problem, Mr President. And its name was Susan Boyle.

That evening at 9 p.m., NBC was showing *America's Got Talent* and the exclusive on the show was an interview with the *Britain's Got Talent* runner-up. Despite the fact that President Obama knew it was a pre-recorded interview with Boyle, he confessed to NBC that he was a fan and didn't want to upset the viewing public by bumping the

Susan Boyle. Photograph: Hugh Stewart.

very popular show back to a later slot. The president talked to the nation about healthcare reform at 8 p.m., before being roundly trounced in the ratings by Susan's Boyle pre-recorded interview at 9 p.m.

By this stage, an estimated 300 million people had watched the now famous YouTube clip of the 48-year-old Scottish singer making her debut on *Britain's Got Talent* on April 11th. The video was a seven-minute hop, skip and jump into global recognition.

On Monday, Susan Boyle's debut album, *I Dreamed A Dream*, will be released internationally (it has been available in Ireland since yesterday). On September 4th of this year, though, when the album was pre-listed on the Amazon website, it very quickly broke all records for pre-sales of an album – any album.

Even before the pre-sales, in a mountain-goes-to-Mohammed scenario, Oprah Winfrey sent a film crew to Boyle's hometown of Blackburn in Scotland to interview the star during the run of *Britain's Got Talent* in April. Boyle couldn't travel to Oprah's studio in Chicago as the producers of the talent show thought it would give her an 'unfair advantage' over other competitors on the show – yes, the logic eludes me too.

In June of this year, while his country's economy was floundering and the ongoing wars in Iraq and Afghanistan were continuing to cause grave concern, UK prime minister Gordon Brown revealed that he made space in his schedule to make two telephone calls to enquire about Boyle's state of health following reports she had been admitted to the Priory Clinic which specialises in addiction and mental health treatments.

Obama, Oprah, Gordon Brown. Three hundred million hits on YouTube. History-making pre-sales on Amazon.

This week sees 'Exclusives!' in *OK!* magazine and various tabloids. Celebrity Twitter users are all tweeting 'til they drop; mainstream news schedules are being cleared for Monday's official release date. All that's missing is that Osama Bin Laden has added her as a friend on his Facebook page and given the album a five-star review.

But why wouldn't the world react in such a manner? This is a beautiful and (in these recession-ravaged times) heart-warming story about how an ugly duckling transformed into a pitch-perfect swan right in front of our very eyes. When she first stepped out in front of the judges on *Britain's Got Talent* (Simon Cowell, Piers Morgan and Amanda Holden) in a nondescript dress that screamed 'frumpy mad aunt', she came across as gauche and deluded. The urbane and sophisticated judges

reacted to her with a distasteful mix of pity and scorn. Audience members are seen rolling their eyes at Boyle's appearance and openly laughing at her as she spoke in wide-eyed excitement about her showbiz dream.

Then she began to sing 'I Dreamed A Dream' from *Les Misérables*. Jaws dropped, the jeers turned to cheers, shock and surprise (and, later, shame) were evident on the judges' faces. The underdog battled through, put it up to the sneering bullies and got a standing ovation. What a story. It would put the plot of any Broadway or West End musical to shame.

Go back to the first two minutes of the famous YouTube clip where she is mini-profiled. The very first image hundreds of millions of people ever see of Susan Boyle is of her stuffing a sandwich into her mouth in a most 'unladylike' manner. The *mise en scène* continues as she is interviewed to camera. We learn that she is unemployed, lives with her cat and has never been kissed. But in classic showbiz fable fashion she has A Dream. This is all presented to us within 35 seconds. The narrative is then ratcheted up further for dramatic effect when she appears in front of the judges and the audience and is immediately judged – in a very negative manner – solely on her appearance. And, watching at home, we are complicit in all of this.

The first question is from Simon Cowell: 'Hi, what's your name, darling?' The suffix here is the most patronising term you can use to address a middle-aged woman. Cowell then rolls his eyes in hurt disbelief when Boyle says she is 47 (because she looks years older) and Piers Morgan visibly winces as his eyes travel up and down her body. Boyle then attempts a raunchy pelvic-thrust but all she can manage is a disturbing and perverse approximation of a pelvic-thrust. Cue laughter and disdainful looks. When Boyle says she'd like to be as successful as Elaine Paige, the camera cuts to an audience member who reacts with distaste bordering on horror that this weird frump on the stage could even dare to emulate the sleek sophistication

Actress Catherine Walker gets up close and personal in **Knives in Hens**, *a play by David Horrower, staged at Dublin's Smock Alley Theatre. Photograph: Pat Redmond.*

of such a glamorous performer. Piers Morgan laughs scornfully as Boyle announces she is going to sing a song from the hugely successful and much admired *Les Misérables* show. We are now at the very top of the garden path.

In his massively influential book *The Hero with a Thousand Faces* (1949), the US mythologist Joseph Campbell wrote about the journey taken by the archetypal hero figure in all mythologies. Campbell details the fixed series of steps taken: the hero starts in the ordinary world; he then receives a call to enter a strange world; the hero must face tasks and trials and survive a severe challenge. If the hero survives, he will receive a great gift.

Campbell called this process the 'monomyth' – the cycle of the journey of the hero. He borrowed the term 'monomyth' from Joyce's *Finnegans Wake*. Campbell's book is perhaps best known now for being the text George Lucas consulted and

borrowed from to create the *Star Wars* films. Lucas freely acknowledges his use of Campbell's work in interviews.

A famous Hollywood producer, Christopher Vogler, advised the Walt Disney studio to use Campbell's book as a guide for scriptwriters – which is why films such as *Aladdin* and *The Lion King* use the 'monomyth' in their stories. The Harry Potter books follow a similar pattern. It is the template for a very large portion of light entertainment shows and is used in its rawest form by reality TV shows. Witness the 'journey' Jade Goody took on Big Brother; the 'journey' Gareth Gates and his debilitating stutter took on Pop Idol.

Curiously, neither Goody, Gates nor Boyle won their respective reality competitions, but all received an even bigger 'gift' afterwards.

If you have ever wondered why so many reality TV contestants over-use the word 'journey' when describing their experience, it's because the producers of the show know it sets off an alert in our minds that a narrative arc is being set up.

Susan Boyle 'started in the ordinary world' (a council house in a small Scottish town); she 'received the call to enter a strange world' (the *Britain's Got Talent* regional heats); she 'faced tasks and trials and survived a great challenge' (the scorn and mocking laughter of the judges and audience on the show) and she 'received a great gift' (worldwide fame and a multimillion pound bank account).

But why Susan Boyle? Why not you or me? Here's why: she uniquely had not only the requisite back story (council house, learning difficulties, never been kissed, etc.) but the talent to unlock the 'reward': her remarkable singing voice. And for what it's worth, her debut album is excellent – as MOR albums go.

She also has a gimlet-eyed ambition. Boyle has been presented to us as an ingénue. She is not. Way before *Britain's Got Talent*, she had a professional vocal coach. In 1999 she cropped up singing on a charity CD which attracted very positive reviews (albeit in the regional Scottish press). Her Wikipedia entry has it that she attended drama school and had previously appeared at the Edinburgh Fringe.

This is not to say she is in any way a fake or a fraud. The producers of *Britain's Got Talent* knew they had something special when she walked in the audition door during the untelevised regional heats.

Here was a compelling narrative arc in-waiting that ticked all the mythological boxes and around which a whole massive-ratings show could be built. They merely – as most in the media do – 'massaged' her story. Crucially, though, in that famous seven-minute YouTube video they gave us a beautifully condensed jump-edit version of Campbell's book.

'I suppose it's a bit of a Cinderella story, isn't it?' Susan Boyle said to reporters last week. Cinderella? Isn't that the 'classic folk tale which

embodies a myth element of unjust oppression and triumphant reward?' The best of luck to her.

Fear not, Flood Victims – the Dáil is to Take Statements!

Miriam Lord

'Bridie, Bridie! Our worries are over!' It's a hopeless scene – the house, and everything in it, is destroyed. It's wet, dark and cold. Plaster is coming off the walls. The furniture is ruined. The kitchen has become the shallow end and granny is floating across the livingroom on a lilo.

Then word comes from Leinster House: the Dáil has decided to take statements on the flooding crisis. Following a major push from Fine Gael and Labour, there will also be a 30-minute question and answer session in the chamber with John Gormley. Bridie heaves a big sigh of relief as she fishes a small trout from the gusset of her waders.

In flooded homes and overcrowded dinghies yesterday, joy was unconfined. The waterlogged and weary wept into their snorkels when the good news from Dublin bobbed up with the sewage and the carpet. For, at last, there was hope on the horizon. The Dáil was going to discuss the floods.

The exchanges were heated, and in a day when the normal Dáil staff was outside the gates on a 24-hour strike, anything could have happened. Thankfully, members didn't take advantage of the lack of ushers. If anything, they were less rowdy. Perhaps they were aware that the Army was on duty in place of the ushers.

The Army personnel on gate duty in Leinster House yesterday looked very smart in their uniforms with their distinctive red caps. For the occasion, they mustered in 'service dress number two'. This, apparently, is one step up for ordinary greens and beret, but one step below the row of 40 medals on the chest.

Because of the strike the Seanad was deemed surplus to requirements. The Dáil bars and restaurants were shut and the public gallery remained closed.

And while the strikes were discussed, there was no doubt that the flooding emergency around the country was the big issue of the day. The wide geographical spread of disaster meant that a large number of deputies wanted to have their say for the local papers. Brian Cowen conducted Leaders' Questions with dry socks and a serenity not usually associated with his Dáil performances in times of crisis. This was because he had donned the Wellingtons of Leadership the day before and moved among the afflicted with words of comfort.

The Dáil was due to discuss the situation at 7 p.m. However, this wasn't enough for Enda Kenny and Eamon Gilmore, who wanted a longer debate. Whether it was held at seven or five in the evening made not one whit of difference, but it gave them an opportunity to come over all Old Testament, blaming the Government for trying to drown the people while evoking vivid images of a sodden citizenry terrified about 'where the next flood might come from'. Enda and Eamon were in full spate, aided by the frothing tributaries of their party colleagues. They demanded an immediate discussion.

'This is an extraordinary day,' said Eamon, not least for those deputies representing constituencies 'that are under water'. Fine Gael's Men from Atlantis nodded their agreement.

They sat in a long line in the second and third

The rising flood water pours through a householder's property at Craughwell, Co. Galway. Photograph: Joe O'Shaughnessy.

An abandoned car on the main road at Caherlea near Claregalway, Co. Galway. In the background is a recently built flooded house. Photograph: Joe O'Shaughnessy.

rows – primarily deputies from Cork, Clare, Galway and Westmeath. It was interesting to note that all the party's TDs in the first-row seats were from Dublin, a place largely unaffected by the flooding. The exception was Big Phil Hogan from Carlow-Kilkenny, but as Phil is the tallest man in the House, he doesn't mind the floods so much.

Under Standing Orders, the Ceann Comhairle said he couldn't give them the sort of debate they wanted. Uproar. 'The river Shannon is now a foot higher than it was in 1954,' bellowed Enda. A debate would be very relevant 'to so many people whose floors are coming up in front of their eyes'.

The Taoiseach did his best to calm matters. 'Minister Mansergh has been out and about,' he soothed. Various projects are 'coming on stream'. Consternation.

'What about Bandon and Skibbereen?' roared PJ Sheehan.

Biffo muttered something about the Shannon. 'Sure Dev promised to drain it 40 years ago,' snorted James Bannon of Athlone.

'We might as well be on strike,' bellowed Padraic McCormack of Galway West. 'The country's up to its ears and you won't allow us debate it,' chimed in Paul Connaughton, of Galway East. 'The Dáil should be dealing with this emergency!' wailed Ciarán Lynch of Cork.

The House argued over the format and timing of the debate. They decided to have a quick adjournment to decide what to do. They had a debate. It's over now. The country is still under water. (But the local newspaper coverage will be great.)

FRIDAY, 27 NOVEMBER 2009

Bishops Lied and Covered up

Mary Raftery

There is one searing, indelible image to be found in the pages of the Dublin diocesan report on clerical child abuse. It is of Fr Noel Reynolds, who admitted sexually abusing dozens of children, towering over a small girl as he brutally inserts an object into her vagina and then her back passage.

That object is his crucifix.

The report details how this man was left as parish priest of Glendalough (and in charge of the local primary school) for almost three years after parents had complained about him to former archbishop of Dublin Desmond Connell during the 1990s.

In 1997, he was finally moved and appointed as chaplain to the National Rehabilitation Hospital in Dún Laoghaire. The report helpfully informs us that there were 94 children aged 18 or under as inpatients here. The hospital authorities were told nothing of Reynolds's past or of suspicions that he was a child abuser.

This kind of callous disregard for the safety of children is found over and over again in the report. Bishops lied, cheated and covered up, almost as a matter of course, in a display of relentless cynicism spanning decades. Children were blithely sacrificed to protect priests, the institution and its assets. It is, consequently, difficult to avoid the conclusion that what lies at the heart of the Catholic Church (at least in Ireland) is a profound and widespread corruption.

The Dublin report divides the bulk of its analysis into chapters devoted to individual priest abusers. But reading through the stomach-churning details of their crimes, another parallel reality appears. Behind almost each one of these paedophiles was at least one bishop (often more) who knew of the abuse, but failed to protect children.

Some of them, Pontius Pilate-like, washed their hands, merely reporting it up the line. Others actively protected the criminals in their midst by destroying files and withholding information. Their handling of complaints is variously described as 'particularly bad', 'disastrous' and 'catastrophic'.

Dermot Ryan stands out as the most callous of the Dublin archbishops. He failed properly to investigate complaints against at least six of the worst offending priests. Kevin MacNamara was little better, but his tenure was considerably briefer, limiting some of the damage he did.

John Charles McQuaid is severely criticised in one case, but it was not within the commission's remit to examine his reign in any significant detail. His response to the pornographic photos of two children taken by one of his priests is a damning indictment of the impact of priestly celibacy. He viewed the criminal act as an expression of 'wonderment' by the priest at the nature of the female body.

And what of Desmond Connell, perhaps the most reviled of them all? A complex picture emerges of a man unsuited to the task facing him, attempting to deal with the enormous scale of abuse in the archdiocese, and ultimately failing. While he did, for instance, engage with the civil authorities, unlike his predecessors, he nonetheless continued to maintain secrecy over much of what the diocese knew of their child-abusing priests.

As for the many Dublin auxiliary bishops, two stand out as being particularly awful. There is arguably enough evidence in this report to send bishops James Kavanagh (now deceased) and Donal O'Mahony (retired) to prison for failing to report crimes. Or at least, there would be if there existed such an offence. Incredibly, there is none.

We certainly used to have one; called misprision of felony, it was conveniently dropped from the statute books in 1998 when the felony laws changed. The effect was that no priest, bishop, or indeed lay person, could be charged with failing to report criminal activity of which they were aware. What a sigh of relief the bishops of Ireland must have breathed.

The report describes Bishop O'Mahony's involvement in the cases of 13 priests from its sample of 46 under investigation. It mentions that he was aware of allegations against several more. His cover-up over his 21 years in office was extensive.

Bishop Kavanagh directly attempted to pervert the course of justice by seeking to influence one Garda investigation and by convincing a family to drop a complaint against another priest. He appears at various stages in a number of other cases, always failing to act to protect children.

Bishop Donal Murray of Limerick is also indicted as having handled a number of complaints badly. He will have very serious questions to answer over the coming days.

Recently retired bishop of Ossory Laurence Forristal equally stands condemned, which is all the more egregious as he was in charge of the archdiocese's efforts during the 1990s to respond to the crisis and draw up child protection guidelines.

Bishop James Moriarty of Kildare and Leighlin, retired Bishop Brendan Comiskey and Auxiliary Bishop of Dublin Eamon Walsh also all knew of complaints of abuse at various stages.

A week before the broadcast in 2002 of RTÉ television's *Prime Time* Cardinal Secrets (which led to the establishment of the Dublin commission), Cardinal Connell engaged in a pre-emptive strike. He had refused to appear on the programme. He chose instead to circulate each of his 200 parishes with a letter read out at every Mass that Sunday. In it, he apologised for the failures of the past, but blamed them on a lack of understanding within the church of paedophilia.

The commission is categorical in its refusal to accept this plea of ignorance as an excuse. It refers bluntly to the inconsistency between such claims

and the decision in 1986 to take out an insurance policy to protect church assets from abuse victims. At that time, we are told, the archdiocese knew of allegations of child sex abuse against 20 of its priests.

The report further notes the documented history of the church's detailed awareness of paedophilia as both crime and sin spanning the past 2,000 years. The first reference dates from AD 153.

Finally, the report refers to the fact that archbishop Ryan displayed as early as 1981 a complete understanding of both the recidivist nature of paedophilia and the devastating damage it caused to child victims. There had been a consistent denial from church authorities that anyone knew anything about either of these key factors until very recently.

Perhaps most damning of all is the report's findings as to the general body of priests in Dublin. While it gives credit to a small few who courageously pursued complaints, it adds that 'the vast majority simply chose to turn a blind eye'.

What emerges most clearly from the report is that priests, bishops, archbishops and cardinals had the greatest difficulty in telling right from wrong, and crucially that their determination of what constituted wrongdoing was vastly different from that of the population at large.

This fact is worthy of reflection on the part of all those who remain connected to the church through its continuing and often central involvement in the provision of services such as education and health throughout the country.

In 2003, ex-governor of Oklahoma Frank Keating drew parallels between the behaviour of some US Catholic bishops and the Cosa Nostra. It drew a storm of protest, and he resigned from his position as chairman of the church-appointed oversight committee on child abuse.

However, it is not too far-fetched a comparison to the Irish church in the light of the three investigations into its behaviour we have had to date. The organised, premeditated pattern of secrecy and concealment of crime is worthy of the world's most notorious criminal fraternity.

Springboks Scalp Sees out Stellar Year

Gerry Thornley

Ireland's most stellar of rugby years could hardly have been rounded off on a more satisfying note. By dint of outmuscling, out-lasting and ultimately outthinking the Springboks, Ireland completed a hat-trick of home wins over South Africa, an all-time record of 11 matches without defeat, and completed a first unbeaten calendar year, comprised of 10 wins and one draw, since 1985 – but that contained just four matches.

Considering where they were at this point last year – grimly clinging on to eighth in the world after a taut win over Argentina had followed the All Blacks' bloodless coup a week before at Croke Park – it's been some turnaround.

Following on from a first Grand Slam in 61 years, this past month has represented further progress, albeit with room for more.

'A coach has to say yes to that one,' joked Declan Kidney. 'Yeah, I think there are little areas that we can look to improve on. Our defence is going pretty well. Les (Kiss, defence coach) won't be happy that there was a try that went in today but that's the standard that the man sets.

'In attack we didn't score a try, so obviously there will be areas that we'll need to do that in.

Ireland's Paul O'Connell clashes with South Africa's Danie Rossouw (left) and Andries Bekker at Croke Park. Photograph: Eric Luke.

Thurles Sarsfields (Tipperary) v Newtownshandrum (Cork) in the AIB Munster GAA Hurling Senior Club Championship quarter final. Newtownshandrum's Ben O'Connor celebrates at the final whistle as Alan Kennedy of Sarsfields lies dejected. Photograph: ©INPHO/James Crombie.

And then there's a whole series of things we'll have to learn by dealing with playing away from home. There are a lot of away matches coming up now – London, Paris, we'll go to New Zealand for a couple of weeks and then finish off in Brisbane in June.'

Ultimately, as one suspected, Ireland not only wanted it more, fortune also favoured the more ambitious side. Ireland showed more of a willingness to keep the ball in hand and counter, whereas South Africa virtually ran out of all ambition until desperation demanded otherwise in the end game.

Aptly in this golden year, no Ireland rugby team has ever been so infused with Gaelic playing roots, and once again no one epitomised this more than Rob Kearney, who was simply sensational. He could surely have played Aussie Rules too, while Tommy Bowe was equally assured under the high ball and, helped by Jonathan Sexton spiralling the ball huge distances, Ireland won the ping-pong too. This was the biter being bit.

That said, South Africa's penchant for aerial bombardment must make them Kearney's favourite opposition. Had the Boks forgotten the Lions tour? Ruan Pienaar is an experienced international, with

35 caps going back four years. On for Morne Steyn and presented with clean scrum ball in the middle of the pitch inside the last 10 minutes, he merely hoofed it down Kearney's throat one more time. Eh, had he not been watching the first hour?

The Springboks were undoubtedly weary and not quite at optimum strength, but they weren't far from it either and were undoubtedly up for this grudge match. At times it felt as if the fog could have been cordite.

Most of the Springboks sullenly made off for the tunnel without returning the guard of honour which the Ireland team afforded them in one of rugby's most cherished age-old customs. There was huge rancour in the Ireland camp over this basic lack of courtesy but then these Boks revel in their hard-man, confrontational image.

Their gracious and articulate captain John Smit – without whom they'd have hardly any PR worth the name – and coach Pieter de Villiers both magnanimously accepted Ireland were worthy winners but it was a disappointing lack of courtesy from a team led by the World Cup-winning captain.

But that couldn't deflect from a memorable, rip-roaring tussle to the backdrop of a mist as heavy as soup. De Villiers was so discommoded by it all he even called it a 'night' game.

Declan Kidney's Ireland have an honesty of effort from one to 15 and play for the full 80 minutes. They showed this memorably in the wins over England and Wales, and underlined it this month with the last-ditch draw against Australia and denying the Boks to the final whistle on Saturday.

Fittingly, in both instances, it was Brian O'Driscoll who had the final say, first with his try against the Wallabies and here with his impression of a human missile when bringing Zane Kirchner and the Boks to a bone-shuddering stop in the game's last play.

Asked for his take on the Kirchner tackle, O'Driscoll grinned and said: 'He was getting hit whether he had the ball or not. That was my take on it.'

Let's be Honest: Lying has Always been Part of our Culture

Ann Marie Hourihane

At last we have it. We've waited for years for an explanation as to why the Irish are so mysterious, creative and spiritual, as well as being such effective communicators. We have had endless discussions about this rather pleasing problem, and books have been written about it, and foreign professors have come over and told us how fabulous we are, without ever really explaining why. The Brits shook their colonial heads in wonder at the Taig capacity both to lie and to charm. We have always blamed imperialism. But now we have the real explanation – it is mental reservation.

You know how it is. We have produced the most wonderful literature in the world – Wilde, Joyce, Beckett, blah, blah, blah. Sure you can fill in the gaps yourselves at this stage, and David McSavage did a nice job on Irish artistic heritage on RTÉ television last Monday night. Yet we do have a couple of tiny blind spots, in areas such as banking, honest politics, running a health service, teaching our children to read, planning, paying taxes and stuff like that.

How to reconcile these two opposing phenomena? Well, this is where mental reservation comes in. Mental reservation is a happy place that you can go to in your head when reality starts to disagree with you. Mental reservation is an elegant and fluid concept as explained in the Murphy report on child abuse in the Dublin diocese: 'It permits a churchman knowingly to convey a misleading impression to another person without being guilty of lying.'

This came as news to quite a lot of people, even some who have theology degrees such as my

Cartoon by Martyn Turner.

colleague Breda O'Brien, who wrote about mental reservation two days ago.

But then the whole slippery genius of mental reservation just goes to show you the endless creativity of the Catholic Church. It is astounding that it can come up with this sort of thing pretty well ad infinitum. The more we learn about the church's contortions around the issue of sexual assault of children, the more it seems to resemble something founded not so much by St Peter as by Lewis Carroll.

Mental reservation could be something that Carroll's Queen came up with in a world where words mean what you want them to mean, and the aristocracy sometimes believes six impossible things before breakfast. The writhing arguments of the church authorities are something to see. It is all quite *Alice in Wonderland*, and the bishops, up until very recently, had the clothes for it. Perhaps a mental reservation is actually a church property, standing in its own well-tended grounds, where

the clergy can shelter from reality forever.

But let's move away from Ireland's Catholic clergy for a moment and look at the idea of mental reservation for a little while longer. Let's stand back and admire it, because it has bled into secular life. Come on, mental reservation covers everything from adultery to tax avoidance. It is a liars' charter. Bill Clinton, that nice Protestant boy, has obviously carved out whole prairies of mental reservation for himself over which he can gallop while pretending he did not have sexual relations with Monica Lewinsky, and also that he had never cheated at golf.

As a nation we have given the glittering jewel of mental reservation to the world, yet it remains strongest at home, where politicians have lied to various tribunals quite shamelessly. But despite all the publicity and the revelations of the various tribunals – or perhaps because of them – we became a bit inured to their findings.

It is the Ryan and Murphy reports on crimes against children and how that issue was dealt with by church and State that have finally proved the poor Northern Loyalists right: Home Rule always was Rome Rule. You were right, lads. We couldn't run the country on our own. We're going to have to import civic virtue on a massive scale for the foreseeable future.

Not only are we unfamiliar with the truth, we also seem to have a problem when it comes to institutions. We are too loyal to them. We seem to like the tribal aspects of belonging to an institution – us against them – and this obsessive love is not confined to members of religious organisations. There is a certain Irish love for circling the wagons, no matter what rot lies inside the circle, or how many decent and distressed people are left outside it.

On Friday, the Religious Affairs Correspondent of this newspaper, Patsy McGarry, highlighted the Murphy commission report's finding that in the face of sexual crimes against children, the church sought to protect itself, its reputation and its assets above everything else. 'It was a case of the institution *uber alles*,' he wrote.

Without in any way minimising the connivance of church authorities in criminal matters, that sentence could be applied to a lot of our political parties – in fact all of them – and many other institutions of the Republic as well. It doesn't matter who gets the job, as long as it is one of ours. That is how our mansion of mediocrity has been built. Let's be honest about it: it's only the phrase mental reservation that is new to us.

SATURDAY, 5 DECEMBER 2009

Tiger Caught by the Tales

George Kimball

The former Elin Nordegren can hardly have been pleased by those photographs of her husband with Rachel Urchitel in the *National Enquirer* two days earlier, but that wasn't what set her on the warpath. Even in the face of evidence to the contrary, Urchitel was still denying everything, but it has been reported that, in search of independent confirmation, Elin picked up Tiger Woods's mobile phone.

Exactly what she found remains unknown, but within hours a panic-stricken Woods was leaving a voicemail on Jaimee Grubbs's answering machine, asking her to remove her name from her voicemail message. By midnight, according to the reports, the row was in full swing, and by 2 a.m., Woods was trying to flee the premises.

We don't want to spoil anyone's illusions, but it should probably be noted that Woods was neither the first nor the last man for whom the life of a professional golfer provided unlimited opportunities for extramarital sex. Woods was engaging in a tradition nearly as old as the tour itself. What has set him apart from his forebears and the Generation X golfers who have followed him is that, technologically speaking, Woods came of age at precisely the wrong time.

The golfers who were chasing women when he joined the professional ranks in 1996 – some of them just a few years his senior – did so without the benefit of mobile phones and laptops. Many of them would, to this day, be befuddled by a text message.

And while those who came along after Woods grew up in the age of multitasking and iPhones, they were also savvy enough to recognise the need for discretion, aware that even erased e-mails and text messages can leave a footprint, and that if push ever came to shove, somebody might subpoena your hard drive.

The 'Tiger' nickname was given to him by his father when he was but a club-swinging toddler. However, in his college days at Stanford, Eldrick Tont Woods was known to his golfing teammates as Urkel, after the socially awkward character who represented the quintessential nerd on the TV sitcom *Family Matters*.

The teenage Woods was far from a ladies' man. He was reputedly the least athletically gifted member of the basketball squad the golf team fielded in a Stanford intra-mural league. His teammate, Notah Begay, also told me Woods was the worst dancer on the Cardinal golf team – not an inconsiderable feat, when one recalls that it also included Casey Martin, who even then suffered from a painful hereditary foot condition that eventually led him to unsuccessfully petition for a waiver which would have allowed him to use a motorised cart on the PGA Tour. And when it came to interaction with the opposite sex, Tiger made his namesake, Steve Urkel, look like Casanova.

Tiger's tenure in Palo Alto lasted but two years. Having abandoned the carefree life of a college student for the world of professional golf, how long did it take the nerd to transform himself into Tiger Woods, horndog? Not long at all, apparently, according to my friend and former colleague Charlie Pierce.

In the spring of 1997, shortly before Woods won the first of his 14 majors at the Masters, Pierce negotiated the labyrinth of red tape his handlers had built around him, and was, for a short time, granted almost unlimited access for an *Esquire* profile.

Six months into his professional career, Woods was like a child in a sweetshop. His zeal in pursuit of young (and some not-so-young) ladies sometimes seemed as obsessively driven as his pursuit of golf perfection.

Even back in 1997, Pierce recalled this week, it was 'one of the worst-kept secrets on the PGA Tour. Everybody knew. Everybody had a story. Occasionally somebody saw it, but nobody wanted to talk about it, except in bar-room whispers late at night. Tiger's people at the International Management Group (IMG) visibly got the vapours if you even implied anything about it.'

Pierce's *Esquire* piece did not detail this emergent aspect of Woods's personality, but it did repeat a couple of off-colour stories he told in the back seat of a limousine. As they ran counter to the image IMG was carefully developing, Pierce was widely excoriated and his became the first name on IMG's informal JEOT (Journalistic Enemies of Tiger) dossier.

Befitting that status, Pierce has now found himself in sudden demand as the go-to guy. 'From that moment on,' Pierce recalled in a blog posted on *Esquire*'s site a few days ago, 'the marketing cocoon around [Woods] became almost impenetrable. The Tiger Woods that was constructed for corporate consumption was spotless and smooth, an edgeless brand easily peddled to sheikhs and shakers.'

Pro golfers have nothing on other professional athletes when it comes to the pursuit Dan Jenkins described as 'chasing wool' (pursuing women), and when the old Cuban-born baseballer Luis Tiant famously joked that 'there's no such thing as an ugly white woman', the witticism played to the worst fear of the racist element.

There are those, no doubt, who have openly rooted for Woods to fail at every turn, and their sentiments can only have been exacerbated five years ago when he married a Scandinavian beauty who could not have been whiter. At the same time, it should probably be noted here that one could comb pretty much the world's entire female population without coming up with a racial match for Eldrick Woods: quarter African-American, quarter Thai, quarter Chinese, one-eighth Cherokee, one-eighth Caucasian (Dutch). In some southern states, Woods would have been violating anti-miscegenation laws no matter who he'd married.

The union with Nordegren was facilitated by Jesper Parnevik, who was employing her as a nanny when Woods asked him to be a conduit in asking her out. Recent events have apparently led the Swedish golfer to reassess the wisdom of that introduction.

'We probably thought he was a better guy than he is,' said Parnevik when the Golf Channel interviewed him this week. 'I would probably need to apologise to her – and to hope she uses a driver next time instead of a three-iron.'

The late-night battle at Windermere resulted in the police being summoned to the gated community in the early hours of November 27th, after Woods managed to hit both a water hazard (a fire hydrant) and a fixed obstacle (a tree). Nordegren's aim was slightly better: she shattered the glass on the back window, supposedly to facilitate her by-then unconscious husband's escape, although even

Golfer Tiger Woods gets a kiss from his wife, Elin, in happier times. Revelations in December 2009 about several affairs threatened his career as well as his marriage. Photograph: Shaun Best/Reuters.

47

the Windermere cops must have been able to figure out what had actually happened.

What Woods really needed right then was one of IMG's spin doctors, because the couple's version appeared so preposterous that it just begged for the journalistic inquiries that followed, to say nothing of the intervention of the Florida Highway Patrol, which felt constrained to take action when the local cops seemed overly intimidated.

Woods might have remained the victim in the eyes of the public, but instead of one unseemly story in the *National Enquirer*, the result has been a veritable flood of mistress tales – at last count, there were at least three.

Grubbs has already made her texts and voice-mail available to a TV programme. Uchitel declined to confirm a sexual relationship with Woods, who allegedly paid for her ticket to Australia when she joined him there a few weeks ago, but it might be noted that though she lives and works in New York, she showed up in Hollywood this week, accompanied by her lawyer.

This whole mess is going to result in a lot of billable hours before it's through, in fact. Even the next-door neighbours whose tree attacked Woods's Escalade are now communicating through their attorney.

Even as he posted his quasi-confessional on his website this week, Woods could not resist throwing a barb at 'the media' for having invaded his privacy and, truth be told, there have been fairly serious internal differences of opinion about the way the sporting press has handled the story.

Once again, Pierce seemed to put it in perspective as he recounted IMG's strategy for keeping the fourth estate in line: 'The golfing press became aware that stories about Tiger's temper, say, or about his ties to unsavoury corporate gifters, would mean the end of access to the only golfer in the world who matters. There is a quick way to tell now which journalists have made this devil's bargain and which ones haven't – the ones insisting that "the accident" is somehow "not a story" are the sopranos in the chorus.'

The metamorphosis of a stumbling kid who didn't know how to ask a girl for a date into a man who believes himself to be God's gift to women is easy to understand. Earning close to a $100 million (€66 million) in purses, as Woods has in 13 years on the Tour, will do that for you – and his on-course earnings pale by comparison with his commercial endorsements from sponsors such as Nike, Buick and EA Sports.

How will Woods's commercial enterprises be affected by the current scandal? They won't be – at least not unless the pressure exacts a toll on Tiger's golf game. As long as he keeps winning, sponsors are going to stay where they are, because they know that their competitors would be happy to leap into the breach.

Kobe Bryant's sponsors dropped him like a hot rock following his arrest on rape charges several years ago, but after that case wound up without a conviction and the Lakers won an NBA title last year, Bryant is a hero again. If things get hot enough over the winter, and if IMG decides it's a good idea, you might even see Woods check himself into some rehab facility to be treated for sex addiction, but we can pretty much promise you this much: whether it's the Masters in April or a subsequent tournament, the moment Woods wins his next major, what seems a nightmare now will become a forgotten memory.

TUESDAY, 8 DECEMBER 2009

Agents of Foreign State should not Control our Schools

Fintan O'Toole

The Vatican, in its refusal to deal with the Murphy commission on child abuse in the Dublin diocese, made it clear that it wishes to be regarded, not as a church

Bishop Donal Murray in St John's Cathedral, Limerick, after announcing his resignation to a congregation including priests of the Diocese, people working in the Diocesan Office and the Diocesan Pastoral Centre, following the publication of the Ryan report into how the Catholic Church handled allegations of clerical sex abuse of children. Photograph: Arthur Ellis/Press22.

organisation, but as a foreign state. Which raises the rather stark question: why do we allow a foreign state to appoint the patrons of our primary schools?

If some weird vestige of colonial times decreed that the British monarch would appoint the ultimate legal controllers of almost 3,200 primary schools in our so-called republic, we would be literally up in arms. Why should we tolerate the weird vestige of an equally colonial mentality that allows a monarch in Rome to do just that?

Last week, Minister for Education Batt O'Keeffe told the Dáil that questions like these are of no importance because 'the current management of schools is working exceptionally well. The patron is in place in terms of ethos but has nothing to do with the overall management of schools. That is the responsibility of the board of management.'

This is wildly inaccurate, not least because the boards of management are themselves both appointed by and accountable to the local bishop. The handbook given to every school principal on his or her appointment spells this out with admirable clarity: 'In appointing the board of management of the school, the bishop delegates to the members certain responsibilities for the Catholic school in the parish. Such delegation carries a duty of accountability by the board of management to the bishop and – where appropriate – to the Department of Education and Science.' (Note that accountability to the State is qualified, that to the bishop is not.)

Batt O'Keeffe misled the Dáil (presumably through sheer ignorance rather than intent) when he claimed that the role of the bishop is confined to the ethos of the school. Again the handbook is unequivocal: 'The bishop, as leader of the Catholic community in the diocese and as patron of the school, has ultimate responsibility for the school. The bishop delegates some of his responsibility to the board of management which is accountable to him. There will be contact between the board and the bishop on a number of specified issues – for instance, the appointment of the board, the appointment, suspension or dismissal of teachers, finance, school ethos.'

While the entire board of management is essentially a servant of the bishop, he has very specific powers in relation to its composition and functioning. The board's chairperson is legally obliged, according to the Education Act (not a medieval statute but passed in 1998), to act on behalf of the bishop: 'The chairperson shall be appointed by the patron and his/her authority shall derive from such appointment.'

There is a timid suggestion in the Act that the bishop in making this key appointment should 'give due consideration to the opportunity to engage in a consultative process within the wider school community'. He may, of course, consider consulting the rest of the school and decide against it, or he may consult everyone and then do what he damn well pleases.

Crucially, the bishop as patron has a legal stranglehold over the appointment and dismissal of teachers. All Catholic schools are subject to what is called Maynooth Statute 262: 'To avoid prejudice against the managership of schools, a clerical manager is forbidden to appoint any teacher or assistant, male or female, in National Schools until he shall have consulted, and obtained the approval of, the bishop: likewise a clerical manager shall not dismiss any teacher or assistant, male or female, or give notice of dismissal, until the bishop be notified, so that the teacher, if he will, may be heard in his own defence by the bishop.' Even the appointment of a special needs assistant requires the 'prior approval' of the bishop.

The current line from both Fianna Fáil and Fine Gael is not to defend the retention of these powers by unelected and unaccountable people who may or may not recognise Irish law, but to insist that they are little used. This is typical of the slithery sleeveenism that still infects Irish politics. Anti-democratic powers are okay so long as they are not used.

There are just two possibilities here. Either the statutory powers of the bishops have fallen into disuse, in which case who can object to the clearing away of this offensive anachronism? Or they have not fallen into disuse, in which case they remain as an affront to a republican democracy.

Even if the bishops were not collectively and institutionally incapable of putting the welfare of children first, the idea that the primary school system of a 21st-century democracy should be ultimately controlled by the appointees of a foreign dictatorship would be shameful.

We need to grow up as a society and that means growing out of our dependence on a 19th-century instrument of power and control. Every intelligent theologian knows that that institution (as opposed to the faith it has distorted and betrayed) is effectively dead. It is long since time that politicians who claim to be republicans stopped prostrating themselves before its corpse.

SATURDAY, 12 DECEMBER 2009

Nature's Solutions to Flooding Need More Respect

Michael Viney

In times like these, one is guiltily glad to be living on a hill above the sea. When the Atlantic unleashes its latest torrents, recycling rain from sky back to ocean, at least the water stays in the ravine beside us, surging downhill under the bridge. The odd clack of colliding rocks echoes up to my window.

To dwell on a glaciated hillside, its fences and meadows merely skin-deep, the old boulders breaking through, is to soak up (sometimes literally) the interface of weather and land. But there are places in Ireland where this becomes obscure, hidden under concrete or beneath the earth itself. Topographic levels, too, can get lost or forgotten once the sea is out of view.

The idea that the Shannon basin could be drained in some way haunted the hopes of generations of farmers. In 1954, after a specially disastrous flood, the government brought in an expert from the US Army Corps of Engineers – tamers of the Mississippi right down to New Orleans – if not always infallible. Colonel Louis E. Rydell spent four years working out the channels to be dredged in the Shannon mainstream and its tributaries. He finally conceded that the problem was immense, needing many further studies, and moved on to tackle the Indus in Pakistan.

Thinking about rivers and floods has changed a lot since then, with a lot more respect for nature's own systems. The arterial drainage by the OPW that canalised so many Irish rivers in the 1960s is now regretted for brutal destruction of bank and riverbed habitats and wildlife: there are better ways of doing it. The EU's Water Framework Directive, compelling the current plans for managing whole river basins – the Shannon among them – sets the needs of wildlife alongside those of human settlement.

The EU's even newer Floods Directive demands flood hazard maps by 2013 and flood risk management plans by 2015. It not only makes the

Shannon floods as seen by Michael Viney.

obvious points about not building new houses in flood-prone areas, but urges, where appropriate, restoring flood plains and wetlands. The OPW, Ireland's lead agency in managing flood risk and remedy, has lifted its head from physical dredging and building walls and weirs to take the more proactive approach, like advising planners and public, shown in websites such as *www.floodmaps.ie*.

The obdurate problems of some landscapes are nowhere more dramatic than in the karst country of the Gort-Ardrahan area of south Galway. Karst is deep bedrock limestone full of holes, from cave systems, surface turloughs and swallow-holes to finger-thick fissures in the rock. Karst has created the botanical treasure of the Burren, Co. Clare, but also, periodically, appalling floods in the farming lowlands to the north. Here, water flowing off the hard sandstone heights of Slieve Aughty disappears underground into the cavernous limestone of the lowlands.

This subterranean labyrinth fills with rain from a vast area, and expels it underwater at Kinvara on the coast. Its deep rocky apertures are fixed and often choked with rubbish, so rainfall backs up inland. There is no surface outlet to Galway Bay. To carve a channel would disrupt turlough habitats prized for European nature conservation, but the huge cost and geological uncertainty of doing so, in such fissured terrain, have been far more decisive – and never more so than in the present recession. In one major investigation, following a flood in 1990, it was thought that once Coillte's young spruce forests on Slieve Aughty had grown to a closed canopy, they should help absorb extreme rainfall. Since then a broad swathe of clearfell – almost 300 hectares – was given over to the big Derrybrien wind farm.

The vegetation of Ireland's upland rim, now recovering from overgrazing, will be crucial to the flow of water in the cascades threatened for the future. As in everything to do with floods, the picture is not simple. Conifers on blanket peat make poor commercial sense: a lot of them grow badly and blow down in storms. Ploughing drains to plant seedlings releases more carbon and methane from the peat, and rushes water downhill. On steep slopes, the stability of the blanket bog itself is threatened by extreme downpours.

Coillte is leaving a few western bog plantations, mostly a tangle of lodgewood pine, to go wild and regenerate as best they can. Loftier notions of reforesting the hills with native trees have their advocates, and research to show which species would do best: sessile oak and birch, holly and rowan, with Scots pines – Ireland's original conifers – as punctuation. It would take a long time, a lot of money, and we're broke. As for 'restoring wetlands' – all those marshy bits at the edge of town, filled with lorryloads of rocks and rubble for foundations. Dig it up again? This isn't China.

FRIDAY, 18 DECEMBER 2009

The Kindness of Strangers Shows Goodness Still Exists

Orna Mulcahy

Buying stocking fillers in Penneys, I left my phone on the counter and wandered off to fondle their famous fleecy pyjamas. People were grabbing armfuls of them while, at the other end of the store, the sequined miniskirts had been slashed to €3 – and still no one was buying. Staying in is the new going out and all that. Who needs sequins anymore?

Anyway, the phone. It was a couple of hours before I noticed it missing and dialled the number, hoping to hear it ring at the bottom of the handbag. Instead a woman answered. Aaaaggghhhh! Now a stranger has my phone and is going to hold me to ransom.

'I took your phone home in case it got lost,' the woman said. Okay. Thank you so much and where is home so I can come and get it? 'Harmonstown.'

John Devlin with his children, Patrick (3) and Dearbhla (4), from Dublin, crossing the newly opened Samuel Beckett Bridge designed by Santiago Calatrava. Photograph: Brenda Fitzsimons.

Now the evening was stretching out in front of me, hopelessly lost in Harmonstown and the Christmas tree still to be bought. 'Don't come all this way,' she went on. 'I'll get my daughter to bring it to you.'

Could this be for real? It was lashing rain and pitch dark, but yes, it seemed Linda, her daughter, was willing to hop in her car and meet me in Fairview by the fire station. She had taken the phone because she didn't trust the security in big shops.

I head for Fairview, thinking this is an elaborate sting, and Linda won't be there but some big lad will be, and money will have to be handed over. *Prime Time Investigates*, eat your heart out.

But, bang on time, Linda arrives and gives me the phone with a smile. Could I take her mother's address to write her a thank-you? Not at all, she said, there's no need. Sure anyone would do the same thing! I was speechless. How kind people are and what a pity that a lot of the kind things they do are so small and everyday that they don't get noticed very much.

Not in these pages at any rate; particularly not in 2009. A year of ferocious self-examination and apportioning of blame has the country semi-exhausted and demoralised. Lying and cheating, thieving, cowardice and hypocrisy have been written about at length. Kindness, decency and good humour a lot less so.

It took just half an hour to regain my vocals, when presented, in the same lashing rain, with the abysmal range of Christmas trees in our local car park. Is there a tree drain going on? Have all the nice fresh bushy firs from the Wicklow hills been exported, leaving the natives with a lot of knobbly, twisty, mutant ones with strange cactus-like tops?

After hauling out one disaster after another we settled on the least ugly one and then managed to screw in the stand in such a way that the whole thing tilts to one side. It doesn't even smell nice, said the eldest later, when it had been wedged into a corner with one branch sticking out about six feet into the room, ready to take the dog's eye out.

No matter, the days of demanding perfection are over. There is, my friend says, a perfect tree for sale in Milltown, but it is €210 and not a bob goes to charity. There are decent trees for sale in the car park of Jurys (what next for the Jurys site – Car boot sales? A horse fair? Fossetts Circus?) but they are €100. A Limerick contact tells me that the trees are equally atrocious down her way and that the county's top families are rumoured to have their trees flown in from Canada.

According to the *New York Times*, the hot new trend is for rentable Christmas trees. In Los Angeles (and maybe next year in Dublin) you can choose your 'temporary tannenbaum' online. It gets delivered in a pot and is taken away to be replanted in a nursery three weeks later.

Drained from the tree debacle, I had to gear up for a big corporate event the next day. The host, who in previous years would have invited his staff, clients and the media to an expensive restaurant and plied them with champagne and fine wines until it was time to stagger to Doheny & Nesbitts, instead opted to have a quieter affair – at home.

Comfort food was on the menu – baked ham, cauliflower in white sauce – served up by colleagues. Carols were sung by beautiful teenagers from his daughter's class. Terrible year but we're still here was the theme of the day. To my left, a former cabinet minister pulled crackers and read out the jokes. Some people were eyeing the biros that came out of the crackers. It was all unexpectedly nice.

I'd stopped off at a wine shop to buy chocolates for the host and could barely get through the door – there were so many wine boxes stacked up ready to be delivered as corporate gifts. Lo and behold, many of them were addressed to people in Anglo Irish Bank.

'I'm so glad they're still being looked after,' I said, aiming for high sarcasm.

'Oh, but there've been big cutbacks,' said the man behind the counter. 'You want to have seen what they were all getting last year!'

FRIDAY, 18 DECEMBER 2009

An Irishman's Diary

Frank McNally

We were discussing here recently Ireland's theft of the song 'Dirty Old Town', a crime on which the many fingerprints include those of The Pogues. Its writer, Ewan MacColl, probably wouldn't have minded much anyway. He had a love-hate relationship with the real DOT, his native Salford. And he believed in reinvention, having been born as Jimmy Miller before adopting a name more in sympathy with his Scottish ancestry.

But The Pogues have in any case handsomely made it up to him for their part in the aforementioned larceny, by means of one of their own compositions. I refer of course to 'Fairytale of New York'. Because when Shane McGowan wrote what for many people is the greatest Christmas song of all in 1987, he incidentally immortalised the woman with whom he performed it: MacColl's daughter, Kirsty.

Not that she needed immortalising at the time. She was still in her prime then and, all things considered, appeared to have a much better life expectancy than her duet partner. But her role in 'Fairytale' acquired an unintended poignancy nine years ago today, a week before Christmas 2000, when she was killed by a rich man's speedboat in Mexico.

Nobody ever went to jail for the incident and, only last week, the MacColl family finally declared the 'Justice for Kirsty' legal fund closed. It had achieved all it could, they said; any remaining money would go to charity.

But even as a line was at last drawn under the tragedy, MacColl and McGowan's famous duet was yet again being dusted off by DJs: its popularity undimmed by the passage of 22 years.

Musical and lyrical beauty aside, part of the song's appeal is the original video which, unusually for something shot in the 1980s, still manages to look classy today. True, the acting is of the ham variety, apart from Matt Dillon's gum-chewing cop and the drunk-tank's unidentified black-man-with-swollen-eye, who both look the part.

McGowan somehow manages to be unconvincing in the performance of a man with drink on him and MacColl is too fresh-faced for the part where the relationship descends into bitterness and recrimination.

There are also such details − technical but inconvenient − that the NYPD choir, as featured in the song and video, was not really singing 'Galway Bay'. This is partly because there is no NYPD choir. But even the pipe band didn't know the tune, apparently. So they had to slow down one of their faster numbers and pretend.

On the plus side, The Pogues' hairstyles have held up surprisingly well. Also, the black-and-white footage, with its rising cigarette smoke and falling snow, still looks great. Thanks to this and the way the central melodrama is counterpointed by the pipe band's relentless bonhomie, the video has attained a classic status to match the music.

As a work of art, the song itself will probably outlive the book that inspired it: JP Donleavy's 1961 play, *Fairytales of New York*, reworked as a 1973 novel with the singularised title. Concerning an Irish-American whose wife dies on arrival in the

Smoke billows from the Guinness brewing plant in Dublin after a section caught fire. Photograph: Cyril Byrne.

Big Apple, and who is then forced to work for the undertaker while paying off the funeral, it was described at the time as a 'funny, lusty and sad novel of comic genius'.

But readers who chance upon the book now probably do so because of the song, not the other way around. Which said, the song is also funny, lusty and sad. And it's partly the fact that it runs this gamut of emotions, from joy to despair, that differentiates it from the multiple saccharine atrocities to which Christmas provokes other musicians.

Unlike many of those, The Pogues' 'Fairytale' is still not quite overplayed. The notorious fact is that on its debut, it was held off the No. 1 spot by some forgettable ditty from The Pet Shop Boys, two of the many unacceptable faces of the 1980s. Yet despite several re-releases in subsequent years and despite topping many favourite-song polls, 'Fairytale' has retained something of a cult status.

The fact that it defies all attempts to dance to it, even while drunk, has undoubtedly helped prevent overexposure. So has its challenging language. Two years ago, BBC Radio One infamously started blanking out the words 'slut' and 'faggot', until shame forced them to abandon the policy.

The song has also inspired many dubious cover versions, including one by a Norwegian band and another by – God help us – Ronan Keating. But it's putting it mildly to say that no cover version I know of is an improvement on the original. Unlike 'Dirty Old Town', 'Fairytale of New York' does not appear to lend itself to borrowing, never mind theft. It remains indelibly the property of The Pogues and MacColl, and to a lesser extent of the members of the NYPD choir, on whom it has also conferred immortality, even if they never existed in the first place.

Members of the first 12 women who graduated from Garda Headquarters on 7 December 1959, pictured in Templemore garda training centre to mark the 50th Anniversary of Women in Policing. Photograph: Brian Arthur/Press 22.

Kalle Eriksson, from Sweden, cheering on runners in the Senior Men's Cross Country event at the Spar European Cross Country Championships at Santry in Dublin. Photograph: Alan Betson.

Later, lying in the recovery room, wallowing in the post-op, morphine-induced fug, waiting to meet my girls properly, I heard the nurse saying that some private rooms in the Merrion Wing had just come free. She was wondering whether there were any semi-private mothers in the recovery room who might like one. I didn't know what the Merrion Wing was but it sounded like my kind of place, so I nearly split my exceptionally neat scar trying to get her attention. And that's how I ended up being wheeled into my own room with an en-suite bathroom and a television. But, and it was a big but, there was only one cot beside my bed, which meant there was only one baby, Priya, to enjoy the five-star luxury with me.

Joya was four pounds when she was born, positively a bruiser compared to some of the pre-mature babies in the neonatal intensive-care unit (NICU) where she was taken directly after the birth. When she arrived, she was found to have a breathing apnea, which meant she was in the habit of turning blue and not breathing for several seconds. (The word apnea comes from the Greek meaning 'without wind', a lack of which she has made up for since in a variety of potent and noisy ways.)

In denial, and out of my head on morphine, I convinced myself they must be exaggerating about the turning-blue part. Until, that is, I hauled myself up to the NICU to visit her for the first time. Beside this mini-baby, an alarm beeped manically, and I watched as her face did indeed turn an unholy shade of greyish blue.

She spent 10 days there being looked after by the people my friend calls 'the best babysitters in Dublin'. One of them, Fleurie, won my eternal gratitude by replying 'Yes, of course' when I asked to take this baby, who seemed to weigh exactly

Taking the plunge on Christmas Day at Blackrock, Co. Galway. Photograph: Joe O'Shaughnessy.

nothing, out of the incubator to feed her. The tubes, alarms, metal and glass all melted away as we locked eyes for the second time. It was a precious moment in an avalanche of precious moments, which included the morning, 10 days later, when we brought our healthy baby home to a house decorated with balloons by the neighbours. Welcome home baby girl, the banner read.

Before Joya was allowed home, we were sent away from the hospital with Priya, because unfortunately my health insurance didn't cover us to stay in the Merrion Wing until her 18th birthday. Five intense days followed while we tried to settle Priya into her new surroundings, returning to Holles Street a few times each day to feed and be with Joya. Priya had patiently taught me how to breastfeed and she was such a good teacher there wasn't a cracked nipple in sight.

Even so, we badly needed help. My own mother had fallen down a hole the day the girls were born, which prevented her from moving in with us for three weeks, as we had planned.

She arrived to see me in the hospital in a wheelchair (I thought this was a morphine-induced hallucination), with two busted-up ankles, and was confined to her apartment for the next month.

So, in those early days, we needed somebody to stay at home with Priya while we went to see Joya, who, having remembered how to breathe properly, had been moved from the incubator to a cot. A new parent, beset by that insides-on-the-outside feeling, wanting to do the best for both girls but not blessed with the gift of bilocation, I rang my boyfriend's mother, Queenie (doyenne of bleach products, bulk buyer of kitchen roll), in tears one day and, like an angel, if angels come dressed from head-to-toe in cut-price clobber from TK Maxx, she answered the call.

Her mercy dash proved to be both a good and a bad thing. Good: Even though she was terrified of being left in charge of such a small baby, she was there for us when we needed her most.

Bad: Hmmmm. How do I put this without being banned from entering the Portadown homestead forever? Let's just say that, like many a mother-in-law figure before her, Queenie didn't agree with a certain aspect of my Keeping The Baby Alive Plan.

To put it in context, Mary of the Merrion Wing, a saint among women, baby whisperer extraordinaire, had told us to feed our premature baby Priya every three hours, whether she was awake or asleep. We clung to this information like drowning people to a life raft. We didn't have a clue what we were doing but we knew we had to feed the baby every three hours. If we did that then we wouldn't sink and everything would be alright.

The first time I woke Priya up to feed her, I didn't mind when Queenie suggested it was wrong and perhaps even a little bit evil to wake a sleeping baby. She had raised six children, she had experience and waking sleeping babies was up there with hanging them out the window by their ankles in the list of things not to do. 'I'd never wake a sleeping baby,' she said, as I blew gently on Priya's face.

With a new serenity bestowed on me by motherhood, I explained to Queenie that we'd been told to do this by the hospital. I thought that would be the end of it, but instead I had to listen to the 'never wake a sleeping baby' mantra every time I went to wake the sleeping baby, who pretty much slept constantly those first couple of weeks.

'I've never heard', she offered on day three as though it was the first and not the 117th time she had broached the subject, 'of waking a sleeping baby.' At this point, Serene Mother went out the window to be quickly replaced by Sleep-Deprived Crazy Mother.

'Please,' I bleated, gritting my teeth. 'Please don't ever say that to me again. I am only doing it because the hospital told me to. I know you wouldn't wake a sleeping baby. But I have to. Please stop saying it.'

She said exactly nothing and I read her silence to mean I had finally broken through. This was a mistake. At lunch later that day, Queenie and I ordered a lemon-meringue pie. I was taking a bite when I noticed it was time for the baby's feed. My boyfriend, Queenie's beloved second son, went to wake her and that's when I heard the words 'I would never wake a sleeping . . . ' She didn't get to finish. I cracked. My outburst – oh, hello there, you must be Psycho Mother; I wondered when you'd surface – sounded something like: 'TOLDyounottosaythatanymore, areyouTRYING toBREAKmewoman, whyyyywhyyyareyoubeing soCRUELamonlydoingwhattheHOSPITALsai, whyyywhyyyyareyouDOINGthis tomeee???'

You'd need to add a few high-pitched shrieks to get the full picture.

I'd never seen Queenie, a consistently animated, vibrant, talkative woman, become so still. When she spoke it was in a tight voice, with wounded words about getting the train home, and having only raised six children, and knowing where she wasn't wanted, and never visiting or helping out again. I am grateful that this dreadful episode, a week after the girls were born, turned out to be the most challenging moment of the past eight months. Part of me still thinks cracked nipples would have been preferable to seeing that strained look on my mother-in-law-in-waiting's face that day.

I apologised. She accepted my apology. She didn't get the train home. The sleeping-baby mantra was never uttered again. She sent word later through her son that a friend of hers told her that premature babies need to be fed every three hours, which meant she accepted that I wasn't making it up. We are closer now because of Lemon Meringuegate. In fact, I am only able to sit writing this because Queenie is wheeling her two grand-daughters around town, lapping up the twin-related comments from the general public, and I hope she knows how grateful I am.

I seem to be bursting with gratitude these days. For the patience of my own mother, who when her ankles healed, came to change nappies and keep me company and sat for two days decoding Gina Ford and Alice Beer's *A Contented House With Twins*. Thanks to my mother and Gina and Alice,

I am in a routine for the first time since secondary school. I know that at 7 p.m. they will be snoring and I will be free to climb into my bed with a good book and give thanks.

I am grateful for that bed. We bought a massive one from Ikea and shared it with the girls over four blissful months. I am grateful for a book about the Montessori method from birth to aged three, which inspired us to think outside the cot. Instead of behind bars, the babies sleep on double mattresses on the floor of their room, and while both our mothers worry about what will happen when they progress from scooting to crawling, they are kind enough not to say it too often.

I am grateful for the thoughtfulness of friends and family. For the sister who brought meals and desserts in the early weeks when cooking dinner or even – and I never thought I'd say this – eating was the furthest thing from my mind. For the other sister who said 'Whatever you do will be the right thing', which gave me strength to trust my own instincts through that first fever, those first teeth and the first time I was convinced one of them had swallowed my earring. Thankful, too, for the friend who gifted us with two slings and introduced us to the joys of babywearing.

Gratitude. For the kindness of strangers, the ones who smile and say 'You've got your hands full', a phrase I hear on average five times a day. It never gets old. For the woman on the packed Dart who knew a stressed first-time mother when she saw one, found a seat so I could breastfeed one screaming baby, kept an eye on the other sleeping baby, told me not to worry and then disappeared before I could thank her properly.

And I am grateful for my boyfriend, for sharing, really sharing the load and for giving me the girls. Ah, those girls. Because of them I can go whole minutes, sometimes several of them in a row, without thinking about myself, my problems or my insecurities. And after a lifetime spent reading self-help books, with all those endless tips about how to live fully in the moment, I've discovered, as most

new parents do, that in this intense new environment it's pretty much impossible to live anywhere else. For that – Christmas, New Year, Ramadan, Hanukkah – I hope I will always be grateful.

SATURDAY, 19 DECEMBER 2009

Last Wake Up Call for 'Old Geezers and Gals'

Mark Hennessy

Shortly before 9.30 a.m. yesterday, the final curtain came down on an institution in British life dating back almost 40 years when Limerick-born broadcaster Terry Wogan spoke to his army of early-morning followers for the last time. 'Now, I'm not going to pretend that this is not a sad day – you can probably hear it in my voice. I'm going to miss the laughter and the fun of our mornings together. I am going to miss you. Thank you. Thank you for being my friend,' he said.

Wogan's departure from his two-hour BBC 2 morning radio show has made the news for weeks in Britain. After 27 years in total on the programme, he is stepping down to make way for Chris Evans.

Everyone had something to say to mark his going, including prime minister Gordon Brown. Though busy at the Copenhagen world climate talks, he taped a message to wish the 72-year-old well. 'Five decades at the very top of British broadcasting is a towering, indeed an unparalleled achievement. I wanted to let you know how very dearly you'll be missed and how delighted we all are you'll be returning with another venture before too long,' said Brown.

Conservative Party leader David Cameron said he first listened to the show with his mother when he was a child, and he applauded the Irishman for his 'great ability to show the funny side of life'.

Wogan, who worked for RTÉ during the 1960s, first hosted The Terry Wogan Show on

BBC Radio 2 favourite Sir Terry Wogan in studio for his last breakfast show after 27 years on air. Photograph: BBC/Press Association.

BBC Radio 2 from 1972 in a run that lasted until 1984, when he left for a thrice-weekly television programme. When that ended he returned to Radio 2 in 1993 in a programme renamed *Wake Up with Wogan*, which attracted eight million listeners – Europe's single largest programme audience.

He stepped down from presenting the UK's coverage of the Eurovision Song Contest last year after four decades, complaining that the contest had become boringly predictable and political.

The final week of his radio show has been marked by many presentations, one being the Freedom of the City of London, which gives him the right to raise Tower Bridge to ship traffic.

But Wogan is not retiring. He will return to Radio 2 on St Valentine's Day with a mid-morning Sunday programme, complete with live music, and he will maintain his ties to Children in Need.

As he ended his programme yesterday, Wogan told his 'old geezers and gals': 'There's nothing to be sad about – we've had wonderful years together. We should be celebrating.'

The show ended with Anthony Newley's 'The Party's Over'.

TUESDAY, 29 DECEMBER 2009

Remembering Loved Ones at Christmas Time

Maurice Neligan

The national goose is being cooked and there is precious little any of us lesser mortals can do about it. Unfortunately, the cook doesn't seem to have much of a clue and God only knows what kind of an unpalatable mess is going to land on our table. Right now I intend to ignore all the problems of the present and retreat into the past. It seems safer there.

My father died on Christmas Day, 30 years ago at four o'clock in the afternoon. Given that we all have to depart some time, he chose to go in an unforgettable manner. My parents had a flat with us in Blackrock and on that morning we had all gone to my sister's house for drinks.

He was in fine form. His three children and all his grandchildren were there. He had his few drinks and smoked a few cigarettes and was in the best of form. I might add that he had smoked 40 a day since going to sea in the merchant marine as a young man. He never had the slightest inclination to stop.

He was a fit man for his years (84) and was still driving competently. He also liked a drink with friends, the odd game of cards and he loved to go fishing. He didn't seem the kind of person who would die and certainly I, as his only son, never thought about a time when he might not be around. He was just there, an immovable fixture, deeply loved by us all. As is often the case of course we did not tell him that; it would have made him deeply uncomfortable and he might have wondered had we some ulterior motive, babysitting duties perhaps.

Christmas dinner was scheduled for four o'clock that afternoon and all was in readiness. About half an hour before the start my mother rang from the granny flat to say that he wasn't well and seemed to have severe abdominal pain. I went up

A member of staff at the National Gallery mounting the annual Turner exhibition 'A Light in the Darkness'. Photograph: Cyril Byrne.

to him and found him *in extremis*. To this day I am not sure if he knew I was there. He tried to slip away quietly but we wouldn't let him. The HA and I tried to resuscitate him and phoned for an ambulance. We knew in our hearts he had left us, but we had to try. God might have made a mistake.

In the midst of our efforts our two elder sons appeared to announce that their electronic Christmas present wasn't working. What are you doing to Grandad? Not enough. What could we do? We were helpless.

The paramedics arrived and took my dad away to St Vincent's. They were great guys, strong and sympathetic; indeed this has been my overriding impression of ambulance personnel over the years. I returned from the hospital after the formalities and we had our Christmas dinner. It was surreal, paper hats, crackers, trying to explain to my mother and to our children what had happened when in truth we couldn't grasp it ourselves. Then a blur of family, of memories, of tears and regrets; we should have told this gentle, nice man how much he had meant to us all and suddenly he was gone and it was too late.

Our Sara was just a little one when her grandfather died and he had been very fond of her. She left just as suddenly and it is our hope that they are together. These are sad memories at Christmas, but you just can't have the happy reflections and ignore the rest of life. What we can do is remember the good times and the real people and the happiness of times past.

I think of my father of course, particularly at this time of year, and of the good times we had. His reluctance to leave the river bank while there was the remotest chance that another trout might be caught was legendary. I remember his unchristian satisfaction at the death of a doctor who some 20 years before had told him that he only had a year to live. This story was worn out by repetition to medical friends and family.

You were a lifestyle nightmare, Dad. You were overweight, had high blood pressure and ate all the wrong things. You worried more than anybody I ever knew about any matter, however trivial. Yet you made it to 84 without serious illness. I hope I carry your genes and I hope I am half the man you were.

WEDNESDAY, 30 DECEMBER 2009

U-turn on Civil Service Pay Cuts Outrageous

Sarah Carey

Apparently the 15 per cent cut wasn't fair. Fair? When did fair suddenly enter into the equation?

Silly me. I thought if we could crawl as far as Christmas Day, we could curl up in front of the fire and eat and sleep for 10 days. Thus restored, we could face into 2010 and the next round of the fight. We finished the pudding, but 2009 hadn't finished with us. The news about Brian Lenihan's illness was the final terrible blow of an awful year.

Despite the fact that he has delivered nothing but bad news and pushed through policies that vary from harsh to high risk, everyone likes him. Though on occasion we are unsure of his policies, we are sure of his integrity. During these bad times, it is a source of comfort. We are desperately sad for the Lenihans, the most likeable and decent of families, and they are in our thoughts and prayers.

But if the man who kept the European Central Bank on board, who persuaded the markets we weren't Iceland, who told the unions to bugger off and who stood between us and the International Monetary Fund is sick, then we must know. TV3 screwed it up, but the Government must take some responsibility. Leo Varadkar said he heard the rumours in Christmas week, so if he knew, then a lot of people did.

If the Minister's health was the subject of gossip among the political and media elite and since it has been beaten into us all year that we mustn't go frightening the international markets with bad behaviour, then the situation called for more management than keeping one's fingers crossed.

Lack of privacy is a high price to pay for high office but there is no shortage of precedents. In a direct parallel, the Japanese finance minister was admitted to hospital on Sunday suffering from high blood pressure and exhaustion. He was in hospital at 10 a.m. and a full statement on his condition and expected treatment issued that evening. I know it's against all our protective instincts towards a family in crisis, but this is how things are done.

We will support the Minister whether he wants to keep working throughout his treatment and give him all the time and privacy he needs to make that decision. But while he's doing that, it's our obligation to keep our eye on the ball. I'm reminded of Naomi Klein's theory of 'Shock Doctrine'. She argues that when a nation is in

shock over a reaction to a disaster, policies to which we'd object to in calmer days are slipped through.

In Christmas week a major policy reversal was introduced and the genuine shock of Lenihan's news mustn't be used to allow it to pass. On December 23rd, when perhaps some hoped no one would notice, a press release was issued from the Department of Finance revealing that just one of the cutbacks made in the Budget would be reversed. There were many hard cases from which to choose: the disabled, the carers, community projects and the low-paid. Which one created such tears and lamentations that the Cabinet was moved to right the wrong?

Why, the pay cuts for senior civil servants, of course. The 15 per cent pay cut for those earning over €200,000 was cut. The 12 per cent pay cut for those earning between €165,000 and €200,000

Cartoon by Martyn Turner.

Winter Reflection . . . A scene on Muckross Lake, Killarney, Co. Kerry, looking towards Torc Mountain.
Photograph: Valerie O'Sullivan.

was also cut. To what figure was the cut, ahem, cut? To between 3 and 5 per cent. A miserable 3 per cent from a couple of hundred grand? Why?

Apparently the 15 per cent cut wasn't fair. Fair? When did fair suddenly enter into the equation? None of this is fair. It's not fair that my children will be paying for the bank recapitalisation. It's not fair to learn that in the prime of your life you've got cancer.

The department mumbled about the loss of performance-related bonuses and 'anomalies' where senior staff might end up being paid less than someone underneath them. I know where I'd shove their anomalies.

The excuses boil down to the point I've made in this column before – the top priority at all times is to preserve the final salary level of senior public servants so that the massive defined-benefit, uncuttable pensions will be protected. It is the most

extraordinary outrage that these people, who issue orders for welfare and public service cuts, spare themselves on the grounds of fairness.

This cannot stand. This must not stand.

The decision was approved by Cabinet in the week Brian Lenihan was receiving his diagnosis. If this was a collective decision, they can collectively cop themselves on.

This is yet another sign of the institutionalisation of a long-standing party of government, so dependent on the 'Sir Humphreys' that they are too quick to identify and sympathise with their unelected colleagues. The danger now is that anyone who opposes the policy reversal will be accused of exploiting the Minister's illness, when in fact the opposite is the case. The Minister is entitled to his privacy, but his moment of weakness must not be ours.

SATURDAY, 2 JANUARY 2010

'Abandoned Cars All Over the Place. It's an Ice-Rink'

Eileen Battersby

On Christmas Eve the roads were so dangerous that we decided to walk the six kilometres to the local shop. We had to, as my station wagon had slid into a ditch the previous night. A man in a four-wheel-drive gave us a lift. Delighting in the dangerous conditions, he said, 'No one is out; this is a test of driving.'

Several hours earlier, on the road below the hill we live on, another four-wheel-drive had crawled by and the driver offered us a lift to the big supermarket. He was bringing three other neighbours, all car-breakdown victims.

It was tempting; the supermarket is fourteen kilometres away. But I had only ventured down the glass-like hill surface on reconnaissance, walking along the ditch, to check the road. My house wasn't even locked. 'You won't get down the road otherwise,' he warned. 'There's abandoned cars all over the place. It's an ice-rink.'

On Christmas morning, all of the high-tech, insulated drinkers in the stables had frozen. I spent hours carrying buckets of hot water down from the kitchen. Horses empty a bucket the way we would a glass. Slipping and sliding and falling, I cursed the ice.

Then, on cue, the electricity went. We had cooked our turkey on Christmas Eve and our gathering had eaten all our food. I was intent on walking sixteen kilometres to friends who had invited us for Christmas dinner. I had the cranberry sauce, but by mid-afternoon my daughter had slipped so often she refused to leave the house. We had banana sandwiches and, crisis of crisis, the chocolate was gone.

Ice is a sinister enemy. It is invisible. For three days, the horses stayed in. Shovelling shavings from

Kevin Cavey, from Cabinteely in suburban Co. Dublin, skiing along the Stillorgan Road. Photograph: Cyril Byrne.

Cartoon by Martyn Turner.

the stables, I made a path for them to cross the frozen yard and stretch their legs in fields so cold they quickly wanted back in.

We thought it had thawed. The road looked wet. Off we went, on foot. I stomped in a puddle and ended up on my back. We began the long trek to the supermarket, the one with the specialist dog and cat food.

The road was so slippery; the few cars were hazards to each other. We walked along the tow path and met an elderly man who wanted to know where we were going. He listened as I told him we were on a mission to fetch gourmet cat food for Nala, whose needs are more complex than our other cats.

At the end of the tow path, a woman called to us from the ditch across the road. Explaining that her husband had phoned her, she offered me turkey 'for the fussy cat'. As she spoke, a car eased into sight; two men asked were we stranded.

On hearing the saga of the cat, they drove us, on a deserted, ice-bound road, all the way to the supermarket, telling us about the numbers filling A&E departments, the crashed cars, the frozen pipes. They had been stranded at a friend's house for two days. 'But then,' said one of them, 'you have to try to make a break for home.'

It was the year of Sea the Stars; it was the year of the death of John Updike; it was the year of the floods; and as a finale, it was the year of the vicious ice that held Christmas hostage.

Yesterday it was different; it was better, possible to walk with your hands in your pockets without negotiating each step like a tightrope walker. Overnight snow had created the ideal postcard effect. Trees laced in white; only the birds were out.

That wonderful, satisfying crunch of snow under foot had replaced the evil slither of ice. New Year's Day spelt survival as the 'Blue Danube', followed by the 'Radetzky March', played on Lyric FM in the stables. The sun was so bright, reflecting off the snow, it must have delivered the country-side the way city people imagine it – peaceful, romantic, stress-free.

On New Year's Eve night, the night after a freak wind had ripped the roof off a stable block, the full moon was as bright as day.

What a difference.

MONDAY, 4 JANUARY 2010

A True Star of Irish Film

Hugh Linehan

Michael Dwyer was more than just a film correspondent. He was an enthusiast, an advocate, a lover of life and of movies. He was also, as many of the tributes that have flowed in, since his death last Friday evening at the age of 58, have noted, a staunch friend to successive generations of young film-makers, film lovers and journalists who crossed his path. Generosity is not a word usually associated with the profession of critic, but it comes up again and again when people talk about Michael.

He was indisputably the most influential Irish film critic of his generation, a fact recognised by the French government when it awarded him the honour of Chevalier des Arts et Lettres in 2006. He chronicled the transformation of international and local film-making over the last three decades: the arrival of home video; the advent of the multiplex; the flowering of Irish film production and of new cinematic voices from around the world.

Along with that he was a natural impresario, a showman with a brilliant sense of timing and a puckish sense of humour who delighted in stand-ing up in front of a packed auditorium to introduce his latest passionate enthusiasm for some film which he had been the first to see in Cannes or Toronto.

He was never afraid to champion the difficult or esoteric, but at heart he was a populist in the best sense of the word, bringing movies of all sorts to the widest audience possible. He loved feeling the keen anticipation of a new title from one of his favourite directors, or the excitement of discover-ing an unheralded gem.

Life never dimmed the boyish enthusiasm he recalled from his schooldays in Tralee in an article for this newspaper: 'From an early age, I engaged in an obsessive ritual whereby I felt impelled to tour around each of the three cinemas every day after school, to peruse the posters and stills and to keep informed of coming attractions. On wet days, my father, Nicholas, would interrupt his working routine as a fruit and vegetable wholesaler to drive me home from school – and regularly had to waste valuable time driving from cinema to cinema to track me down.'

That youthful passion inevitably led him to Tralee's film society, which he rapidly expanded from seven screenings a year to weekly screenings every Monday night from October to March, fill-ing all 620 seats in the Ashe Hall. At that time, film societies provided the only alternative to the often stale mainstream Hollywood fare provided by the established cinema chains and, because in theory they were private clubs, were able to avoid the worst strictures of what was still a draconian censorship regime.

But, with glacial slowness, official attitudes to film in this country were changing. In Tralee, as in other parts of the country, increasing numbers of people wanted to see the best of world cinema. A new organisation, the Federation of Irish Film Societies, had been set up to co-ordinate the distri-bution of these films to clubs around the country. In 1978, an enthusiastic and hugely knowledgeable young Kerryman became its first employee.

At the same time, he began working as a jour-nalist and critic, first for *In Dublin* magazine, later for the *Sunday Tribune* and the *Sunday Press*.

As Gene Kerrigan has noted, he was part of a

spoken out with such force. That's no justification for her opinions. But it does indicate why DUP voters have not – yet – stood up en masse and excoriated her. It helps, too, that Robinson is well-liked for her assiduous constituency work, which she performed with great glamour and panache, zipping around in her black and cream convertible Mini Cooper, clouds of expensive perfume trailing behind.

While sins of sexuality are easily understandable from an evangelical Christian standpoint, for whom every day is a tight-rope walk between good and evil, other potential transgressions may prove harder to swallow.

It has emerged that the public confession may have been in part prompted by a BBC investigation into Iris Robinson's finances. Sex is one thing to the canny, hard-nosed but fundamentally upstanding unionist heartlands. Money is quite another. If there are questions to be answered here, invoking God may not be enough to redeem the Robinson name.

SATURDAY, 9 JANUARY 2010

How to Bring Down Public Sector Using the Weapon of Complaint

Newton Emerson

As an ordinary citizen, what are your options for a long and sustained campaign of resistance against the public sector unions? At first sight it might seem that your options are limited. Public sector workers keep their jobs no matter what they do, let alone what you do.

There are laws against refusing to pay taxes and fees, and unlike the laws against Gardaí going on strike you cannot get around them by phoning in sick. You are required to deal with the public sector to obtain the various permits, papers and licences which it in turn requires you to hold. Finally, there are certain essential services that only the public sector can provide, such as seaweed harvesting, 2FM and prosecuting sexist golf clubs.

However, there is still one guaranteed means of counterattack. All public sector jobs are subject to Kafkaesque complaints procedures, which pass personal responsibility upwards and outwards until it has been diluted to the point of irrelevance and dispersed to the point of incomprehensibility.

Most people see little point in complaining as a result. But public sector workers still live in constant fear of being caught in these soul-destroying mechanisms, which often take years to grind through the motions. The slightest suggestion of prejudice or discrimination is raked over in excruciating detail and there is never any real comeback for making a complaint later found to be groundless, vexatious or even transparently mendacious.

Using the public sector's own culture against it brings the fight to the enemy and evens up what has until now been a very uneven score. Criminals and layabouts have always known this – which is why, after the public sector takes most of your money, the underclass gets the rest. So it is important that ordinary citizens learn how to complain in order to make themselves heard.

Research the relevant complaints procedures online or ask to speak to someone in person. You can complain about them later as well. Is there a dedicated ombudsman, commissioner or regulator whose existence you can help to justify? Is there a rights, equality or campaign group you can involve before they realise a taxpayer is exploiting them for a change?

Find out the current obsession of the institution you are targeting. Is it poverty, social exclusion or just racism as usual? Consider how you might 'minoritise' yourself before filing a complaint. Are you on any medication? Can you speak a foreign language? Have you ever considered another religion?

Conjoined twins from Cork, Hassan and Hussein Benhaffaf, with their mother, Angie, and father, Azzedine, and sisters, Malika and Iman, photographed at Great Ormond Street Hospital for Children in London. Photograph: Daragh McSweeney/Provision.

Insist the way you were initially dealt with was 'offensive', especially if you cannot say why. Keep a record of each complaint you have made and make a follow-up phone call every two weeks. Should the opportunity arise, complain about the way your complaint has been handled.

The unions have accused the Government of pursuing a divide-and-conquer strategy by setting public and private sector workers against each other. In this regard they have a point. Only militant public sector workers should be divided from the rest of us and conquered.

Identify the union activists in your local school, hospital, Garda station and social welfare office and subject them to a long and sustained campaign of resistance.

The whole of Ireland is complaining anyway. Make your next complaint official.

SATURDAY, 16 JANUARY 2010

'We Dug for Five Hours, then We no Longer Heard Him'

Lara Marlowe, in Port au Prince

'Ca commence ici,' says Claude, the Haitian driver. It starts here, at Ganthier, 50 km from the Haitian capital. Just one roof caved in, glimpsed behind a garden wall. Lush vines and banana groves, bougainvillea, framed by the stark mountain range to the north. Every few minutes, another collapsed wall, a staircase that has fallen off a building.

Brightly painted 'taxis tap-tap' with names like 'Jesus Saves' and 'God be Praised' still ply the highway, an impossible number of passengers clinging to the sides. Then more and more houses, as if they'd been bombed from the air, or dynamited.

Claude thinks a curse has fallen upon his country. 'If not, why us and not the others? It's because Haitians have no conscience. After Baby Doc left, we did terrible things. We threw petrol on people and burned them alive, because they'd been *ton-tons macoutes* (agents of Duvalier's secret police). God must do his work. This is the anger of God.'

We have reached the outskirts of the city, and there is more and more devastation. A crowd presses in around a water tanker, brandishing jerricans. People pace up and down the streets, purposefully, as if they had somewhere to go. But no one, not one of them, is smiling. About a third of them wear surgical face masks or bandanas, to keep out the cement dust, and the smell of rotting flesh. Those who do not wear masks smear a stripe of white toothpaste on their upper lip, to attenuate the stench.

'We're a people who resign themselves; who accept everything, like innocent children. I was educated by Salesian fathers in Pétionville. I am the oldest in my family. I understand things,' Claude continues wearily.

Buildings in every stage of demolition. Some appear untouched. Others are piles of rubble. No rhyme or reason. The arbitrariness of it. 'Why us and not the others?'

At an intersection, the handpainted sign over the ground floor shop can still be read: 'Where the customer is king.' Upstairs, the shopkeeper's apartment has been shaved off like a doll's house. A red armchair faces the television. A floral picture hangs in a gilt frame. The wrought iron gates on the ground floor are twisted and tossed into the street, bound by a useless padlock.

A crowd has formed on the slanting slabs of a collapsed building. Two men wear hardhats, and they hack away uselessly at the concrete with sledge hammers. That smell again, of decomposing flesh.

Cars in driveways crushed by fallen balconies. A man sits on the back fender of a 'tap-tap', his head dropped down between his knees in desolation. In Delmas 33, the road is closed because they're clearing the ruins of the police commissariat where some 30 police died. A girl hobbles by on a crutch. A child sits on the ground, her right hand wrapped in a bandage the size of a football.

From a distance, it looks like a colourful picnic. But closer up, one reads only desolation on the faces of these thousand or more Haitians who have crowded onto the lawn of the School of the Brothers of Saint Louis de Gonzague. The Collège Dieudonné l'Hérisson, the top sliced off and leaning backwards, opened like an oyster, a flag fluttering from the top.

At an intersection in Delmas, two Haitians play cards at a folding table on the pavement. A shiny, brand new bus, sparkling clean, glides by, surreal. It is filled with US Marines in full combat gear, wearing ray-bans, from a contingent of 5,000, just landed.

But the heroes are the Mexican rescue team I meet in their dust-covered red jumpsuits, exhausted from a day of battling broken buildings. They throw their shovels on the ground, sink down, exhausted, to smoke a cigarette. Oscar Oliva (36) from Cancún, is a giant of a man, with arms and neck as thick as tree-trunks.

'The nuns asked us to go to the archbishop's office, next to the cathedral. This morning, we heard Father Benedict's voice – Father Benedict, like the Pope – from under the rubble. We dug for five hours, and we couldn't get to him. This afternoon, we no longer heard him.' Oscar Oliva is crying.

THURSDAY, 28 JANUARY 2010

An Irishman's Diary

Frank McNally

We were talking here last week about the unfortunate Irish Christian name, Fechin, and the double misfortune that might arise were this to be combined with certain Anglicised surnames, viz: 'Thank you for flying with us today. We'll be hearing from the captain, Fechin Looney, shortly. But first I'll take you through the emergency evacuation procedures . . .'

The good thing about Fechin, however, is that being phonetically controversial in itself, parents who choose it for a son will at least be on guard against such troublesome combinations. Or so you would hope. Whereas other forenames, innocuous in their own right, might be innocently combined with surnames whose incompatibility is not noticed until it's too late.

My thanks to several readers who, for example, have drawn attention to the old Irish forename, Sonabha. It's a girl's name: a small mercy in the circumstances. And it is rather lovely on its own. But to get a mild (and hypothetical) flavour of the potential complications, imagine if those well-known Irish estate agents, the Gunne family, had a child called Sonabha.

There are worse combinations than that, I'm told: not all fictional. And although I won't go into further examples here, in case of adding to any-one's pain, they do at least help explain the famous case of the former governor of Texas, James 'Big Jim' Hogg who, distracted by joy at the birth of his first-born daughter, decided to call her 'Ima'.

But back to Fechin; and my thanks also to Pádraic de Bhaldraithe for explaining that, although anglicisation of Irish names can cause problems, they sometimes solve them too.

Pádraic recalls a professor of psychology in UCD in the 1960s, a priest named Feichín

Ó Dochartaigh, 'whose elderly female relative used refer to him as the man with the unfortunate name'. But he adds, 'in the English-speaking part of Connemara', people get around the Fechin problem 'by anglicising the name as Festus and more familiarly as Festy'.

In the Ballyconneely area, apparently, there is even a Frenchman so named. He was awarded the distinction by locals after he arrived in the 1970s to do a course in thatching and stayed.

Which begs the thought, incidentally, of what might have happened had it been another 7th-century Irish saint, rather than Fiacre, who went to France and gave his name to Parisian cabs. Rugby fans wandering that city next month might be complaining about how hard it is to get a 'fechin taxi' after midnight, without anyone having to pardon their French.

Perhaps the best known Festy was Festy Mortimer, a boat-builder and fisherman who features in Tim Robinson's book *Connemara – The last Pool of Darkness*. Aside from his local renown, Mortimer became an interesting footnote in the history of European philosophy, when for a period in the late 1940s he was a neighbour to the temporary Connemara resident Ludwig Wittgenstein.

The latter is widely considered the greatest philosopher of the 20th century. Bertrand Russell called him 'the most perfect example I have ever known of genius'. And that genius was still at work when in 1948, Wittgenstein spent time living in Rosroe, near Killary Harbour. He was probably exploring new ideas in the philosophy of mathematics there.

But of what exactly, we don't know, because Festy Mortimer did some cleaning work in the house where Wittgenstein stayed. And in an interview (for another book) 45 years later, Mortimer recalled burning – at Wittgenstein's request – 'a very large pile of used manuscript papers, many of which [. . .] had mathematical writing on them'. Which, even if he was only obeying orders, is the

Rebecca O'Connor, Hollie Payne and Nadia Burke, from Scoil Caitríona, Baggot Street, using interactive Microsoft technology to view rare and valuable collections, at the opening of the Discover your National Library exhibition in Dublin's Kildare Street. Photograph: Alan Betson.

sort of detail that might make scholars of philosophy want to Gaelicise his name again.

The embarrassment caused by certain Anglicisations is not unique to Ireland. Even once respectable English names have evolved, due to vagaries in spelling, in unfortunate ways. And perhaps the classic example is that of a Yorkshireman who died 100 years ago this week.

Contrary to popular belief, Thomas Crapper did not invent the flush toilet, versions of which had existed for centuries. But the confusion is understandable because he was a plumber – a master one at that – and he was also a major innovator in the field of sanitary hardware. Indeed, his company is credited with the world's first showroom of bathroom fittings, window displays of which are said to have made Victorian ladies faint with shock.

But back to his name, which bears no etymological relationship to his chosen line of work. On the contrary, it derives from the good old Anglo-Saxon verb 'cropp', meaning 'to cut'. Thus, England's original 'Croppers' would have been mowers or farm labourers.

As for 'crap', that came from old Dutch, meaning 'chaff'. And it was already a rude verb in English by the 1840s, when the plumber was only a boy. So although he did probably give his name to the American slang for toilet, the related verb at least seems to have predated him.

We still speak of someone 'coming a cropper'. The crop here is a riding whip and, according to Brewer's Dictionary, the expression refers to a bad fall, in which a rider hits the ground, 'neck and crop' first. Well, the English surname Cropper could probably be said to have 'come a Crapper'. But a century after the aforementioned plumber's death, his company still bears it proudly – on among other things crests, some of which display the legend: 'Crapper, by royal appointment.'

SATURDAY, 30 JANUARY 2010

Passion and the Playwright

Hilary Fannin

Lady Antonia Fraser, the willowy ash-blond daughter of Lord Longford, the former wife of the late Conservative MP Hugh Fraser and the second wife of Harold Pinter, has, a year after the death from cancer of Britain's most famous and influential modern playwright (on Christmas Eve 2008), written a paean to their enduring love affair and marriage. With unarguable dignity and a marked lack of irony or self-doubt, Fraser has produced a long, graceful, albeit at times cloying account of their seemingly extraordinarily happy life together.

Must You Go?: My Life with Harold Pinter a memoir by Antonia Fraser is based on Fraser's diaries, in which she virtuously charted their busy, fulfilling and deeply loving relationship, interspersed with her elegantly written and occasionally moving retrospective musings. A strangely persistent book, this memoir, like the historical biographies Fraser has been writing since her early 20s, illuminates an era, with its court of characters – the likes of Samuel Beckett, Arthur Miller, Laurence Olivier, John Fowles and Edna O'Brien, who somehow seem as distant as the men in frocks who more usually populate the author's work.

Fraser and Pinter's relationship began after a dinner party hosted by her brother-in-law, Kevin Billington, who had directed Pinter's *The Birthday Party*. 'I was slightly disappointed not to sit next to the playwright, who looked full of energy, with

black curly hair and pointed ears, like a satyr,' Fraser recalls.

The seating arrangements did not prevent the star-crossed couple from finding each other, despite both being encumbered by other spouses. Pinter was in an apparently difficult marriage to the actor Vivien Merchant (the couple had one son), while Fraser was firmly ensconced in her rambling west London home with her Tory MP husband, six children and various cats. Leaving the dinner party that evening, Fraser stopped by Pinter's chair to congratulate him on his theatrical success:

'Must you go?' he asked.

'I thought of home, my lift, taking the children to school the next morning, the exhausting past night in the sleeper from Scotland, my projected biography of King Charles II . . . "No, it's not absolutely essential," I said.'

Pinter, having escorted Fraser home in his chauffeur-driven car, remained in her house until dawn. 'He stayed until six o'clock in the morning with extraordinary recklessness, but of course the real recklessness was mine.'

This is the point when one casts the book aside in a state of bleak incomprehension. Not that Fraser chooses to cavort with a married man but that she would have the energy for such an endeavour at all, with six bleating offspring to care for. Presumably, her domestic life, already propped up by boarding schools, was also staffed by people who grilled the fish fingers and sorted the socks.

By the time the press eventually got its inky mitts on the scandalous story of Harold and Antonia, the couple were sweeping their lives clean of impediments and had embarked on a relationship that would last for 33 years. Fraser's description, written with her trademark aristo-cratic understatement, of breaking the news of her passion for the saturnine playwright to her husband, Hugh, borders on high comedy: 'It was beyond ghastly – I fetched him inside from the garden, where he was smoking and reading the *FT*.'

English playwright Harold Pinter in 1985 with his wife, Antonia Fraser, who has written a memoir of their life together. Photograph: David Montgomery/Getty Images.

Later, Fraser fetches Pinter around to help sort out the domestic situation. 'Hugh and Harold discussed cricket at length, then the West Indies, then Proust. I started to go to sleep on the sofa. Harold politely went home. Nothing was decided.'

Despite the unintentional comedy, Fraser's benign tome to her raven-haired lover is, at times, as irritating as getting the silver spoon stuck in one's craw. Fraser describes herself, the Catholic aristocrat, and Pinter, the Jewish boy made good from London's East End, as 'bohemians', backing up this unconvincing thesis with such lines as: 'In various fish restaurants in Dubrovnik, money worries are discussed.'

Having jettisoned the spouses – Hugh Fraser went off amicably to shoot grouse in the Highlands while Merchant, described by Fraser as an alcoholic, clung on to the corpse of her marriage until shortly before her early death – Pinter moved into Fraser's Holland Park home. Later, he purchased an adjoining mews to write in, away from the holler of the children during the hols.

The middle section of the book roves from Caribbean vacations to Parisian readings, to play openings in New York City, to sipping Corvo Biancos under a Venetian winter sun, to sojourns in eastern Europe and South America. Everywhere the couple go they are feted by the artistic community and the intellectual elite, due to their political activism as well as to Pinter's stunning dramatic canon. The names Vaclav Havel and Daniel Ortega (the Sandinista leader in Nicaragua) are scattered among the guest lists to the couple's home, along with just about every successful actor, director and film-maker of the past half-century.

Despite the occasional pomposity and the sheer privilege that permeate the pages, you can't help but feel deeply impressed by Pinter and Fraser's energy, their political engagement and intellectual rigour. Pinter may have shouted louder and more vociferously, but Fraser, although instinctively more conservative, was no lightweight.

Strangely, despite its being embroidered throughout with Fraser's abiding love for her husband, this book has an absence at its centre. Somehow Pinter goes missing: his moodiness and bouts of depression are touched on, the green shoots of his ideas for new work are documented, his political views are revealed (we discover that, at one stage, he even voted Conservative and supported the Falklands War), his gentle domesticity and uxorious nature are painted in sharp relief to his more truculent and volatile public persona, but ultimately his character remains abstruse, somehow untouchable. It is as if Fraser loved him so

instinctively and so entirely that she had no need to analyse the man.

The final section of *Must You Go?* is the strongest and most affecting, an account of Pinter's ill health, his 75th-birthday celebrations in Dublin, his Nobel Prize, his struggle to make his political voice heard and Fraser's gradual realisation that her time with Pinter is running out.

This is a moving account of carefully crafted and cherished love, a theme that is, in itself, unusual.

SATURDAY, 30 JANUARY 2010

Case Gave Insight into Marriage of Contrasting Characters

Kathy Sheridan

When childhood friends of Eamonn Lillis read the story about the burglar in the balaclava, they knew instantly it was fiction. As a boy in Terenure on Dublin's south side, young Lillis was the only one they ever knew who owned a balaclava. 'When we were out pretending to be shootin' up the street, he'd be there in his balaclava being James Bond . . . That story was a total throwback to his childhood.'

When he wasn't being James Bond, he was devouring Ian Fleming's books about 007 on her majesty's secret service, or writing short stories or sketching brilliantly realistic images. A vast mural of an action-packed Battle of Britain inside the garage of their immaculately kept house in Wainsfort Park was his. He was a dreamer, a doodler, an exceptionally quiet, rather detached, slightly built boy, who had little in common with his peers in Templeogue College and none of the usual interests in street kickabouts.

He was one of three children of Séamus Lillis, an Irish Army officer (with the transport division) who moved on to become transport manager for

Beamish & Crawford. His mother, Mairéad, from Rossnowlagh, Co. Donegal, died when he was 18, about the time he went to UCD. His father was a 'nice person but unbelievably regimented', says one who knew him in later years. 'His routines were so precise you could set your watch by him. He was not an affectionate man.' He was apt to refer to his only son Eamonn as 'George', in tones that implied the boy was beyond his understanding and floated on a loftier plane: 'George? He's up there, his head stuck in a book.'

To the few who got to know Lillis as an adult, it was clear he had always fallen well short of his father's expectations. He went to UCD to study Arts and told the court he spent four years there, although it is not clear if he graduated.

His chosen career in art directing was also a long way from his father's world. He went on to work for DDFHB, the advertising and marketing agency, in a pitiless industry. 'It's a fairly merciless meritocracy . . . If things aren't working out, you're gone,' says an industry source. In September 1990, the career of the 33-year-old Eamonn Lillis was waning when he met 28-year-old dynamo Celine Cawley, a driven, ambitious producer with GPA, a television commercials production company.

The pair worked in the same industry and shared a love of dogs. But there the similarities ended. Her relationship with her father, James, a high-flying solicitor, was one of mutual adoration. The contrast between her passion, energy and ambition and Lillis's passive, dreamy, almost disconnected persona was stark. But to one who cared deeply for Cawley and grew close to both of them,

Eamonn Lillis leaving the Criminal Courts of Justice in Dublin after being found guilty of the manslaughter of his wife, Celine Cawley. Photograph: Alan Betson.

'they were the perfect fit. I thought he was a nice guy. I really liked him.'

To another who knew him well in recent years, 'the reality is that he was and is an oddball. He seemed to have no friends. He was easy to talk to – if you talked to him – but you'd never remember him again. He seemed to have no opinions of his own'. Another suggests that the marriage suited both of them, 'Celine would never have married someone who would stand up to her formidable authority. It would take a brave man or woman to say "No" to Celine once she set her mind on something.'

To one of Cawley's closest friends, 'they were good friends. They got on.' They met in September, were engaged by Christmas, and married the following July, in Howth church with a reception in her parents' home at the Baily in Howth. With Celine, once she made up her mind, 'everything was done quickly', says an old friend, wistfully.

People who were close to her personally talk about her almost reverently as a force of nature. A jolly, outgoing, funny child who went to Scoil Íosa in Malahide, followed by boarding school in Rathnew, they say some of her happiest days were between the ages of about nine to 13, when she and Juliette Hussey, her first cousin and lifelong friend, spent holidays in Hossegor, in southwest France, where Juliette's mother took a house.

At 17, to her father's consternation, she announced she wanted to be a model, although her mother, Brenda, played along, suggesting she go to a London training college. Spotted by Johnny Casanova of the Elite modelling agency, she went to New York, where she lived with John McEnroe's family for a time – the tennis star's father and Celine's were business associates and friends – and travelled the world. There were a couple of 'significant relationships, not flashy types – cheeky maybe'. A deeply tanned Texan fireman is particularly remembered from this period.

In her early 20s 'she was beginning to see the nonsense of the modelling life', had her Bond girl moment in *A View to a Kill*, and returned to Ireland, aiming herself at the film production world. She could have done it the easy way, with the help of her father and brother Chris, with their blue-chip industry contacts and funding possibilities. But she started from scratch, going to work as a receptionist in Windmill Lane, where Gerry Poulson, head of GPA productions, spotted her potential, employed her as his personal assistant and taught her everything he knew.

In court, the bald evidence was that she founded Toytown Films, gave her husband a job when his own work had dried up two years into the marriage, made him a director and trained him in as a producer. In the good times, she was earning half a million a year and he one-fifth of that.

No one mentioned her bravery, determination and capacity for hard work. She started the company at home while pregnant with their daughter in 1992, effectively acquiring the goodwill of GPA and becoming the first company to set up in the newly deregulated market.

She was also an extraordinarily well-organised woman – 'She'd have her taxes paid three months in advance' – but she could hardly have chosen a more ruthlessly competitive, male-dominated industry.

Her standards were high, she deemed nothing impossible, and there is no doubt she could be difficult, says one who worked closely with her. 'She really knew her business and she didn't suffer fools gladly . . . If she didn't like somebody or thought they weren't up to scratch, she wouldn't have them hanging around. She wasn't afraid to get rid of people. But she was no drama queen going around firing people either.'

Toytown thrived, producing commercials for world markets and its prestigious client list came to include Carlsberg, Guinness, Volkswagen and Volvo. A memorable campaign was for Walker Crisps, starring Roy Keane. There were many personality clashes; she knew well that she wasn't universally loved. A highly unusual feature of this murder trial was that almost everyone in court and around Dublin appeared to know someone who knew her. The picture was rarely flattering. A long line of sources talked of business meetings and scenes where she came across like a 'tyrant', including to her husband.

An image emerged of the victim as harridan, a woman who shouted and bullied her way to success, a ball-breaker who treated her husband as a lapdog. The tone of Garda questioning of her husband supported the picture of a domineering, emasculating woman. 'Celine was the breadwinner, wasn't she?' 'I believe she was bossy enough?' 'Did you always do what she told you?' 'You were more of a gofer, weren't you?' 'She'd say jump, you'd say how high?'

It was obviously intended to spark a visceral reaction in her husband, in fairness. It is evident that the Cawley family hold the Gardaí involved in the highest regard. And the officer in charge was a woman – Det. Insp. Angela Willis, promoted early in a man's world, so who better to understand Celine Cawley?

Nonetheless, the line of questioning bolstered a sense that there was provocation in the mere fact of her bullish ambition and earning power. Would similar traits in a successful man elicit such comment? What might be described as 'ambitious', 'driven' and 'focused' in a man can translate to 'ball-breaker', 'hard-nosed' and 'thundering bitch' in a woman. 'Isn't that what they say about a woman who's successful in business?' a friend of Cawley remarks sadly. 'You wouldn't hear it about a woman doctor . . .'

And there are other, quieter sources who insist there was plenty of smooth with the tough. For Celine Cawley, it was an article of faith to pay people properly and on time. Crews working up to the early hours would still get paid before heading home, with Cawley personally handing out the cheques. There is plenty of evidence that she had a gift for loyalty, for recognising raw talent and nurturing it. She might have been loud and bullish but

Celine Cawley. Photograph: **Irish Daily Star.**

she was never patronising or demeaning, says one who worked closely with her; she gave responsibility beyond their years to people she had faith in.

The condemnatory chatter and line of questioning contrasted sharply with the official status accorded the other prominent woman in the case, Jean Treacy, the 31-year-old massage and beauty therapist from Nenagh, Co. Tipperary. Her clandestine sexual trysts with her client in car parks and her place of work won her the kind of treatment normally accorded to terrorised participants in the witness protection programme. The day before her evidence, to make her fully comfortable with her environment, she received a familiarisation tour of the courthouse from a Garda, as is the right of any witness. Then, on her evidence day, shrouded celebrity-style in large scarf and sunglasses, she was driven to court in a police vehicle, escorted through a side entrance and buffered by detectives in court.

Evidence revealed that Jean Treacy – who was introduced to Lillis by Celine – was herself engaged to be married when she invited Lillis to feel her racing pulse while he lay on her massage table; that she had fancied him for months beforehand and re-established contact with him many weeks after the killing with drink on her, seeking 'closure', as she put it. After gentle handling in the witness stand, she was smuggled out of the court and driven away at speed in a Garda vehicle up North Brunswick Street, where a road block was set up to halt pursuers.

That was the deal agreed, and Gardaí kept their end of it. 'How else are we to persuade people to give evidence voluntarily?' asked a detective unconnected to the case, recalling police discomfort at the relentless media pursuit of Nicky Pelley, the mistress in the Rachel O'Reilly murder trial. Meanwhile, Jean Treacy's wedding arrangements are said to be back on track.

The Garda treatment of Treacy triggered larger questions about who in such a case merits this level of protection, and why, and who decides. After all, every day, family, friends and witnesses on both sides, however aged, distressed or humiliated, are forced to negotiate the courts' main entrance, a bank of cameras and a curious public. If this is a precedent and a future witness thus shielded wishes to sell his or her story, obviously the pay-off will be significantly greater thanks to the rarity of the photographs. Is this desirable?

Sources close to the Cawley family found many other aspects of the trial distressing, perceiving a system that allows itself to be 'manipulated outrageously' by the accused. 'The power you have to paint yourself as innocent, meek, kind, someone who wouldn't hurt a fly . . . At times, it was like listening to a combination of a Mills & Boon novel

The family of Celine Cawley, (from left) her sister, Susanna; father, James; brother, Chris Cawley (far right) and his wife, Sorcha, leaving the Criminal Courts after the verdict on Eamonn Lillis. Photograph: Alan Betson.

and the kind of horror movie a 10-year-old would make – a very bad one.'

Another source of distress was the requirement at short notice for the couple's 17-year-old daughter to give evidence (by video link, from a room in the courts complex), a request understood to have come from the defence. It was hard to see the value of it or of the cross-examination. Usually, such statements are simply read to the court. Friends were aghast. 'Above all else, Celine was a wonderful mother. Her daughter was everything to her, the light of her life.'

Among her close family – her brother Chris and his wife Sorcha, her sister Susanna and her husband Andrew Coonan, her brother-in-law Rory Quigley who was married to her late sister, Barbara – Celine's hugely practical, vigilant, humorous presence is profoundly missed. Despite suggestions in court that her husband handled the domestic side of things, a friend insists she ran the home and was 'incredibly house-proud'.

She was the kind who would suddenly appear in your chaotic house, take command of your newborn baby and other squealing children and order you up to bed. She had several godchildren and kept a loving, beady eye on all her nieces and nephews. A nephew who wanted to dress like Jim Morrison (of The Doors) circa 1968, for his 18th birthday party had only to mention it and the skin-tight leather trousers, cowboy boots – real leather and properly vintage – and all the rest were couriered around.

'She was a bit of a bossy-boots at times but they all knew she was there for them . . . She really loved them and cared about them individually, and she helped several of them to get going in life in very important ways. When they went to her for work experience, she'd talk to the parents and would take time to figure out how they were. She'd take her guidance role very seriously.'

A source close to Rory Quigley and his children speaks in virtual tears at her unstinting devotion, generosity and vigilance through the years following her late sister Barbara's death. While others stepped back delicately to give them space, Celine barrelled in, leaving a legacy of sustained care, love, fun and organisation: 'There wasn't anybody else in the world like her. She was a giant.' Every year, the Christmas trees of her loved ones would have a 'mountain' of presents from the Lillis household. 'There would be individual presents for each person and one from each of the dogs and the cat for every family member – and the present from the cat would not be insignificant. Even the Christmas after she died, there were presents from her; they'd already been bought and wrapped.'

Her Christmas Eve parties were much anticipated, especially by the children. But one old friend suggests that she had become less inclined in recent times to socialise outside of her own parties – 'great, memorable parties', says one regular – because she was acutely conscious of her weight problem, referred to several times in court as 'marked' obesity. 'Look, 32 per cent of women are obese and 50 per cent of men,' comments a friend, with finality.

More important to this friend was that Cawley's long-term loyalty and gift of friendship were reflected in the attendance at her memorial Mass last year when almost her entire class from Rathnew turned up and Moira Healy recited Christina Rosetti's touching poem 'Remember'. 'She was a great storyteller, so clever and witty . . . You always felt the better for having spoken to her. She was such a big presence in our lives, such a loved presence.' Her social circle were her family, her friends – particularly Juliette Hussey and old school friends such as Moira Healy, Irene Meagher and Miriam Hamilton, her small team in Toytown who had soldiered with her for years, people such as the fashion designer and stylist Helen Cody, and others in the industry she nurtured such as the director John Hayes.

'She was an extraordinarily good and close friend, a proper good friend in the true sense. I have so much to thank her for,' said Cody after her death.

If the passive, dreamy Eamonn Lillis felt like a passenger beside this dynamo, it would hardly be surprising. The fund of unflattering impressions about her public treatment of him is complemented by unflattering impressions of the energy he brought to the marriage or the company of which she made him a director. But some suggest they had worked things out: 'They weren't that young when they met, so they met each other as they were and accepted each other as they were . . . She was the leader, the strong one . . . They were very affectionate towards one another . . . The idea portrayed over the past few weeks that he was downtrodden is not borne out by the facts. She always spoke about him with the highest regard; she never said a bad word about him. And no one in the family would have dreamt of saying a negative word about Eamonn to her.'

This 'fierce defensiveness' of Eamonn within the family is raised by several sources close to them, although some concede that arguments between them were not unusual.

In fact, they suggest she was Eamonn's great protector, and went to battle for him in many quiet ways. She worried about him. A few weeks before her death, she was ringing family members discreetly to discuss his cholesterol levels. When he complained of a bad back, it was Celine who introduced him to Jean Treacy for massage. She bought him gifts of centre-court tickets in Wimbledon and season tickets to Old Trafford. When he wanted to pursue his military interests by touring the Normandy battle fields or the walled town of Carcassonne – each time with her father – it was Celine who organised it. When James Cawley, his son and three sons-in-law attended a Davis Cup match in Madrid on October 18th (less than two months before the killing), Eamonn was already embarked on the affair with Jean Treacy, says a friend. 'I think that affair just completely unbalanced him.'

In losing his wife, Eamonn Lillis also appears to have lost almost his entire social circle. It was evident after her death – when he was sheltered by Chris and Sorcha Cawley – that the Cawley family were his main support, his strongest pillar then being Celine's grief-stricken father. Others observe that there was no one around the Garda station for him when he was interviewed or under arrest. His sisters Elaine and Carmel, who live in England, were his daily supporters during the trial and it was a measure of them and the Cawley family that they were regularly seen chatting to one another.

His other trial companion was Gerry Kennedy who went surety for him, an old friend from his UCD days, now a freelance advertising copywriter, and on occasion, David Cassidy, another UCD alumnus.

The media have come under criticism in some quarters for the vast coverage given to this trial. Why this one, when other tragic cases around the courts attract no interest? As one sturdy regular in the queue for the public seats put it: 'Ah look, this had the X factor . . . It had everything.' It's human nature. It involved wealthy Dubliners with a hot tub, a life-size ornamental cow, a mistress and multiple houses. The small troupe of rather mortified civilian witnesses was quintessentially middle-class, of a kind that prefer to lead utterly private lives and are never sighted in the Central Criminal Court. It's what made the trial so compelling for those who thronged Court 19, a fact that didn't escape Mr Justice Barry White.

When the court was shown a 20-minute guided tour of the expansive Howth home, courtesy of a Garda video, he sent the jury out, saying angrily it was reminiscent of something from the OJ Simpson trial and demanding to know what the video had added, other than 'whetting the ghoulish appetites of some members of the public'. Not to mention the rather sensational admission at the start (one even Gardaí were not expecting) that the accused had concocted the story about the burglar in the garden.

Yet, as one hard-chaw journalist put it, was 'it just another domestic', another cautionary tale? After all, there was no Joe O'Reilly-style figure or gangster boss plotting the 'perfect' crime. For all the media emphasis on Lillis's designer garments (Ralph Lauren, Abercrombie Fitch) and prestigious vehicles, there was nothing that isn't available at an outlet store somewhere. If nothing else, the video demonstrated that there was nothing ostentatious about the much-vaunted luxury home either. 'With Celine, it would have been the opposite,' says a friend. Her 'only indulgence' was a French property acquired five years ago, a beautiful four-bedroomed house just off the beach in Hossegor, the surfing haven in southwest France, where she had spent some of her happiest childhood years.

MONDAY, 8 FEBRUARY 2010

Little Cash for a Lot of Gold

Conor Pope

It's a cold morning and I'm in a shockingly decorated hotel room on a leafy road in Dublin, trying to sell my wedding ring to a man who is not exactly busy. He's been in this place for more than five hours waiting for a gold rush which has yet to materialise. Despite the fact that fliers offering to buy unwanted gold for cold hard cash have been posted through every letterbox in the neighbourhood, I'm his first customer of the day – very bad news for a man who works exclusively on commission.

I hand him the ring. He looks for the carat – 18 – weighs it – 6.6 grams – and punches a few numbers into a cheap desk calculator before offering me €80 for the ring. I'm horrified, as it's nearly 90 per cent less than the ring cost when bought in a moment of madness from an upmarket jewellers in the city centre several years ago.

I tell him I am not here to sell but to find out more about the growing trade in recycled gold. The news that he's not even going to make this – very modest – buy is plainly not welcome news. He is, however, willing to talk about his business although unwilling to identify himself by anything more than his first name, Martin.

He's been in the gold-buying business for six years, the last three of which he has spent in Ireland. He says that while it has been quiet since

Model Baiba Gaile strikes a pose at the launch in Dublin of the Marks & Spencer Spring/Summer Collection. Photograph: Brenda Fitzsimons.

Daire Lydon, aged 5, from Sandymount in Dublin and his brother Cathal, aged 3, at the 2010 Hennessy Gold Cup at Leopardstown, Co. Dublin. Photograph: Alan Betson.

Christmas, before then he was dealing with between 20 and 30 customers with gold to sell daily. 'There are too many people in the business now and too many websites. At least in here you can see what I'm doing. I can offer €14 a gram while the best price many of the websites will give you is €4.'

Over the last year, daytime television ad breaks have been taken over by mostly web-based companies offering to buy unwanted gold off cash-strapped punters laid low by the global economic malaise.

Martin is right on the money when he says that some of these companies offer consumers shockingly bad value.

The magazine *Which?* recently sent three pieces of brand-new gold jewellery to four gold buyers that advertise on TV. It also sent the same items to three independent jewellers and three pawnbrokers and it found that TV gold buyers consistently gave the worst quotes.

CashMyGold offered just £38.57 (€44) for the three pieces of new jewellery which had been purchased for £729 (€834). One of the poorest deals from CashMyGold was an offer of just under £10 (€11.40) for a £215 (€246) 9ct gold bangle – an independent jeweller quoted £54 (€62) for the same piece.

Another site, Money4Gold, effectively held a 9ct necklace to ransom telling the *Which?* researcher that the necklace, which cost £399 (€456), was 'not gold' and insisted the customer pay £10.95 (€12.50) to have it returned. The magazine's investigation found that on average the TV gold buyers offered only around 6 per cent of the retail price for gold, but British high street retailers paid around 25 per cent.

'The poor value for money that these TV gold buyers are providing is simply shocking. The cash for gold market is unregulated, and this investigation has raised some serious concerns about the fair treatment of consumers,' says Peter Vicary-Smith, *Which?* chief executive. 'People should be wary of buyers' adverts as they could almost certainly get more money for their gold elsewhere.'

One place might be Martin Gear's jewellers on Dublin's Dorset Street. He opened seven years ago and the 'We Buy Gold' sign is nearly as big as the name over the door. He offers me €90 for my wedding ring if I am simply scrapping it but says he'll give me €130 if I trade it in for a new piece.

He says that while the gold-buying business is good, there is a misconception that the recession has seen desperate people beat a path to his door. 'We have seen an upsurge in recent months and I think that is thanks to the television ads more than the recession. People have suddenly realised how much money they might be sitting on. We might get around 15 people in a week. Mostly they are just having a clear out or a spring clean – there are loads of places that take CDs or books so why not gold?'

When I express dismay at the offer of €90 for my ring, he points out that I paid a premium because the ring was unusual and highlights VAT at 21 per cent and the jeweller's mark up. 'Some of the big stores would work on a 300 per cent mark up but they have to because they might be paying €10,000 a week in rent as well as up to a million in key money.'

Niall Marren is the MD of *forgottengold.com*, an Irish-based, gold recycling website. The site has staked its claim to be the first entirely Irish-owned such website and he says that since they started trading 12 months ago, they have bought gold from 7,000 people. There has, however, been a stiffening of competition in recent months and, in addition to a handful of other Irish operators, US and UK sites are looking towards Ireland to boost trade.

He offers €82.67 for the ring. 'We determine how much we can sell it for on the gold markets and we work out how long it will take to get it on to those markets. We pay between 65 and 80 per cent of the market value. We are in the business to make a profit but the profit margins are not high; they are in the single digits,' says Marren. He describes the typical seller as 'an astute person' who recognises the value of things. 'My impression is that people see this as an opportunity because of gold prices,' he says.

Since August this year, the value of gold has risen steadily on international markets, reaching an all-time high of $1,226 (€879) an ounce on 3 December, up from $255 (€183) an ounce in December 1999. He says that 90 per cent of the business is from women selling jewellery they received from old boyfriends or because it has simply gone out of fashion.

'The one thing that people don't sell is the stuff that has sentimental value, not unless they are really on their uppers. Very often we get rubbish bits of old pieces that people just have lying about the place, stuff that would be of no use to anyone unless it is melted down and recycled.'

He accepts that the *Which?* study did come to some very grim conclusions about the websites trading in gold but is understandably anxious to distance himself from their findings. 'I don't believe that it would come to the same conclusions about the Irish market.'

I also tried to flog the ring on a US-based website where I was offered just €53, but the worst price offered came not from one of the new gold traders but from a considerably more old-school operation. In one of Dublin's dwindling number of pawnshops, a man behind the thick glass panel could hardly have been less interested as he casually threw the ring onto a scales and barked '50 quid' at me. I made my excuses and left, ring on hand.

Planet Dáil in Turmoil as Fine Gael's Shooting Star Turns Out to be an Alien

Miriam Lord

I rish politics is in deep shock. A blue fireball blazed across the political firmament yesterday and plummeted into the heart of Leinster House. Everyone was stunned. Politicians from all sides couldn't believe what happened.

'Is it true?' they asked each other. 'It's incredible!' they cried.

And so it was that the meteoric career of George Lee fell to earth. It was blinding, it was brilliant and it was over in a flash. Fine Gael's shooting star shines no more.

They were utterly astounded. Because for politicians – who would sell their grannies for a safe seat in the Dáil – what George did defies reason.

TDs couldn't understand why a newly-elected deputy, with an adoring public and a national profile they can only dream about, upped and walked away. The idea of doing such a thing is alien to them. George and his principles? No, they will never get it because it is beyond their ken. And as the smoke cleared, and Fine Gael prepared to assess the damage and Fianna Fáil danced, all parties agreed on one thing: George Lee was never really one of them. Which is why he got elected in the first place.

The news broke at lunchtime. Few deputies and Senators were about, for the House doesn't sit

George Lee speaking to reporters outside Leinster House, after he announced his resignation as a TD for Dublin South and as a member of Fine Gael after just eight months. Photograph: Brenda Fitzsimons.

on Monday. For those Fine Gaelers who were there, the same word kept cropping up: 'Gutted.' George – The People's Princess – had buoyed their spirits and cheered them. And now he was gone. Maybe they should have minded him a bit more. He said they never included him in their plans. He was Inda's plaything, paraded around the country for his celebrity status. But he had 'zero impact or influence' on formulating economic policy.

As George put it in one of his many interviews yesterday: 'If this was a relationship, it would be irretrievably broken down – I'm off!' He stopped short of saying there were three people in the marriage – George, Enda and a clutch of front-bench heavyweights who are no respecters of Georgie Come Latelys, even if they arrive on the scene with an excellent pedigree, a stellar TV career and a landslide majority.

Now, in the wake of the departure of his South Dublin rose, all a devastated Inda can do is take comfort in the words of Sir Elton John: 'Goodbye Georgie Lee, although I never knew you at all . . .' He issued a brief e-mail to mark the embarrassing departure, then stayed behind closed doors back in Castlebar. House private.

But George was talking. A lot. He looked despondent. He sounded shattered. His dream – the one he spoke about so eloquently nine months ago – was dead. 'I had to be true to myself . . . I've decided I'm not going to be fake . . . I am not prepared to live a lie.'

Congratulations to all those interviewers who resisted the urge to ask: 'But what about the children, George?'

A bit late for that now. And did nobody in Fine Gael see this coming? Everybody else did.

The novelty of his new job would have kept deputy Lee going in the early months. But as time passed, that eagerness and enthusiasm visibly waned. Many commented on the regular sight in the Dáil chamber of finance spokesman Richard Bruton, in conclave with his deputy, Ciarán O'Donnell, while George, weighed down with folders and documents, looked on from a few rows behind. Deputy Lee's resignation will be no surprise to the 'I told you so' brigade. They forecast it would end in tears from the start, knowing how the system works. 'He'll need counselling within the month,' commented one Leinster House sage after George was received in triumph on his first day.

From the afternoon he was first unveiled to the public, Fine Gael treated Lee like a trophy wife. At the time, the party leader joked they would have to employ a tour manager to organise George's diary, such was the clamour from the grassroots to meet him. They put together an economic roadshow, with George as chairman, and blitzed the country.

But it was Richard and Ciarán, along with Leo Varadkar and Simon Coveney, who got to deliver the speeches. And when the platform speakers did their thing, they departed to continue formulating policy and thinking deep thoughts while economist George was left behind to press the flesh, sign autographs and pose for photos. He didn't like it. He wanted to have an input into that policy. He said his sole purpose for putting himself forward for election was to get his teeth stuck into shaping the party's economic strategy.

What made him go? Innocence and ego or courage and principle? It's probably somewhere in between. But George did a brave thing nonetheless.

Ironically, in those starry-eyed days, he said he went into politics because he felt 'constrained' by his job in television. Little did he know. We wished him the best when he said, 'I am going to speak out and I don't care if they don't like it.' Noting the raised eyebrow he insisted: 'I will!' It didn't happen.

George Lee says Enda Kenny misjudged him. He wanted to be involved in formulating policy, but he was cold-shouldered. His boss was more interested in using him as a show pony. 'I'm not there to be used just for my celebrity or [to] draw a crowd.'

The jokes have started already: RTÉ is to air a new reality show starring Charlie Bird and George

Lee. It'll be called Celebrity Big Baby. It's a cruel world outside Montrose.

TUESDAY, 9 FEBRUARY 2010

Lee's Betrayal Adds to Cynicism he Intended to Fight

Fintan O'Toole

If you've had the chance to go around the country in the last few months discussing the state of the nation, you will have felt the rage that is out there in middle-class Ireland. You will have realised that things are so desperate that even media types are objects of some kind of hope. This has happened not because the public has lost its suspicion of the media but because there is no one else to look to. The need for someone to trust is as palpable as the fury at those who have previously betrayed it.

George Lee's sweeping victory in the Dublin South by-election last June was, of course, the most spectacular evidence of this phenomenon. It was an expression both of profound rage and of almost touching trust. There was, on the one hand, a desire for someone outside the system to get in there and give it a kick. And on the other, there was the notion that we needed someone who knew what was going on, who could make sense of the acronyms and unfathomable numbers that were buzzing around our heads like venomous hornets.

The union of these two forces was, for Fine Gael, a marriage made in heaven. It was a perfectly polite revolution, a radical gesture that was also a cry, not so much for an overturning of the established order, as for intelligence, integrity, competence and decency.

That this project has exploded in clouds of mutual bewilderment, sending jagged shards of shattered egos flying in all directions, tells us two things. The most important of them is that the political system has no idea what is happening. Even while the ground is shaking, it continues to run along the established tracks of thought.

Fine Gael, we realise, actually thought that George Lee's apotheosis was about Fine Gael. They saw his triumph as being essentially nothing more than a particularly brilliant political stroke. Beyond its immediate nature as a morale-booster for the party and a beautifully embroidered pillow to shove over the mouths of those who whisper that Enda Kenny isn't up to it, it had no larger meaning. Its concrete manifestation – George Lee TD – was just another bumptious backbencher. Beyond his celebrity function in recruitment and fundraising, he was simply a rival foot on the greasy poll. He must learn to serve his time, pay his dues and work the system.

This says a great deal about Enda Kenny's ultimate unfitness for leadership, the leadenness that marks him, not as an alternative to a political culture that has failed us so disastrously but as part of it. The unwillingness to use Lee's obvious intellectual talents and to build on the trust he has built with the public points to a small-minded nexus of jealousy, caution and smugness.

It reveals a party assuming that it will be in power after the next election and need do nothing except avoid trouble. But the failure of the whole project also points to a lack of imagination on George Lee's part. There was a certain naïvety in believing, in the first instance, that a classic catch-all, conservative party like Fine Gael is particularly interested in a cutting-edge economic analysis that acknowledges what Lee surely knows – that the old orthodoxies cannot provide solutions to the crisis that they caused.

But there is also an apparent lack of understanding on Lee's part of his own power. He seems barely to have understood what it was that made 27,000 people vote for him. They didn't vote for him to be an economic adviser to Enda Kenny.

Richard Bruton on the day of George Lee's resignation. Photograph: Eric Luke.

They know very well that there are good and honest economists who could be hired for that role without being elected to anything. They voted for George Lee to change Irish politics. The two qualities they looked for and found in him were simple – he was an outsider and he could be trusted to speak the truth as he saw it.

This gave him immense power – and it also in part explains why Fine Gael couldn't handle him. He was much bigger than the party and in a sense almost completely independent of it. No one gave a damn whether he did constituency work or sat on committees examining the minutiae of legislation. In particular, no one gave two hoots whether or not he was expounding Fine Gael policy. He was George Lee, tribune of the enraged and disorientated middle classes.

Walking away from Fine Gael is fine but walking away from this much bigger, freer, more exciting job is not. He should have been thrilled to be free of a party that had begun to regard him as an exotic pet that it had been given for Christmas and wasn't sure quite what to feed it.

Paradoxically, the party's misuse of him gave him the excuse he needed to leave it and actually represent the people who trusted him with their votes. They elected him to embody a new kind of politics – free-thinking, plain-speaking, honest, uninvolved in clientelism. By betraying that trust, he has added to the cynicism he intended to fight.

Gardaí at the fire-damaged west wing (left) of Russborough House in Blessington, Co. Wicklow. Photograph: Bryan O'Brien.

SATURDAY, 13 FEBRUARY 2010

Looking for Love

Eoin Butler

The lighting is soft – that's the first thing you notice when you arrive downstairs at the Turk's Head pub in Dublin city centre. If it were any softer, in fact, you might pull up a chair by one of those old flower pots and ask her what she looks for in a man. The organisers of tonight's speed dating event asked participants to assemble at 7.45 p.m. sharp. I arrive at 7.49 p.m., so flustered I almost sign up for salsa dancing lessons by mistake. But nothing actually happens until almost 9 p.m.

The ladies have, by and large, shown up in pairs. They sit awkwardly at the bar, fixing their hair and stealing furtive glances at the latest arrivals. The guys have almost all come alone. But as with any group of men, thrown together in any

circumstances, anywhere in the world, we pick up the conversation almost without missing a beat. Robbie Keane to Celtic, huh? How'll that pan out? Risky move on Spurs' part. He scores goals, the boy scores goals. . .

The concept of speed dating was developed in California in the late 1990s by Rabbi Yaacov Deyo as a means to help Jewish singles meet. Since whether or not one is attracted to another person is decided almost instantaneously, Rabbi Deyo reasoned, 12 short, face-to-face encounters with members of the opposite sex in a single night might prove more conducive to matrimony than a string of dates, with often incompatible partners.

Another possibility, which the Rabbi may not have considered, is that a dozen crushing rejections on a single evening could prove more mortifying (and, in the long term, more traumatic) than the same number of rejections spread out over as many months. But who's to say? I'll have to take my chances, I suppose.

Frank McDonald peers warily up the stairwell of a Georgian house on Dublin's Henrietta Street that is badly in need of refurbishment. Photograph: Brenda Fitzsimons.

Tonight's event was pitched at singles in the 25–35 age bracket. The females in attendance seem broadly representative of that demographic. But the male contingent, as far as I can tell, ranges from guys in their early 30s to veterans practically of the showband era. No one seems to mind. We stand at the far end of the bar, swingers young and old, buying each other pints and guffawing to beat the band.

The only bum note at this stage comes when I tell an affable plumber from the midlands that I have a couple of friends from the same parish as him. His bonhomie vanishes in an instant. 'You better not tell anyone you met me here, right?' he warns. I couldn't if I wanted to – I don't even know his name.

Eventually, our compère for the evening, Hugh Redmond from *GetOut.ie*, calls us all to attention and explains how things are going to proceed. Each female has been assigned a table. The men will rotate tables, spending three minutes in conversation with each woman.

It's about now that my nerves begin to fray. Only three minutes? Dear God, what can I possibly convey in three minutes that won't send them running for the hills? Looks. Grooming. Hygiene. Personality. Prospects. None are exactly strong suits of mine. No, I'm more like a Don DeLillo novel. You have to read at least five or six hundred pages before you know why the hell you've bothered to begin with. Forget 'speed dating', I reckon, I should have signed up for 'static dating'. Prospective romantic partners should be contractually obliged to stay with me for a year at least, to give me a decent shot at winning them around.

It's a minor wobble, but I get past it. As long as I don't meet anyone I know, I tell myself. I take a seat.

'Well, long time no see, Eoin!' What are the odds? My very first date is a girl I went to college with. Karen and I don't even bother going through the motions. We just exchange gossip about old acquaintances. Such-and-such just got married. Such-and-such is a miserable failure. Such-and-such is doing really well for himself. (Really? Yeah, I hated him, too.)

My next date is Grace who is cool and funny. She seems to have a pretty face, although in this light she could also have a broomstick and cauldron beneath that table too, for all I know. She's an accountant. My father was an accountant, I tell her, unloading an arsenal of accountant jokes. If I could have any idea just how many accountants I'm about to meet, I'd probably elect to keep some of that powder dry. But that's another matter. She takes them in good spirits and fires back a couple of her own.

After Tracey, there's Sandra – another accountant. Then there's Mary – yet another accountant. Then Irene – payments department. Then there's Patricia – works for Volkswagen. 'Crash Test Dummy department?' 'No, accounts actually.' None of them, though, launch the sort of Lady Bracknell-esque cross-examination I had feared having to endure. One girl asks what my ambitions for the future are. I tell her I'm still waiting on a call-up from the Mayo football team. She seems okay with that.

The conversations, by and large, flow free and easy and with just 180 seconds to make your pitch, there aren't too many awkward silences to fill. One girl is drunk, which makes attempting meaningful communication a wasted effort. Another notes approvingly that I don't drink. Actually, I'm in the throes of a pretty nasty vomiting and going-to-the-bathroom-more-frequently-than-I-would-wish bug. But I choose not to correct her misconception.

All in all, I'd have to say that this evening is turning out to be a much more enjoyable experience than I had anticipated.

After seven dates there's a 10 minute interval, during which the women decamp to the toilets to gossip about the men, while all the men decamp to the bar to check the latest soccer scores on their mobile phones.

It's hard to get back into the full swing of things after the break. Churning out the same autobiographical information for the tenth or eleventh time becomes a little tedious. I grew up in Mayo . . . went to university in Galway . . . have lived in Dublin for X number of years . . . It's one thing to tune out of a conversation when the other person is talking – quite another when the person speaking is yourself.

Things don't really come back into focus for me until I meet my last date. Rebecca is a doctor in her mid-20s and, even in this light, she's clearly very attractive. She inveigles from me that I'm a journalist and deduces pretty quickly that I'm probably here on an assignment. It's the end of the night. I don't bother denying it. We hit it off though and, when time is called, repair upstairs together for a drink. She tells me she works in A&E in a Dublin hospital and proceeds to share all sorts of indiscreet anecdotes about the proctological 'mishaps' that seem to befall the citizens of this city on a nightly basis.

Do I feel bad, she asks eventually, that I met all these girls tonight under false pretences? I'm single, I tell her. There were no false pretences. But you're a journalist, she replies, with a friendly shove. They gave us each some sort of a score card this evening when we arrived. At this point, I'm about ready to throw mine out the window. I protest, as suavely as I can, I'm only doing my job.

I'm joking with you, she smiles. 'Sure, I'm in the same boat. I've got a boyfriend at home. I'm only here to keep a friend company.' 'Really?' I ask. She nods. 'Yeah, she's downstairs talking to one of those Kerry lads.' 'Really?' I ask again. Yes, she nods. She isn't joking either. Wow. I've just tasted my own medicine and I'm not so sure I like it.

An Irishman's Diary

Frank McNally

'Property seller goes into matchmaking business' (Headline in *The Irish Times* Property supplement, 11 February, over a story about how the slowdown is forcing estate agents to diversify, in one case by setting up a dating agency).

Just imagine.

Liam, 47, Dublin 6. Mature male in much sought-after location, close to Luas green line, schools, shops and all amenities. Presented in superb condition, following recent upgrading work at gym. Non-smoker, GSOH. WLTM female 36-45 for fun and friendship. Viewing by appointment. Box No. 1062.

Katie, 38, Dún Laoghaire. Utterly charming, bijou female (4ft 11, extending to 5ft 2 with high heels), located in cosy bedsit close to sea, Dart, etc. Katie is lovingly maintained, with many surprise features. Currently double-glazed, pending laser eye surgery. Would like to meet male, 35-45, with view to friendship and maybe more. Viewing highly recommended. Box No. 1761.

Seán, 39, Navan. Good-looking, semi-detached

American actor Samuel L. Jackson, photographed at the American Ambassador's Residence in the Phoenix Park in Dublin, with members of the New York City based Soul Stepdance singers, who were in Ireland for Irish American History month. Jackson was in Dublin for a charity event and to help raise awareness on behalf of Irish Autism. Photograph: Brenda Fitzsimons.

male (divorce proceedings pending), likely soon to be homeless. In excellent condition, located very close to fitness and only a 20-minute daily run from athleticism. WLTM similar female, but with own house. On view, O'Malley's Bar, every night from 9 p.m. Or contact Box No. 2074.

Margaret, Leixlip. Curvy fortysomething female, firm-bodied but deceptively spacious. GSOH. Social drinker, loves dining out, socialising and having fun!!?! WLTM male with energy rating certificate B1, or higher!!! Box No. 3546.

Brian, 50s, Clontarf. Imposing double-fronted businessman, full of character, situated in leafy corner of prestigious Dublin suburb. Returning to the market for the first time in decades and might benefit from some modernisation. But a small investment by the right female would repay handsome dividends! Box No. 2351.

Siobhán, 42, Galway. Highly desirable female, located in prime area of life, combining breathtaking frontal views with spectacular, secluded rear (south-facing). One of the most stunning properties to come on the Galway market in years. Would suit discerning mature male or sincere toy-boy. No time-wasters please. Viewing by appointment. Box No. 1623.

George, 60s, Rathgar. Old world charm meets new world excitement in this lively, superbly preserved widow. Constructed in the late Edwardian style, with listed façade and many original features, he also offers all the modern conveniences, including full-time Lithuanian housemaid and chauffeur-driven Bentley. A bon-viveur, George enjoys all of life's pleasures, from the best Cuban cigars to vintage malts. A property simply boozing – er, oozing – character, he would like to meet women aged 18-58 with a sense of fun. Short-term rentals considered. Box No. 3429.

Angela, 29, north Cork. An ex-nun, her phased release onto the dating market for the first time represents the most exciting development in the Montenotte/St Luke's area for many years. Set on a dramatic, spiritually elevated site, she is

presented in pristine condition throughout. Seeks soulmate. Age and looks of no importance. Unveiling Saturday noon-1 p.m. Box No. 1262.

Stephen, Dundalk. Middle-aged accountant, currently located in career cul-de-sac, just around the corner from success. Enjoys pre-1963 designation but in need of total refurbishment. Obvious potential for mix of residential and commercial activities. This is a superb investment opportunity for an imaginative female with the creative touch. Box No. 1317.

Lucy, 37, west Dublin. Originally advertised in 2005, and then 2007, but now returning to the market with a greatly reduced reserve and even lower expectations. Would still prefer to meet a single, heterosexual male, with working pulse. But all reasonable offers will be considered. Box No. 3765.

Mick, 32, Clondalkin. Just released (from a private, gated community boasting state-of-the-art security and 24-hour supervision), Mick is a high-spirited and adventurous individual seeking a new start in life. His characterful street-frontage belies an interesting, split-level interior with hidden depths. Façade features a number of interesting relief carvings and many original tattoos. Viewing recommended. Box No. 6103.

Debbie, 27, north Dublin. Former soccer-star groupie, blonde, currently resident in penthouse at Belmayne apartment complex, where 'gorgeous living comes to Dublin'. Combines sunny, light-filled head with state-of-the-art accessorisation. Is now a bit tired of gorgeous living and footballers, however. Would like something a little less exciting and more sustainable as, for example, the wife of a surgeon in Clontarf. Box No. 2445.

Alexandru, 28, Moldova. Ever considered investing in Eastern Europe? Alexandru, an up-and-coming businessman currently overlooking the Black Sea, offers guaranteed short-term returns to an Irish-resident female in return for instant marriage. Looks and age unimportant. Box No. 2338.

Cartoon by Martyn Turner.

Michael, west Cork. Location, Location, Location! That is the watchword with this superb late middle-aged man: now a picturesque ruin but magnificently sited on his own property overlooking the majestic Bantry Bay. This is a unique opportunity for a woman with some money and endless patience to put her own stamp on a timeless classic. But act now, while he's still standing. Box No. 4035.

FRIDAY, 19 FEBRUARY 2010

How a Slur Led

Harry McGee

On a Monday afternoon in early January 2009, gardaí forced their way into an apartment in the Clancy Strand area of Limerick and arrested three Brazilian women, whom they suspected of running a brothel.

The following day, Tuesday 13 January, all three appeared before Limerick District Court. Judge Tom O'Donnell convicted the women and imposed suspended six-month sentences. He also directed them to leave Limerick within three days.

The raid on the brothel would set off an unusual sequence of events over 13 months that would eventually force the city's best-known politician, Minister for Defence Willie O'Dea, to the brink of resignation.

Later that week, the *Limerick Leader* reported a new angle to the story. The registered owner of the apartment on Clancy Strand was one Nessan Quinlivan. The name was immediately recognisable. He was one of two IRA men who had escaped from Brixton Prison in July 1991. The other was Pearse McAuley, who was later convicted for

Ronan O'Gara, of the Irish rugby team, about to go on to the pitch at the Stade de France in Paris, for a training session before the Six Nations game against France. Photograph: Billy Stickland/INPHO.

the manslaughter of Det. Jerry McCabe in Adare in 1996.

Nessan Quinlivan said that he had no knowledge the apartment was being used as a brothel, an assertion that has never been questioned.

Quinlivan's younger brother Maurice was an aspiring politician in Limerick, a declared candidate for the June 2009 local elections in the North Ward. Two months after the event, on 9 March, Fianna Fáil launched its local election campaign in the Clarion Hotel. Mike Dwane, a reporter for the *Limerick Leader*, attended the event and approached O'Dea after the speeches. Dwane had a digital voice recorder which he held up visibly.

Quinlivan had criticised O'Dea that week for sending out letters to planning applicants using Department of Defence stationery. He also criticised the cost of the six civil servants who were employed to help O'Dea with constituency affairs. The criticisms prompted a ferocious attack from the Minister, which began with a swipe at Sinn Féin.

'They are running a big campaign. The money from the Northern Bank must be stretching fairly far. Quote me on that.

'While occasionally we send out letters to planning applicants on the wrong paper, we have never been involved with anyone who shot anybody, or robbed banks, or kidnapped people.'

He moved on to a new line of attack: 'I suppose I'm going a bit too far when I say this but I'd like to ask Mr Quinlivan is the brothel still closed?' he asked.

Dwane had been on holidays during January and was unaware of the story about the brothel.

'Do you know the brothel they found in his name and in his brother's name down in Clancy

Strand? . . . Did you not hear that? You better check with your sources. There was a house owned by him that was rented out and they found two ladies of the night operating in there in the last couple of weeks,' said O'Dea.

Dwane contacted Quinlivan seeking a response to O'Dea's claim and also checked it out with the gardaí. Quinlivan was reported in the newspaper the next day saying he was considering legal action against O'Dea 'after the Minister for Defence claimed he part-owned a Clancy Strand apartment where a brothel was discovered'. The only part of the interview quoted was the question to Quinlivan as to whether the brothel was still closed.

On 9 April, Quinlivan issued proceedings against O'Dea. He sought an injunction restraining O'Dea from repeating the allegation. He sought it under the provisions of a 1923 Act, the Prevention of Electoral Abuses Act, which created a criminal act of making a false statement about a candidate. Quinlivan also indicated that he was bringing separate proceedings against O'Dea, claiming defamation.

On 14 April, O'Dea swore an affidavit for the injunction. While accepting he made the reported quote, he went on to say: 'I must categorically and emphatically deny that I said to Mr Dwane that the plaintiff was a part-owner of the said apartment.' He also said that there was not a shred of evidence to support Quinlivan's claim that he was involved in a dirty tricks campaign.

At the hearing on 20 April, Quinlivan's application was rejected by Mr Justice Cooke on the basis that a repetition of the claim was unlikely and also noted O'Dea's denial that he claimed Quinlivan part-owned the apartment.

Dwane read the affidavit within 24 hours of the case and immediately realised that it did not tally with the O'Dea interview. 'I suddenly had a credibility problem, which if I had not recorded the interview might have hung on my word against a Minister's in a court case,' he wrote this week.

The affidavit, he recalled, was effectively 'accusing me of making up the allegation'.

Within hours of reading the affidavit, Dwane brought his concern to Alan English, the editor of the *Limerick Leader*. English ordered a transcript of the interview.

The timing of this first contact assumed a huge importance yesterday. It emerged that the first formal correspondence Quinlivan's legal team received was on 11 August, some four months after O'Dea swore the affidavit.

Yesterday, English says that he made an initial, unsuccessful attempt to contact O'Dea to point out the difficulty. Initially, yesterday, he said he may have contacted O'Dea in late May. If that were the case, O'Dea had two problems. There would have been an onus on him under the 1923 Act to immediately correct the false statement to avoid a prosecution. And if his solicitors had been contacted in May, it would have meant a delay of almost three months in contacting the other side, which would have made nonsense of O'Dea's statements this week that he had acted immediately upon learning of the error.

Later yesterday, however, both English and O'Dea confirmed, after checking their records, that the first contact was on 24 July. English said that the paper's delay in contacting the Minister was due to the fact that it also faced legal action.

O'Dea, recalled Dwane, was 'taken aback' by the transcript when he read it and said he had made a genuine mistake. O'Dea said this week that he immediately corrected his affidavit. He was wrong in that respect – affidavits cannot be corrected.

What happened was that O'Dea's solicitors wrote to Quinlivan's legal team on 11 August stating that 'important information has now come to light in relation to an interview with the *Limerick Leader* journalist.

'Having considered this information which is a partial transcript of the interview, [O'Dea] is happy to confirm that his memory of the interview was incorrect and he did in fact state to the journalist that your client was an owner or part-owner of the premises in question.

'. . . He readily and willingly concedes that in the heat of the moment he said something that he had not meant to say and which subsequently escaped his memory.'

It was a total concession and also clear that O'Dea was no longer in a position to defend the defamation proceedings. The matter was concluded on 21 December without going to hearing. The Minister accepted he had defamed Quinlivan and paid damages and costs to the Sinn Féin councillor. The *Limerick Leader* made the recordings available to both sides that day.

In his explanations to the Dáil this week, O'Dea and Fianna Fáil relied heavily on a paragraph in the statement which stated: 'It is not suggested by Mr Quinlivan that Mr O'Dea acted other

Tiger Woods making a statement at TPC Sawgrass, home of the Professional Golfers Association Tour, in Ponte Vedra Beach, Florida, during which he admitted cheating on his wife, Elin Nordegren. Photograph: Sam Greenwood/Getty.

than innocently in making such denial' in his affidavit. But it has been pointed out since then that Mr Justice MacMenamin in the High Court approved the settlement but was never expected, or asked, to rule on an affidavit used in an earlier injunction proceeding.

The case was reported in late December but subsequently fell from prominence. It returned to public attention in early February when Senator Eugene Regan accused O'Dea of perjury in the Seanad, reigniting a controversy that greatly gathered momentum this week.

In the Dáil this week, O'Dea accepted he made a mistake in the affidavit but could not bring himself to apologise for his slur against Quinlivan. He was finally forced into doing that by Seán O'Rourke on the *News at One* yesterday. By that stage, many colleagues in Fianna Fáil thought it was too late. Last night's resignation proved them right.

SATURDAY, 20 FEBRUARY 2010

Flagellation of Presidential Proportions

Mary Hennigan

Cripes, it made for uncomfortable viewing, kind of leaving you torn between feeling half-sorry for the auld rake and having divil an ounce of sympathy. He did, though, seem repentant.

'I must take complete responsibility for all my actions . . . [this was] a personal failure on my part for which I am solely and completely responsible,' he said, looking straight into our eyes, making it seem like he was talking to us individually, begging each one of us for forgiveness and for a second chance.

He spoke of how much he'd hurt his wife and that nothing mattered more than repairing that relationship. 'I am prepared to do whatever it takes

Tiger Woods making that statement. Photograph: Lori Moffett-Pool/Getty Images.

to do so,' he said, 'nothing is more important to me personally. But it is private, and I intend to reclaim my family life for my family. It's nobody's business but ours.'

Hear, hear. But enough about Bill Clinton's post-Monica address to the nation in 1998, how did Tiger do yesterday? Well, to be honest, if he'd had a Presidential seal on his lectern, the Stars and Stripes over his shoulder, spoke with an Arkansas drawl and mentioned God instead of Buddha, we'd have said: 'Ah Bill, not again.'

What Bill said back then that Tiger didn't, but probably should have, was: 'Our country has been distracted by this matter for too long . . . now it is time – in fact, it is past time – to move on.'

But, it was ordained, there'd be no moving on until Tiger spoke publicly about his private mis-deeds; what was needed was not a quiet chat with his wife but a global address to those gazillions,

from Ballybunion to Bangalore and Bogota to Boston, waiting to hear if that story about him and the pancake waitress was true. We had a right to know, apparently.

Kay Burley was on *Sky News* duty for the main event, having regained her poise from her mishap earlier in the week ('What's happened to his head? It looks like he's walked in to a door,' she'd said when she saw a black mark on Joe Biden's forehead . . . on Ash Wednesday). For close on three hours Kay asked her colleague Enda Brady what he thought Tiger might say, to the point where an exasperated Enda came close to suggesting he'd declare: 'I like hot chicks, okay!' That line, incidentally, was 150 to 1 in one book-makers' list of things Tiger might say. Alas, we lost our fiver.

Show time. Out he came to an eerie silence, looking suitably sombre. This, we had to remind ourselves, was a golfer, not the leader of the free world. He ripped up his carefully crafted script, forgot those many hours of practising in front of a team of PR folk, resisted looking directly into the camera for the Big moments, declared he didn't give a fig about his 'business partners', laughed at the notion that he was a role model and declared: 'Listen dudes, my private life is none of your damn business – I hit golf balls for a living, end of.'

Na, he didn't. There followed 'three sorries, two apologies, one failure, one shame – the most extraordinary 15-minute self-flagellation', as Krishnan Guru-Murthy put it on Channel 4.

True, after the public flogging he'd meted out to himself, Tiger hugged his Ma and limped away, his sponsors high-fiving in the background. It had the feel of the relaunch of Coca-Cola after their New Coke fiasco, a brand apologising to its customers for letting them down, promising to be good from here on. Surreal and excruciating.

Back in the Sky studio, 'PR Guru' Phil Hall warned that 'you can over-analyse these situations'. Kay nodded in agreement, before asking Enda, Robert Nisbet (Sky's man in Florida), sports psychologist Amanda Owens, the *London Times* golf correspondent John Hopkins, *Golf Monthly* assistant editor Alex Narey, Graeme McDowell (on the phone) and 'Showbiz' writer Martel Maxwell to analyse the situation.

Robert was a bit unimpressed. 'You can tell he's been in therapy, can't you? It was like he stood up and said "My name is Tiger Woods and I'm a sex addict".'

Kay chuckled. Phil didn't. 'Your reporter is being very cynical. I think it was absolutely spell-binding, the most amazing *mea culpa* I've ever seen from any public figure.' (Phil was hired by John Terry recently to handle his 'difficulties', so he knows about these things.)

Over on Channel 4, Buzz Bissinger of the

Tiger says sorry, hand on heart... Photograph: Lori Moffett/AP.

Ballybunion Bugle – kidding, he's with *Vanity Fair* – noted that 'this is Tiger doing what he's done all his career – control, control, control'. But why, asked Krishnan, was this 'news' conference even necessary? 'Great question,' said Buzz, but he, like the rest of us, didn't have the answer.

It's not like Tiger was facing impeachment. Mind you, he is the commander-in-chief of the multi-billion-dollar golf business.

TUESDAY, 23 FEBRUARY 2010

Belgium's Sunday Opening Rules Take Some Getting Used To

Arthur Beesley

It was time for a trim, my hair had grown a little unruly. New in town, I dropped into the first barber I found. No joy. The guy was a dozer.

'Bonjour. Where will I sit?'

'Have you an appointment?'

'No.'

'Then I can't do it. I only do appointments.'

'But your shop is empty.'

'I have an appointment at 1.30.'

'It's five past one!'

'I only do appointments.'

Anyone can have a bad day, of course, but this fellow was champion of the slow lane. He was open for business, but only to the extent that he was taking appointments.

Brussels is like everywhere else; customer service varies. When it's good – and it frequently is – it's very good indeed. Some places we've been to could hardly be matched for helpfulness and spontaneous kindness. As buggy-pushing parents of tiny kids, we've seen this again and again.

When customer service is bad, however, it's grim. No matter where you go in the world, you'll always find surly staff. In New York, for instance, the worst are too cool to care. In Brussels, they might snarl or snap at the most basic questions.

Important here is a certain attachment to rules and procedure, which knows few bounds. Nowhere is this more so than in the case of Sunday shopping, which is limited in Belgium as elsewhere on the continent. A legacy of more religious times, the rules owe much to industrial relations and find expression in a legal code of strong-willed rigour.

On this particular issue, one's own finely-honed sense of hypocrisy thrives. In principle, I'm all for a day of rest and a chance to cleanse the self of filthy consumerism. In real life, however, it can be a dreadful inconvenience.

Navigation is tricky. When first encountered, the system led to certain pressures at evening time on Saturday. Yes, a local Sunday market provides limitless options in the realm of veg, fruit, bread, cheese and cold meat. But it's not much use if nappy supplies are running ominously low.

Certain small supermarkets open on Sunday, a blessing when discovered. Strangely, though, some of them stay closed throughout Saturday. While the city also boasts an extensive range of night shops, they are obliged to shut their doors between 7 a.m. and 6 p.m.

All shopkeepers must take an uninterrupted rest period of 24 hours each week. They can determine this rest period independently and, if they wish, can open on Sunday – but they are not allowed to employ any personnel on Sunday. Exceptions are made for bakeries, butchers, small food stores, florists and the like, who can open until 1 p.m.

Moves to relax the regime have proved contentious. In the face of opposition three years ago, the government forced through a modest reform when it extended to six or nine Sundays per year a three-Sunday exception to the general rule. Pay must be at least double the normal wage and companies that do not recognise trade unions are bound by sectoral deals made by unions.

Fine Gael leader Enda Kenny (left) and the party's health spokesman, James Reilly, in front of a poster at the launch of their new Faircare campaign. Photograph: Arthur Carron/Collins.

A minority group of small shop owners, the Liberal Association of Self-Employed, has campaigned for a total liberalisation of opening hours. Yet bigger retail lobbies have resisted the push, their members in fear of being overwhelmed by large corporations if the floodgates open.

However, the question has gone away politically. 'There's no big debate anymore, so it's a fact of life,' says Guy Van Gyes, an academic in the Research Institute for Work and Society at the Catholic University of Leuvan. 'Maybe there are some people who'd like more opening on Sundays, but I don't think it's an issue any more.'

None of this is to imply overbearing exactitude in Brussels life; far from it. I know of café-bars here that don't sell food but invite people to bring in their own from an outdoor take-away nearby, Belgium's answer to Leo Burdock. The sense of conviviality is palpable. There's charm on tap, too, in the bakeries of Brussels, pinpointed by friends who are a key source of local intelligence. They were right.

Then there are the things that are rarely seen at home anymore. In central Dublin, for example, filling stations are virtually extinct. Although some sites were sold off at vast profit during the property mania, an industry chief told me long ago that fuel pumps in town centres had been regulated out of existence due to health and safety rules and other concerns.

Now, the reflex might well be to pin the blame for this state of affairs on 'Brussels'. Over here, however, there seems to be a station on every other corner.

WEDNESDAY, 24 FEBRUARY 2010

Epitome of a Professional Hit – Ruthless, Clinical, Clean

Miriam Lord

This was a professional hit – ruthless, clinical, clean. But the big question today is: Whodunnit? The next-of-kin trooped solemnly on to the plinth last night to face the media. 'We are pretty shell-shocked at the moment,' said John Gormley, still trying to come to terms with the tragic loss of Trevor Sargent's ministerial career.

Dispatched by an unknown hand, but reading between the lines, John and his party have their suspicions. Under questioning, he refused to rule out his Coalition partner as the possible assassin. Clustered around him in a show of solidarity, his stony-faced TDs and Senators looked into the distance. These champions of the new media looked like a living Facebook page. Title? Justice for Trevor.

So whodunnit, John? 'We don't want to give any hostages to fortune . . . I'm not going to jump to any conclusions.'

Labour's Pat Rabbitte wasn't quite so circumspect. Short of holding up his name in big letters, Pat insinuated that the pawprints of Minister for Justice Dermot Ahern were all over the hit.

If not Dermot, well then, his party. Stung by the loss of one of their own, Rabbitte described the

Green Party former junior minister Trevor Sargent following his resignation. Photograph: Dara Mac Dónaill.

Members of the County Wexford Youth Orchestra, backstage at the Irish Aviation Authority's 15th festival of Youth Orchestras held at the National Concert Hall in Dublin. Photograph: Marc O'Sullivan.

swift and surprise dispatch of the former minister for food as 'the empire strikes back'. Trevor never stood a chance. The end came quickly. He was gone in 100 seconds. On his feet one minute. Career toppled the next.

Never, but never, had they witnessed the like before in Fianna Fáil, where resignations last as long as an old-fashioned wake. All shrieking and keening and rending of garments, with raucous displays of anger and denial, followed by dark intimations of revenge further down the road.

Sargent, on the other hand, took just one minute and 40 seconds to resign. Sorry. Didn't mean it. Error of judgment. Goodbye.

Last week, it was death by tweet. This week, it is death by leak. (Or should that be leek?) Life in Leinster House is beginning to resemble the plot of an Agatha Christie novel.

And now there are four: George, Déirdre, Willie and Trevor.

What next? A political body in the library, yet another knifing in the back in mysterious circumstances? Curiouser and curiouser.

Forget about George Lee. And Déirdre de Búrca. O'Dea is the key. Fianna Fáil lose a minister. They fight hard to keep him, he fights hard to survive, but in the end he is brought down by a fit of conscience from the Greens. Never mind that Willie was the author of his own destruction. It wasn't the Greens who brought him to court, or forced him to swear a false affidavit, or implied that a journalist fabricated a story about him, or said that a political rival was operating a brothel.

They didn't wind up Senator Eugene Regan and let him off in the Seanad. They didn't write the Sunday newspaper articles that ignited the

O'Dea controversy. In fact, the Greens held their noses and stood well back. They didn't make the running at all. Instead, events caught up with them. By last Thursday, if they were to be left with any shred of credibility, they had no choice but to demand the former defence minister's moustache on a plate.

No, Willie's downfall was not the fault of the Greens. But they played a part in his downfall, and that, it seems, was reason enough to extract revenge. So it came to pass that Brian Cowen, acting Minister for Defence, lost a Sargent yesterday. He didn't bat an eyelid. Brigadier Biffo knows that war ain't pretty. Particularly when Fianna Fáil is manning the trenches.

Then again, maybe the sudden surfacing of a letter that spelled certain resignation for Trevor Sargent, not a week after his party was responsible for the end of O'Dea's ministerial career, was mere coincidence. But that's hard to swallow. 'It's too much of a coincidence,' said Pat Rabbitte, the Hercule Poirot of the Labour Party. 'When you look at it circumstantially, I think it points in one direction.' And to think, he added, that Minister for Justice Dermot Ahern was threatening Sinn Féin's Caoimhghín Ó Caoláin with the files during last week's confidence motion in O'Dea. 'It occurs to me that someone was rooting in the files at the weekend . . .' But it's all conjecture.

Dermot Ahern seems rather pained that he seems to be the man in the frame. He said yesterday evening that the first he heard of Trevor's inappropriate communication with the gardaí was on the lunchtime news. In fact, he sees Sargent as 'a friend'.

The beginning of the end for decent, honourable Trevor came at midday, with the publication of the *Evening Herald* and its front page headline: 'Minister Asked Gardaí to Drop Case'. Almost immediately, Sargent confirmed he had written such a letter on behalf of a constituent, three years ago. His fate was sealed. A Dáil statement scheduled for 5 p.m.

He spoke before the appointed time, his fellow Green TDs in the chamber to witness the moment. Trevor stood and began his statement. There wasn't a peep from anyone, on any side of the house. Ahern sat, expressionless. A far cry from his exploits of the previous week.

Soon to be former food minister Sargent was brief and to the point. He did wrong. He resigned. He left the chamber, his colleagues leaving with him. There was silence. They seemed stunned on the Fianna Fáil benches. They couldn't manage one gratuitous vegetable joke between them. What? No blood? No recrimination? No fingers gouging out the wooden desk nor heels burning rubber as the condemned man is dragged, roaring innocence, from the chamber?

They were supposed to be discussing the Petroleum Bill. Nothing happened. Deputies whispered quietly to each other. Brian Cowen looked pensive. Eventually, Minister Conor Lenihan screeched in and got the debate under way. As a Fianna Fáil man, he mustn't have been expecting Trevor to have gone so quickly, or as quietly.

But is this the end? Probably not. What happened yesterday stinks of dirty tricks. The Greens couldn't bring themselves to absolve their partners of any complicity in Trevor's downfall. If nothing else, it appears the trust is gone. They may never know whodunnit – but that doesn't stop them thinking they do.

MONDAY, 1 MARCH 2010

Plot Behind Passport Scandal yet to be Told

Mary Fitzgerald

It began, as is so often the case in the Middle East, with whisperings. Rumours that European passports had been used by the alleged assassins of Mahmoud al-Mabhouh, a senior Hamas official suspected by Israel of smuggling arms from Iran, first surfaced just days after the Palestinian's body was found in his Dubai hotel room. Before long the speculation made it to print, and on 4 February, the first mention that Irish passports were implicated appeared in the *Khaleej Times*, an English-language newspaper distributed throughout the Gulf.

But it wasn't until 15 February – when Dubai's police chief named 11 suspects, including three ostensible Irish passport holders, and hinted at further revelations to come – that the scale of the operation began to become apparent. Last week, true to their 'drip, drip' approach to releasing information about the assassination, the Dubai authorities named a further 15 people they believe were involved, bringing the total number of suspects to 26.

The case has developed into a major international intrigue worthy of a John Le Carré spy thriller. The alleged hit squad used cloned passports from five countries: 12 British, six Irish, four French, three Australian and one German; and credit cards issued by a US bank.

From the outset, the finger of blame has been pointed at Israel and its intelligence service Mossad. After all, Mossad has plenty of form when it comes to what Israelis call 'targeted killings'. And jubilant media coverage of the assassination in Israel, working on the assumption that this was a Mossad job, was telling. As was opposition leader Tzipi Livni's cheering of the assassination as 'good news to those fighting terrorism'.

But Israel still refuses to confirm or deny involvement. After Dubai's police chief declared he was '99 per cent' certain that the spy agency orchestrated the hit, Israeli officials merely responded that there was no hard evidence this was the case.

What is known is that a number of the 15 new suspects named last week travelled to Dubai on passports bearing the names of people resident in Israel. Several of the eight – like the six British-Israeli dual nationals whose names were used by the first 11 suspects – have said their identities were used without their permission.

Late last week Israeli media claimed the passport photographs used by the alleged assassination team were subtly doctored to ensure they could not be recognised later. This revelation was interpreted by some as an attempt to deflect mounting criticism of Mossad within Israel for exposing both its agents and those whose identities they had assumed.

Israel's bullish foreign minister Avigdor Lieberman appears to have shrugged off the concerns of the five countries implicated, citing Israel's 'policy of ambiguity' on intelligence and security matters. In Brussels last week, after meeting EU counterparts including Minister for Foreign Affairs Micheál Martin, Lieberman appeared quite blasé about what some have described as a serious diplomatic rift. 'I think you have all seen too many James Bond movies,' he quipped to reporters.

A member of the Hamas politburo griped to *The Irish Times* that the response from the European countries whose passports had been implicated had been too 'shy' and he argued that if any other country had been suspected of fraudulently using the documentation of another to carry out an assassination the reaction would be very different. Opposition deputies here have accused the Government of being too timid in the way it has handled allegations of Israeli complicity.

The most robust response yet to the entire debacle, and the most explicit in implying that Israel was likely to have been responsible, has come from Australia. Its foreign minister Stephen Smith has demanded co-operation from Israel in investigating the identity theft: 'If the results of that investigation cause us to come to the conclusion that the abuse of Australian passports was sponsored or condoned by Israeli officials, then Australia would not regard that as the act of a friend.' Prime minister Kevin Rudd later said he was 'not satisfied' with the Israeli ambassador's responses to

Australian concerns and warned his government would be taking an 'absolutely hard line' in defending its passports' integrity.

All this is unfolding against a background of creeping anxiety within Israel that a point has been reached where it can no longer take international support and goodwill for granted. The damning UN-commissioned Goldstone report, which alleged war crimes were committed during Israel's military offensive in Gaza last year, came on the heels of boycott calls and widespread protests over the deaths of 1,200 Gazans during the fighting. In Britain, arrest warrants have been issued against Israeli politicians.

Israeli officials admit that, while support remains at government level in Europe, public opinion of their country has plummeted to an all-time low.

Moshe Feiglin, president of Manhigut Yehudit, the largest faction inside Israel's ruling Likud party, acknowledged these new realities in an acerbic commentary on the Mabhouh killing. 'Somebody in the Mossad and the echelon that authorised the Mabhouh mission is still living in the 1980s. They didn't notice that the Western world, and particularly the British, no longer sees Israel as the good guy in the story,' Feiglin wrote. 'In the eyes of much of the world, Israel is no more than a pirate ship sailing on borrowed time . . . The world has changed . . . Israel can no longer expect the international community to wink its eye and look the other way.'

Israel is not likely to lose sleep over a chilling of relations with Ireland as a result of the passports controversy. Israeli officials, after all, are pretty much resigned to what they view as Irish antipathy. 'Ireland . . . is currently one of the European countries most antagonistic to Israel, and a country where the hostility of the press is matched by the tone of the Government,' a columnist in the *Jerusalem Post* wrote during the conflict in Gaza last year. Earlier this month, another writer at the paper described Ireland as a country where 'Israel's name is routinely dragged through the mud'.

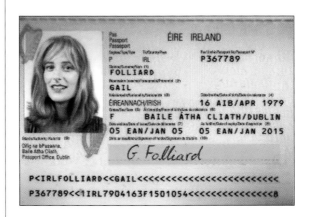

Three of the fake Irish passports which are thought to have been made by Mossad, the Israeli intelligence service, which is believed to have been behind the assassination in Dubai of Mahmoud al-Mabhouh, a senior Hamas official. Photographs: Dubai police.

So far European focus has been on the fraudulent use of passports, but Dubai police say the trails of the alleged killers begin and end in five European states: France, Germany, Italy, Switzerland and the Netherlands. Why the apparent reluctance to investigate? Mahmoud al-Mabhouh may have been an unsavoury character in the eyes of many but Philip Alston, the UN's special *rapporteur* on extrajudicial executions, argues that European countries would be wrong to ignore or wish away the wider implications of his assassination. 'If a foreign intelligence agency was responsible . . . the matter should clearly be classified as an extrajudicial execution,' he said. 'All states have an unquestioned obligation to investigate and prosecute anyone accused of a killing who they have reason to believe is within their jurisdiction. Political considerations can never be invoked to avoid taking the necessary action.'

WEDNESDAY, 3 MARCH 2010

Four-Minute Frenzy as Deep Pocketed Bidders Push Chinese Vase to €110,000

Michael Parsons

'People collect everything – the weirdest stuff, thank God,' said Philip Sheppard, ahead of a sale yesterday of antiques and collectibles at his family-run business in Co. Laois.

Sheppards Irish Auction House in the village of Durrow, off the main Dublin-Cork road, was established after the second World War, and has been selling to a loyal – and increasingly international clientele – ever since.

Amid the 984 lots at yesterday's auction was a number of items of Chinese porcelain which had been consigned for sale by a Co. Carlow family who had 'inherited the collection'.

Most of the items had a pre-sale estimate of €100–€150. During the sale preview on Monday, Mr Sheppard mentioned casually that a Chinese woman had flown from Beijing via Heathrow to Dublin and 'then straight down to Co. Laois'. But there was no sense of the drama about to unfold.

Rong Chen (48), a fluent English speaker, told *The Irish Times* that her husband Xing Chen, an accountant and antiques collector in Beijing, had seen the auction advertised on Sheppards' website. She agreed to travel to Ireland to bid on his behalf.

The auction, which began at 10.30 a.m., was progressing quietly when the Chinese lots began to appear shortly after noon. Some of the early lots sold

Richard Peters holding the Chinese vase for which he paid €110,000 at an auction in Laois. The vase was given a pre-sale value of €100 to €150. Photograph: David Sleator.

within or slightly above estimate, but gradually prices began to rise. When Lot 258, a pair of Chinese polychrome vases estimated at €100-€150 sold for €41,000, the mood in the saleroom changed dramatically.

Bids had flooded in by telephone and the internet, but the buyer was London dealer Richard Peters, a renowned oriental ceramics expert, who had also come over to attend the sale.

He and Ms Chen then went head-to-head in an intense battle of nerves for the next item: a 12-inch high 'Chinese blue and white vase' of 'bulbous form'. An opening offer of €50 was followed by four minutes of frenzied bidding, which ended in victory for Mr Peters at €110,000.

He later said he had 'got a bargain', while Ms Chen said she was 'very disappointed'. She said she had been taking instructions on her mobile phone from her husband in Beijing and, as the bidding spiralled upwards, he 'was saying go, go go' before asking her to stop at €100,000.

Mr Peters, who runs an antiques business on London's Kensington Church Street, said the vase was from the Peking palace of the Emperor Qianlong, and was made in the 18th century. He hoped to sell it to a 'private client in China or London'. Mr Peters, who flew back to London last night, paid a total of €129,965 for the vase when the buyer's premium and VAT were added to his final bid of €110,000.

Describing herself as 'disappointed and tired', Ms Chen also left Co. Laois yesterday afternoon on the first leg of her long journey to Beijing. She bought a number of lesser items, spending about €3,000.

Mr Sheppard said the vase and the other Chinese porcelain items in the auction formed part of a collection amassed by 'two Carlow sisters' who had lived in the United States during the 1940s and 1950s. He believed the vase had been bought in the city of Philadelphia.

The ladies were 'now deceased' and the collection had been inherited by a family in Co.

Carlow. He called the family yesterday afternoon with news of the sale and said they were 'delighted and chuffed'. Asked why the estimated price had been so low he said the firm specialised in 18th century furniture rather than ceramics, but had 'the expertise to market a sale to the right people'.

His uncle, company founder Christy Sheppard (87), was also delighted with the result. He said he had survived 'numerous recessions', adding: 'We've never had a flop' in over 60 years of auctions.

SATURDAY, 6 MARCH 2010

Poetic Licence

Fiona McCann

Few people have the required mix of chutzpah and creativity to make an appointment with a revered dead poet. Neither is a problem for Mike Scott, however, at least if his upcoming Abbey show, *An Appointment with Mr Yeats*, is anything to go by.

It's an 'appointment' that has been pending for some time – 19 years, to be precise, since he first took part in a tribute night to W.B. Yeats at the Abbey Theatre back in 1991.

'I'd set some Yeats poems to music specially for the show, thinking everyone else would do the same . . . And when I got there, nobody had done that at all! I was the only person who did any Yeats songs. They all did their own numbers. And I thought, "There's something untapped here". There should be a whole concert that is all Yeats's lyrics set to music.' He smiles wryly, his face creasing under his trademark cap. 'I didn't realise then that I would have to do it all myself.'

As it turns out, he won't be entirely alone. Scott will be joined onstage with the latest Waterboys line-up, which extends to a 10-piece band playing a range of instruments including a trombone and an oboe. They'll all be playing along to the words of W.B. Yeats, around whose poems Scott has crafted the songs that make up the set.

Mike Scott of The Waterboys, in front of a portrait of W.B. Yeats, whose poetry inspired Scott's show,
An Appointment with Mr Yeats, at the Abbey Theatre in Dublin. Photograph: Paul MacManus.

It has been a long gestation. 'I've got my book, *Yeats's Complete Poems*, which somebody gave me as a wedding present, for my first marriage in 1990, and I've always kept that book close. I'd put it on the piano and go through it, and if a poem suggested a tune in my mind, I would wrestle with it and try and get a whole melody for it,' he says.

Over the years since the idea of a Yeats concert first occurred, he has written enough songs to make up a full set. 'Suddenly I was sitting on a concert's worth.'

Where he would perform it was never in question. 'In my mind, if I'm going to make a radical statement with Yeats's lyrics and put them into contexts that are unusual, then I'd rather do it in his own theatre. And I feel that the music I've written is very in tune with Yeats's intentions, as far as someone 100 years later can discern those, so I feel quite confident about playing in the Abbey.'

There's the *chutzpah*, then. Scott has no compunction about taking on one of the literary greats and even tinkering with the words themselves. 'Once I've decided to work on one of the lyrics, I treat it like one of my own lyrics. I'll be totally ruthless with it. And if I have to change it very slightly, I will do. If I have to replace a word because a word that Yeats used has fallen out of common currency, I'll do it.'

Scott is matter-of-fact about making alterations to words that are sacred to so many. 'He'll use a rhyme pattern, like A–B–B–A, and it sounds rubbish with music, so I'll flip it around. I'll make sure it doesn't corrupt anything that Yeats is intending. As long as it still keeps the integrity of the poem and the meaning, if I have to change it, I will.' He shrugs.

'I'm not intimidated by him being the great W.B. Yeats. Of course, it's because he's great that it's such a pleasure to work with, but I'm not going to be overwhelmed by that.'

Not every Yeats poem suits his purpose, however. 'Speaking from my own experience, I find the ones that scan and rhyme, unsurprisingly, are the ones that work best with music. But where they do scan and rhyme, clearly there's a lot of music within the poetry.' So how does he make his choices? 'When I sit at the piano or with my guitar, the first line, if I hear it in my head with a melody . . . bang. Off I go. And sometimes they work out, and sometimes they don't.'

It's not the first time Scott has taken on the master either. A musical version of Yeats's 'The Stolen Child' appeared on The Waterboys album *Fisherman's Blues* back in 1988. 'I'm fortunate,' he says, by way of explanation of his unjaded approach to the Irish poet. 'I didn't "get" Yeats at school.' He did, however, get plenty of Robert Burns,

which didn't stop him putting Burns's words to music either. Yet over the years, he has kept returning to Yeats, whose poetry he first encountered when he was growing up in Edinburgh.

'I enjoy Yeats's subjects,' he explains. 'His subject set, if you like. Politics. Love. The mystic. Ireland. Myth and legend. I like that set of subjects.' The notion of the mystic, the occult, or 'just spirituality, that's what we call it now' is one dear to Scott's own heart and a part of Yeats he'd like to see reclaimed. 'I'm hugely interested in that. Have been for decades. I also think that Yeats's interest in the unseen is misunderstood,' he says, taking issue with a wealth of scholarly work on the poet without any hesitation. 'Yeats's interest in the unseen was very serious indeed . . . And, judging from his poetry, he got it. He understood.'

There was another practical advantage to working Yeats's words into his own music. He admits to struggling with the lyrical content of his work far more than the musical composition. 'Music happens almost instantly. It is as simple as hearing a tune in the head and then just expanding it. But the words of a thing, I'll slave over. So working with Yeats is great – it's like I get a bye to the next round. I'm working with world-class lyrics. Fantastic.'

Though the music might come easy, Scott is not classically trained and had always played by ear. For his Yeats show, however, he decided to address this. 'I taught myself to read and write music for this project. When I started writing the string arrangements for some of these songs, I realised it's not enough to just have them on a tape recorder and play the tape recorder to a transcriber. I need to score these myself, learn how to do it.'

So he did. With the help of Waterboys constant Steve Wickham, he taught himself to score music and began to write down the music he'd been hearing in his head. It was a laborious process. 'It would take a day to do a page.' The pages mounted up, and though he says it hasn't changed how he approaches songwriting, 'the manuscripting gives me more authority over it somehow, and it gives me some more confidence as well'.

'I've always been fairly confident as a musician anyway, but when I'd be working with trained musicians and they'd be talking in terms of bars and crotchets and minims, I'd be completely lost. But I'm not lost now.'

He does hope for record company interest, or some funding for an album of the Yeats songs once the run of concerts is complete. Yet, this being Mike Scott, who admits he is inseparable from The Waterboys – 'if it's me, it's The Waterboys, if it's The Waterboys, it's me' – there is more, non-Yeatsian material in the pipeline, too. Not to mention several other projects. 'I've also written a book.' It's a memoir of his life in music, and there are several more where that came from. 'I've got

three – I don't know if I'd call them books – but three shorter things ready to go.'

His energy is impressive. Though now in his fifties and three decades into his musical career, he's all fired up about his latest project, content to live it all again. And though other musicians have put Yeats to music – Van Morrison, Shane McGowan, even French First Lady Carla Bruni – Scott is more than ready to do battle.

'I quite like doing the ones that other people have done and doing my own take on them. I'm a competitive bastard,' he admits and, smiling, adds, 'I take on Christy Moore's version of "The Song of Wandering Aengus"'. He's taking on more than one Irish giant, then? 'Yeah,' he grins. 'Someone can come and knock me over after that, you see.'

A skateboarder displays his skills during Gravitation 2010, at the Skate Park at Monkstown Pool and Fitness Centre in Dublin. Photograph: Eric Luke.

Fitzgerald tried to run the company as if apartheid did not exist. 'We had completely integrated facilities; we paid equal wages to people of any colour; we moved people around the country in ways that were illegal.' He also went for a drink in a township shebeen with his opposite number in union negotiations, Cyril Ramaphosa, and through him developed links to the African National Congress leadership. Tricky as it was, Fitzgerald's strategy was at least retrospectively endorsed when Nelson Mandela subsequently asked him to head the UK branch of his charitable foundation.

After his return to London, however, his rapid rise seemed to be the prelude to a dramatic fall. 'In 1994,' he says with a rueful grin, 'I was personally responsible for Unilever's biggest ever marketing disaster. We launched a product called Persil Power. Persil Power was the most effective detergent that's ever been made – to this day. Because we'd had this technological breakthrough I decided we'd launch it across Europe simultaneously – never been done before. A huge investment. It failed dramatically, not because it didn't wash the clothes, but because if used slightly outside the specified conditions, it also washed the clothes away. I still have the pictures from the *Financial Times* of the clothes line with the rotting underpants – that was me.' Unilever lost hundreds of millions of pounds, market share and some of its hard-won reputation.

At the time, he was widely assumed to be the designated successor to the chairman and chief executive of Unilever. He offered his resignation, asking only for a few months to rebuild the morale of the team he had led and which he felt he had let down. The then chairman told him, however, that 'you are now much better equipped to be the CEO of this business. You have gained two things – a degree of humility, which you didn't have before, and a greater tolerance for the errors or inadequacies of others.'

Having achieved the top job, however, Fitzgerald found himself in the midst of a personal and professional crisis. 'My marriage was breaking up, but I didn't recognise that because I was someone to whom these things didn't happen. I could control these things. And, very largely, I was the person who was responsible for this. But I was trying to control how it happened in an orderly fashion, which of course is a disaster.'

At the same time, he was losing some of the very qualities that had made him such an effective manager in the first place. 'It's very easy, running a huge international company, to begin to believe in your own grandeur. You begin to become the role rather than the individual. I wasn't really conscious of it, but the more it happened, the more I became distant from people, the less I was approachable, and the less I was effective at the job. I wasn't enjoying it anymore, because I wasn't being me.'

Two 'searing' moments forced him to take stock. His eldest daughter, Tara, then aged 22, shattered his illusions that he could protect his children from the crisis in his marriage and told him, 'Dad, we all know what's happening. We don't approve of it, we don't like it, but you're trying to get our approval for it and you ain't going to get that. So you have to decide what you want to do and live with the consequences.' And he spent a lot of time with an old friend from Limerick who was dying. On the night before his death, he told Fitzgerald that 'you are currently living a lie, and it is diminishing you, and the people around you are suffering as a consequence.'

His friend's warning that 'this life is not a rehearsal, it is the only performance' galvanised Fitzgerald into facing up to the breakdown of his marriage. (He has since remarried and has a young daughter by his second wife.) He also gathered together his management team and told them that 'I think I've been kind of absent for a while, so I'm going to try and come back.'

What he took from this episode was the need for authenticity. 'If you're not authentic, people can't relate to you – you with all the warts, you with all the failings, all the weaknesses. If you try to hold yourself up as some kind of icon of perfection who has all the answers, you will fail.' Authenticity, as he sees it, also involves responsibility and accountability. He is highly critical of those in the banking industry who insist that the bonus culture can go on as before.

'I have been genuinely amazed at what I would regard – because I know most of them – as very bright, able leaders of international banks, that they just haven't got it. They don't realise the degree of rage and anger that's around, and that they have to make significant personal sacrifices to rebuild society's trust in them and their institutions. There's too much of "we can't do this because our competitors will grab our best people away". Fine, let them grab them away. You mean, these terribly valuable people who either didn't understand the risks they were running, or understood them and continued anyway without thought for the consequences? You know what? I could do without those valuable people.'

Nor has he much sympathy for those of the super-rich who flee to tax havens rather than pay their taxes. 'I had a conversation the other day with a well-known international banker who's bothered by what's happening in London with tax and so forth, and he's decided he's going to live in Zug in Switzerland. I asked him, "Have you ever been in Zug?" He said, "No, but it's got a very good tax regime." I said, "Well, you'll have a real ball with all that extra money, spending it in Zug. I find it really, deeply sad that you've got yourself into a position where you think the only thing that matters is how you avoid at almost any cost to yourself and your family being a supportive member of the wider society in which you live."'

He does not believe, however, that the current crisis can be solved simply with more regulation. 'We shouldn't think that by introducing more regulation, we solve a problem which is about lack of accountability in the boardroom. Where it went wrong is that there was an undervaluing of true independence, of somebody who has no vested interest in anything that's going on in this board,

has an interest only in his or her own reputation. And who is prepared to say "this is not right".'

He is unconvinced that Ireland has yet learned this lesson. 'The thing that really worries me, if I was losing sleep about it on behalf of Ireland, is that there are too many people who have a vested interest in there being no accountability. If the leaders of a society are not prepared to hold themselves accountable, or there are not the institutions which are sufficiently independent to hold them accountable, then I think you have a very serious problem on your hands.'

TUESDAY, 16 MARCH 2010

Church in Ireland Sinking as Rot Goes Right to the Top

Patsy McGarry

It did not seem possible that it could get any worse. It has. The clerical child sex abuse scandal has now spread to the very top in Ireland and in Rome. We heard at the weekend, through the German press, that in January 1980 the then Archbishop of Munich Joseph Ratzinger approved the transfer of Father 'H', a suspected paedophile, to Munich to undergo therapy.

Despite his record Father 'H' was assigned work in pastoral care where he again abused minors. In June 1986 he was convicted of sexually abusing minors, fined DM4,000 and given an 18-month suspended sentence. Father 'H' is, apparently, still serving as a priest in Bavaria.

At the weekend priest Gerhard Gruber, who was at the time vicar general in Munich, assumed total responsibility for the decision to readmit Father 'H' to pastoral care work, expressing regret and seeming to suggest that Archbishop Ratzinger had not been fully informed.

Few who are aware of the meticulous working methods of Joseph Ratzinger throughout his long

Twins Hugh (left) and Arthur O'Rahilly, from Glasnevin, enjoying themselves in the giant's kitchen during a preview of the National Leprechaun Museum in Jervis Street, Dublin. Photograph: Matt Kavanagh.

career, right up to and including the current papacy, are convinced, however, that such a significant matter would have escaped his notice.

As the well-known US clerical child sex abuse activist Fr Tom Doyle said at the weekend: 'Tell the vicar general to find a better line. What he's trying to do, obviously, is protect the pope.'

We heard at the weekend also, through the Irish press, that in 1975 as a 35-year-old priest of Kilmore diocese, Cardinal Seán Brady conducted canonical investigations, involving a 10-year-old boy and a 14-year-old girl, into clerical child sex abuse allegations against Fr Brendan Smyth.

He bound the children to secrecy, believed what they said and, acting on the information they supplied, recommended to his bishop that his priestly faculties be removed from Fr Smyth where diocesan work was concerned.

He told no garda and no one in the then health board of what he had uncovered, nor did any of his superiors. And none of them told the two children at any time, either before, during, or after the inquiry, that they were free to tell the Garda or health board. No, the only people they were told they could talk to about their abuse were authorised clergy. Not just any old priest.

Whether intended or not, the oath these children were asked to take ensured their complete silence. Some would suggest that putting young children through such an exercise in enforced silence was in itself a form of abuse by adults.

Cardinal Brady feels none of this is a resigning matter and that such would be a matter for the pope anyhow. Considering the pope's own current troubles in this area, one has to wonder just what authority still remains to Benedict XVI on the subject.

But whether Cardinal Brady resigns or does not is really a moot point. Similarly with the resignations, offered or otherwise, of bishops Moriarty,

Walsh, Field, Drennan or Murray. It doesn't matter anymore. It is too late.

The Catholic Church in Ireland, as we have known it, is seriously damaged and probably beyond repair. It is sinking and sinking fast. And, as indicated from recent revelations on the European continent, the Irish Catholic Church may have company on that journey down. And what seems to be missing in this process of decline and fall is any awareness of the truly great damage all of this is doing to Christianity itself, whether in Ireland and abroad.

But, be sure of one thing, such damage will not stop Ireland's Catholic bishops rallying to the side of Cardinal Brady in the coming days, as he and they did where Bishop John Magee was concerned early last year and indeed where bishops Murray, Moriarty, Walsh, Field and Drennan were/are concerned since publication of the Murphy report at the end of November.

The only exception where such rallying around a beleaguered colleague (whatever the circumstances!) was concerned has been the Archbishop of Dublin Diarmuid Martin.

He was silent on the matter of Bishop Magee. He challenged those bishops named in the Murphy report to explain themselves. When Bishop Eamonn Walsh circulated a letter last December saying he had his (archbishop's) support following publication of the Murphy report, Archbishop Martin responded with 'a clarification'. That was followed quickly by Bishop Walsh's and Bishop Field's offers of resignation.

But of late Archbishop Martin has dropped very far below the radar. He was very much to the fore following publication of the Ryan report last May and again following publication of the Murphy report last November. He has gone to ground since Christmas, having suffered the slings and arrows of some outraged colleagues and clergy, it seems. He must rediscover his mojo. Otherwise the Irish Catholic Church has no future.

Either that, or he sinks with it.

SATURDAY, 13 MARCH 2010

How Johnny's Jaunt Came Back to Haunt him

Kathy Sheridan

It was billed in one paper as a 'Magnificent Obsession'. However, readers expecting a modern take on the 1929 story about a waster's dramatic conversion to the care of others may have needed a lie-down afterwards. The only dramatic turnaround in this version was the speed at which a street brawl between a 52-year-old property developer and father of three, and a celebrity-show presenter 23 years younger than him, was parlayed into a searing *Romeo and Juliet* tragedy for our time.

Only when the 'doings' – as John S. Doyle put it – of Johnny Ronan, Glenda Gilson and a former Miss World, Rosanna Davison, made it on to *Morning Ireland*'s It Says in the Papers early this week was it evident that the story had entered the mainstream.

Time for Treasury Holdings, half-owned by Ronan, Nama-bound and with two publicly quoted tentacles, to become concerned. There was little surprise when it was announced yesterday that Ronan 'is to take a break from his business activities for the next few months arising from the recent high-profile media coverage of aspects of his personal life which he believes has the potential to distract attention from his business interests. His decision will not affect the day-to-day operation of Treasury Holdings, of which he is a director and shareholder, and which has operated under a management team and board of directors headed by managing director John Bruder for the past five years. His own personal business interests will continue to be managed by their entirely separate management team.'

This week, the number of 'friends' claiming to have witnessed the fight between Ronan and

Gilson outside McSorley's pub in Ranelagh after the England-Ireland rugby match threatened to equal the throng crowding the GPO in 1916. The potted version of the story is that Gilson kicked a glass out of Ronan's hand, then made sharp contact with his groin area before receiving a kick on her rear end from him. Not quite the denouement of a Shakespearean tragedy or a magnificent obsession; more like the dying throes of an out-of-time, brazenly public Celtic Tiger lifestyle.

Some date the volatile Ronan-Gilson relationship back to 2006. In view of the intense media courtship by certain players, the scarcity of photographic evidence of the two together is startling. Few beyond the gossip columns knew or cared until a press statement, issued by Ronan, pinged onto newsdesks last spring announcing that the three-year relationship had ended.

In more recent times, a picture of an intimate kiss between the pair emerged, suggesting a situation not quite settled or perhaps an attempt by someone to rekindle interest. Then came what the tabloids call the 'Rumble in Ranelagh', preceded by a flurry of texts between the pair while each watched the rugby match in different parts of the south city, and then a decision by Ronan to leave the Four Seasons in his chauffeur-driven, €640,000 Maybach and drive to McSorley's.

This only matters because of what transpired the following day, when Ronan joined a neighbour's child, 25-year-old Rosanna Davison, former Miss World (2003), model and daughter of Chris de Burgh, at lunch in the Treasury-controlled Ritz-Carlton Hotel in Enniskerry. At an increasingly excitable table for four, Ronan whistled up his private plane to fly three of the party – the third believed to be a college pal of Davison's – to Marrakech for the night. For the crack.

It was sometime early on Monday, 1 March, when they checked in, according to the La Mamounia hotel bill published in the *Sun*, with obligingly itemised services, such as €2,140 for rooms, €668.60 for drink and €532 for food, in a

Johnny Ronan of Treasury Holdings ... in the news for all the wrong reasons. Photograph: Bryan O'Brien.

24-hour stay, all covered by Ronan's credit card. The newspaper also estimated private plane costs at €56,000, bringing the estimated grand total for the jaunt to a neat €60,000 or so (a figure some dispute).

The vulgar, ill-conceived flashiness of it – the boozy lunch at the Ritz-Carlton, the impulsive flight to Morocco, the night at possibly the dearest hotel in north Africa – could well have remained below the radar but for the timely emergence of yet more photographs, this time of Ronan and Davison, at a glass-and-bottle-strewn table in the Ritz-Carlton and a few hours later in Marrakech.

The immediate upshot was a lively tabloid 'feud' between Davison and Gilson, liberally

Model Glenda Gilson (left) with former Miss World Rosanna Davison — both of whom were linked to Treasury Holdings property developer Johnny Ronan. Photograph: Mark Doyle.

ornamented with pictures of both, and kept studiously on the boil throughout the week by 'friends' who gave interviews about how one was feeling about the other right now, whether the other could ever be forgiven and, above all, whether the sheer magnitude of events would permit the two to walk the same red carpet at an awards show last night.

Since neither claims to have been bosom buddies with the other in the first place and Ronan, presumably, was history in Gilson's life after the Ranelagh brawl, it's hard to see what the

'feud' is about. What or whose purpose is served by the dissemination of those photographs? After all, this wasn't untypical behaviour by Johnny Ronan's flamboyant standards. Although he is said to have a 'big heart', he could never be mistaken for a man of quiet dignity. 'Explosive', 'light on manners and the social niceties', with a penchant for 'fucking and blinding people out of it' are comments from people who know him. He cuts a starkly contrasting figure with the polished and intellectual co-owner of Treasury Holdings, Richard Barrett, whose social perambulations are a study in discretion.

Married with three children, Ronan has a mini-palazzo dubbed 'Saddam's Palace' on Burlington Road in Dublin 4, complete with painted 'sky' in the domed master bedroom, and a splendid country estate in Co. Wicklow, with a glass-and-steel summer house/party pad cantilevered out over the River Dargle. He makes a lot of noise wherever he finds himself, usually in the company of men such as Robbie Fox (whose Renards nightclub closed with debts of €1.8 million and whose wife, Martina, is now employed by Ronan to run the Bridge Bar Grill), impresario Denis Desmond, music publisher Dave Kavanagh and Abrakebabra founder Graham Beere.

The Maybach, with waiting chauffeur, can usually be spotted outside a select few haunts in the south city, such as the Expresso Bar in Ballsbridge, the Merrion Hotel (where he frequents Patrick Guilbaud's restaurant), the Town Bar Grill (which Treasury kept afloat by putting in half a million euro, but only after paying creditors off at just 20 cent in the euro) or the Residence on St Stephen's Green (Treasury owns the building).

The now public trip to Marrakech, and the resulting media swarm, will have triggered much dismay in Treasury Holdings, a multi-armed international company (two of those arms publicly quoted) which employs some 900 people. While observers suggest that – unlike some others in the Nama top 10 – Treasury is going into Nama because of its size and as an instrument of market strategy rather than because of any default on its part, the tough gents in Treasury will be aware that public sentiment is a vital factor in any business. At the very least, this story illustrates the abyss between the powermongers who guard the knowledge of the workings of Nama and the taxpayers saddled with the final bill.

A property source, talking about the business plans being presented to Nama by the top entrants, reports that one developer, for example, is demanding a €500,000 salary in exchange for running his empire on the taxpayers' behalf. 'Well, what's the CEO of a billion-euro company worth?' he asks. 'What's Johnny Ronan worth, for instance, if you want him and Richard Barrett to continue to run Treasury Holdings?'

However, following the deeply unwelcome attention focused on Ronan's flights of whimsy, it has been made clear by various sources that his public skites are covered by his personal investment assets, which are quite separate from Treasury. And while those assets will also be going into Nama, they are not in default at this stage.

The plane is also his personal property and is run as a business by Ronan's own company, also unrelated to Treasury. In this version of events, the plane was idle on the ground on the Sunday concerned and, that being the case, the cost to him of the Marrakech trip would have been more like €12,000 than €56,000, paid for out of his own deposit account.

Meanwhile, his role in Treasury is said to be quite limited compared to Barrett's or the other heads of Treasury's various companies. Other than being a co-owner, a board director and assisting in development projects, he has no executive function, no role in management or administration and is not a director of either of the publicly quoted companies.

This was underlined in yesterday's statement, which said that Ronan's 'decision will not affect the day-to-day operation of Treasury Holdings, of which he is a director and shareholder, and which has operated under a management team and board of directors headed by managing director John Bruder for the past five years'.

People who know both men sigh deeply at Ronan's 'deeply inappropriate' behaviour, while arguing that there are worse offenders out there, throwing lavish parties and living in exile on money that rightly belongs to Nama and the taxpayer. 'Ronan and Barrett don't play golf, they don't own racehorses . . . You won't see them at the American Ryder Cup and they won't be going to Cheltenham next week, unlike some others,' says one.

Former Anglo Irish Bank chairman and chief executive Seán FitzPatrick, leaving Bray Garda Station in Co. Wicklow, following his arrest and questioning by garda fraud officers probing financial irregularities at the bank during his tenure in charge. Photograph: Alan Betson.

Meanwhile, as Ronan steps down to spend more time in quiet contemplation, perhaps in the cantilevered summer house/party pad or somewhere far from Irish models at any rate, questions remain about the media coverage which, he claims, led him to his current situation.

Who wins out of this? Industry insiders suggest that such mutually exploitative tabloid games, whereby pages are fashioned out of model/celebrity 'feuds' that can continue indefinitely, fuelled by anonymous 'friends', are commonplace. Photographers' numbers are on speed-dial for photo opportunities. The end result may be a briefly

raised profile and premium appearance fees for the model/celebrity, whatever the price in terms of dignity or notoriety.

The late Katy French's 'feud' with restaurateur Marcus Sweeney, when deeply abusive text messages found their way into the public domain, constantly fed by provocative quotes from 'friends', was a first step on the ladder for her as a young model/promotions girl in a competitive, poorly paid arena.

That 'feud' began, we were told, when Sweeney discovered French draped across his restaurant tables in skimpy lingerie for a photo-shoot. The pictures, published in the *Sunday Independent* magazine, coincided with the well-publicised 'feud', and a 'star' was born, with bonus publicity for the restaurant and magazine. Other sexually provocative photo-shoots in the magazine have included Gilson posing between male thighs and Davison in risqué positions with her on-off boyfriend.

Those in the industry insist that a distinction should be drawn between fashion models – for whom this country has limited, seasonal use – and glamour/promotions girls – whose regular beat is St Stephen's Green or Grafton Street, and who are increasingly to be seen in bikinis, whatever the product. Only five years ago, says one insider, if a girl posed on the street in a bikini, it was probably to advertise a beach holiday, whereas 'now it's bikinis and nothing else – it's just ridiculous to see them in bikinis for everything'. The model who posed in a bikini with a platter of food next to a chef in full whites, at a restaurant awards function, kept Liveline listeners in heated argument for days.

Davison is said to be doing most of her work now in Germany, where her father is also a big box-office attraction. She is also said to do a lot of charity work, free of charge. Gilson, meanwhile, has moved away from modelling to become a presenter on TV3's *Exposé* show, 'again not a highly paid area at all and more hard-working than you'd ever think', according to another insider. Whether either of these protagonists has suffered collateral damage in Johnny Ronan's excesses is for others to decide.

Professional caterers handing out free tea and coffee to people queuing at the Passport Office in Dublin.
Photograph: Matt Kavanagh.

WEDNESDAY, 24 MARCH 2010

Queue Leaves 'Hopping Mad' Passport Seekers Enraged but no Solution in Sight

Pamela Newenham

'I'm hopping mad,' said Dubliner Billie Traynor, one of hundreds of people queuing for a passport on Dublin's Molesworth Street yesterday. 'I have little sympathy for the workers . . . I work in the arts and we're affected too,' she added. Hers was one of 40,000 applications that were backlogged. Some of those with immediate travel plans queued outside the office from as early as 3 a.m., staying as close as they could to the door, even through a lunchtime bomb scare.

Noreen Tierney from Castlebar, Co. Mayo, left her home at 4 a.m. to travel to the office in Dublin. 'My passport isn't out of date but I was told to renew it for six months . . . It was supposed to be processed and ready to go on March 11th, but I still haven't heard anything.'

Angela Reville travelled from Wexford after being told not to apply via 'passport express'. 'Somebody's going to have to cover the cost of my flights if I don't get my passport,' she said. 'My brother's a teacher and my sister-in-law is a nurse so I have sympathy with them, but at the same time we're suffering the follies of others. People are losing money on holidays; it's disgraceful.'

133

Deirdre Keogh, Ratoath, Co. Meath, said she had been queuing for a passport for her son since 6.50 a.m. 'I just discovered my son's passport is out of date and he's due to go on a school trip to Italy on Thursday.'

Paula Hicks, due to go to Zurich on a business trip on Thursday morning, was also queuing. 'I applied for a new passport on March 8th via passport express, which is only supposed to take 10 days. I don't feel very hopeful, but . . . I really feel for all those families who paid their hard-earned cash to go on holidays and now they can't.'

Orderly queues turned to angry scenes at lunchtime, when a bomb scare led to the evacuation of people from the building. Some 50 to 60 people were evacuated shortly before 1 p.m., with a section of this group refusing to move from the door, chanting: 'What do we want? We want our passports now!'

As tensions mounted, a visibly distressed Thomas Sherlock, who had travelled from Ballaghaderreen, Co. Roscommon, told reporters

People queuing outside the Passport Office in Dublin. Photograph: Bryan O'Brien.

he was threatened with arrest after refusing to leave the building without his passport. Mr Sherlock said he needed a passport in order to fly with his partner to the Czech Republic at 6 a.m. this morning. 'My partner's dad died . . . she will have to bury her dad without me for support if I can't go.' Criticising the industrial action by Passport Office workers, he said: 'I work in car sales. If I didn't answer my phone I'd be told to go home.'

Shortly before 2 p.m., a security official announced that a sweep of the building had been completed, the bomb scare had been declared a hoax and the processing of applications would recommence. A round of applause erupted throughout the queue a short time later as one woman exiting the building shouted: 'Yes! We got it!' Encouraging people queuing, the woman said: 'How dare they hold what is legally mine? I sat in there and I fought for my passport until I got it.'

Relief was the word of the day for another tired member of the public as he exited the Passport Office, passport in hand, after queuing since 5 a.m. in order to attend a family wedding in Durban, South Africa.

A bomb scare that closed the Passport Office for almost an hour yesterday is under investigation, gardaí have said. Gardaí said they were investigating a report of an alleged suspect device at the building. A spokesman said they couldn't reveal whether the report had been telephoned in, or received by another means, 'for operational reasons'. The security alert was declared a hoax shortly before 2 p.m. after a sweep of the building. A security official said: 'We've done a sweep . . . It was a hoax.'

The alert triggered the evacuation of more than 50 people who were in the building at the time. Consequently, the evacuation led to angry scenes, with people anxious not to lose their place in the queue. Molesworth Street, which had been closed to traffic, reopened after lunch following the sweep of the premises.

FRIDAY, 26 MARCH 2010

It's Crystal Clear

Brian Boyd

Two indie music fans walk into a bar. Adjusting their Urban Outfitters shirts to show off their vintage T-shirts, they put down their iPhones and take a break from tweeting links to YouTube videos to talk about music.

There is a bit of hand-wringing about the fact that one of their current fave bands is in a new ad for an Apple product. They conclude that no ideological damage has been done because Apple make cool stuff. They're on safe ground with talk of Arcade Fire and the pre-eminence of the Montreal music scene. They swoon once again over Joanna Newsom, name-check The Hype Machine, give out about Pitchfork and fret a bit about if it's still okay to like Ryan Adams.

They're both wary about talking about new music because of 'The Rules'. These are: if you mention a band you like and the other person has heard of them, you lose. The other person owns you. The above is paraphrased from Christian Lander's *Stuff White People Like*. The book grew out of a blog that took satirical swipes at 'left-leaning, city-dwelling white folk'. It was the rigid cultural diktats of these anti-corporate, environmentally and socially aware urbanites that prompted Lander into sardonic action.

This self-appointed liberal elite tend to cluster around the media and feel an obsessive need to inform everyone, in a peremptory manner, of their cultural loves. *The Wire*, Arrested Development, Fleet Foxes, Broken Social Scene et al. are all solemnly approved of in a self-aggrandising manner. Their voices now carry a technological echo thanks to the profusion of social networking sites such as Twitter and Facebook. And you daren't fall foul of their inflexible aesthetic. You will be sneered at, derided and bullied. Culturally, you become an 'unperson'.

Then in wanders Crystal Swing. This hard-working band from Lisgoold, Co. Cork, are like thousands of others, looking to break into the world of light entertainment. But theirs isn't Choice Music Prize music, they don't look like The Strokes and there's not a scintilla of bespoke urban angst about them. So sneer at them on your Twitter feed, blog your embarrassment, set up the 'post-ironic' Facebook fan page. Add in the nudge nudge references, evoke the imagery of Irish 'duelling banjos', and even allude to 'Outsider Art'.

The treatment meted out to Crystal Swing by those who believe themselves to be culturally enlightened, socially aware media commentators is a disgrace. Sneering at and ridiculing a family pop band who don't tick their right-on boxes is a type of bullying.

In his book, Lander refers to how the self-appointed cultural/liberal elite hate and mock anything that's 'mainstream' because they're so desperate to find things that are 'more genuine, more unique and reflective of their experiences'. It would therefore have been consistent for the ridiculers to dismiss Crystal Swing as an unwelcome throwback to the showband era, but that hasn't happened in Ireland.

Instead, we get excited reminders that a leading US chat show host, Ellen DeGeneres, has played the Crystal Swing video on her show – DeGeneres being sophisticated and urbane enough to be in on the 'joke', of course.

Members of the Crystal Guggen brass band, from Menieres in Switzerland, performing at the St Patrick's Festival Big Day Out on Merrion Square in Dublin. Photograph: Matt Kavanagh.

So sophisticated and urbane is DeGeneres that, moments after playing the video, she quipped: 'Most people in Ireland wear green on St Patrick's Day, so when they pass out on their lawn, they'll be camouflaged and their neighbours won't see them.' This zinger was followed by: 'I'm good at Riverdancing but I can't show you now because I've sprained my shillelagh.' Jaysus.

There are also calls for Crystal Swing to be added to the Oxegen bill. Wouldn't that be the coolest thing? Once you're done with the 'more genuine, more unique and reflective of your experiences' indie bands on the bill, you could deign to culturally slum it a bit with Crystal Swing, as if they're some sort of rural Irish freak show. If, as has been stated numerous times on blog posts and Twitter feeds, Crystal Swing make some of these people 'embarrassed to call themselves Irish', might we not at least ask Mary Murray-Burke and her children Dervla and Derek how they feel about sharing the same nationality as their mocking detractors?

I know which side I'm embarrassed by.

MONDAY, 29 MARCH 2010

How is State to Unlock Perilous Embrace of the Quinn Group?

John McManus

Considerable effort has been expended in recent days to prepare the ground for the injection of a staggering €9 billion of additional taxpayers' money into Anglo Irish Bank.

The chief executive of the bank, Mike Aynsley, has publicly pleaded the case for reinventing Anglo as a business bank. He has argued that the alternatives – shutting down the bank immediately or running it down gradually over 10 years – would cost substantially more than the €13 billion (which includes the €4 billion already injected by the State) required for his plan.

You could easily get sidetracked into a debate about the veracity or otherwise of Mr Aynsley's analysis, but there is little to be gained from this.

As anyone who has ever played with a spreadsheet can testify, it is very easy to generate the numbers you need in these situations if you also write the spreadsheet and make the underlying assumptions about factors such as economic growth and interest rates. One suspects that if a few assumptions were changed on whatever spreadsheet Mr Aynsley is using, you could easily enough generate the numbers you need to support the case for pursuing one of the other courses of action open to the Government. These assumptions could be just as valid as those used by Mr Aynsley, given the level of uncertainty on what the economic landscape will look like 18 months hence, never mind 10 years.

No. The simple truth is that it has been decided by the Government that Anglo will be kept going and that is pretty much the end of the matter. The reasons for this dogmatism, however, are becoming a little clearer. A clue lies in the answer to the question: if Anglo Irish Bank is going to be a business bank once it has dumped its €36 billion worth of toxic loans into the National Asset Management Agency (Nama), then who will be its biggest customer?

The answer is the Quinn Group. Once the bank has been 'cleansed' of its land and development loans, its loan book will shrink to €36 billion. A good portion of this – perhaps up to €10 billion – will be hived off into a run-off vehicle and the remainder will form the basis of the new business bank. Quinn Group – which owes Anglo about €2.8 billion – will account for well over 10 per cent of the new bank's loan book.

Anglo's single biggest activity under Aynsley's plan will be to provide finance to the Quinn Group, and its loans to Quinn will exceed the bank's capital base. If you were serious about setting up a business bank, you would not do it this way. And this raises the question of whether or not a large part of the rationale for keeping Anglo going is fear over the possible collateral damage to the Quinn Group of closing it down.

The Quinn Group has written health insurance policies for some 400,000 Irish people and is the second largest general insurer in the Irish market. It employs thousands of people in these two businesses as well as in its original building materials and cement business. It is simply too big

to fail. So: is the real systemic importance of Anglo its role as financier to the Quinn Group?

It is certainly open to question whether – in the current climate – Quinn Group could find another bank to step into Anglo's shoes on the same terms. It already has additional borrowings of €1.3 billion from other banks and bond holders which must be refinanced later this year. The group is confident it will succeed in doing so, but the appetite for further lending by international banks to a business so heavily exposed to the Irish economy must be limited.

What you could buy with

€21,800,000,000

1 Large Hadron Collider
€4 billion
(Cost of building the Cern Large Hadron Collider)

1 space shuttle €1.26 billion
(Cost of building the Endeavour space shuttle)

1 metro €5 billion
(Projected cost of the Dublin Metro North)

1 3D movie
€370,000
(Budget for Avatar)

2 very expensive paintings
€167 million & €107 million
(Prices fetched by Jackson Pollock's No. 5, 1948 and Gustav Klimt's Portrait of Adele Bloch-Bauer I, both sold in 2006)

1 tribunal of inquiry
€222 million
(Cost of the Saville Bloody Sunday inquiry)

2 Luas lines €770 million
Cost of building the Red and Green Luas lines

2 jackpots €250 million
(Recent Euromillions jackpot was €125 million)

3 hotels (in Celtic Tiger money)
€260 million
(Price paid by Sean Dunne for three Ballsbridge hotels in 2005)

23 pupils per class
€30 million
(Annual cost of reducing the primary school class size by one pupil. The figure has been estimated at between 18 million and 30 million per annum)

3 million swine flu vaccines
€12.8 million
(Price paid by the State for swine-flu vaccines)

1 mayor
€1.5 billion
(Proposed annual budget that the new Dublin Mayor will oversee)

1 year's supply of alcohol
€6.55 billion
(Estimated national expenditure on alcohol in 2009)

1 better Limerick
€1.7 billion
(Cost of phase one of Limerick Regeneration)

© IRISH TIMES PREMEDIA

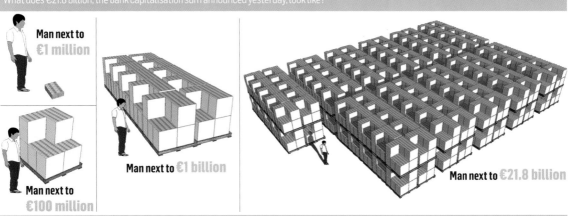

About the size of it
What does €21.8 billion, the bank capitalisation sum announced yesterday, look like?

Man next to
€1 million

Man next to
€100 million

Man next to **€1 billion**

Man next to €21.8 billion

© IRISH TIMES PREMEDIA

On top of this, the Quinn Group and its owners, the Quinn family, have very seriously dirtied their bib over the last few years. We have yet to have anything approaching a proper explanation from the Quinns of why they built a secret 28 per cent stake in their company's main banker, Anglo, with catastrophic consequences. The fallout from the affair does not amount to a corporate governance record a prospective lender would put a lot of store by.

The truth is that we really don't know what would happen to Quinn Group if Anglo Irish was shut down, but it's safe to say that no one really wants to find out.

The Government, via Anglo, is, for the time being, locked in a desperate embrace with Quinn.

The question is, how do they get out of it? It is worrying that Quinn Group seems reluctant to engage with a number of proposals put on the table by Anglo aimed at reducing its debt. It's not necessarily surprising, as they involve debt-for-equity swaps and asset sales. All of which are anathema to Seán Quinn, who built the company from nothing over 36 years. Mr Quinn's feelings are not the issue here though. It's taxpayers' money.

(On 30 March, the High Court appointed administrators to Quinn Insurance at the request of the Financial Regulator, Matthew Elderfield, on the same day Brian Lenihan announced the taxpayer was pumping some €21.8 billion into Anglo.)

FRIDAY, 2 APRIL 2010

She Stared and Said: 'You're Really off the Wall, Man'

Michael Harding

I saw a mink last week, on my way to the train; black and shiny, its gorgeous coat far superior to even the most beautiful black cat I ever had. It was running across the road that leads down to Lough Ennell, where the swans live. There was something about its wild nature that I envied.

Later in the day I met Natalie, a Russian friend, on Grafton Street, and she was wearing a big black fur coat, so I began thinking of her, too, as wild. I rubbed the fur on her shoulders and asked her if it was real.

She said: 'Of course it is real!' I said: 'Have you ever been to the fur shop down the street?' 'Yes,'

A girl carries her sister on her back as she breaks rocks into smaller pieces for use in construction in Juba, south of Khartoum. Photograph: Goran Tomasevic/Reuters.

she said, 'I love that shop; but I not go there any-more, because of recession.'

'What kind of animal are you wearing today?' I wondered. 'Rabbit,' she said, apologetically, as if perhaps she might be more comfortable in the skin of a white tiger, or a Siberian wolf. 'Well, that's not too offensive,' I said. 'In fact, Irish people actually eat rabbits.' 'Oh,' she said, 'you must come to my house tonight, and I will cook you rabbit.' I declined the offer, explaining that I had a prior engagement.

That night I was scheduled to partake in a panel discussion on the radio with two other people, a young man and a woman, both of whom are known as entertainment journalists. We were

going to talk about movies.

When the programme began I tried to sound as if I knew something about Hollywood. 'Apparently Sandra Bullock is having personal problems,' I declared, but everybody already knew that.

The young man beside me explained how the movie under review was not very good, and was the same as half a dozen other movies, and how the storyline was silly, but that Sandra looked good. 'If you like Sandra,' he said, 'you will like this.' He sounded like he knew her intimately.

The presenter was just off a plane from New York, and he was sporting an impressive tan, and the young woman on the panel was all giggles, like

Marilyn Monroe on the verge of ecstasy, as if this was the happiest day of her life.

I just didn't know enough about movies, and I couldn't keep up with the eloquence of the other two. I was amazed at how much they knew about celebrities and at all the hot gossip they had about Hollywood.

At one stage I asked them if there was a danger that we might be losing the run of ourselves, that perhaps our over-familiarity with American culture was a sign that we were, as a nation, still colonised. They looked at me as if I had two heads.

I left the studio a bit dazed and wandered into a nearby pub. A young woman in gothic evening wear was leaning against the bar and holding her head, like she had a migraine. I asked her if anything was wrong. She said she had been in the back of a taxi and she had heard an old geezer on the radio trying to say something intelligent about movies.

'The old fart probably wasn't at a movie for decades,' she said. 'He was going on about being colonised or something. He said he was from Mullingar, wherever that is! Probably on Planet Zog!' 'No,' I said, 'Mullingar is in Westmeath. It's an hour away on the train.' 'How do you know?' she asked. I said: 'The fart on the radio was me.' 'Jesus,' she exclaimed, 'that's cool.'

We didn't have much of a vocabulary in common, so I tried to use words judiciously. When she asked me if I would like to join her for a drink, I said: 'That would be cool.' And she said I was cool. And then the drinks arrived – my wine and her vodka – which is when she realised that she had left her money in the taxi, and she was all distressed about that, so I paid, and she thanked me, and I said: 'Don't worry, it's cool.'

Then, for the sake of conversation, I said that I had seen a sleek black mink that morning, on the road to Lough Ennell, where the swans live, and that it was utterly wild and beautiful. She stared at me with some unease, and said: 'You're really off the wall, man.'

SATURDAY, 3 APRIL 2010

Upfront

Róisín Ingle

Hello. My name is Róisín Ingle. You may remember me from such columns as 'My Mother-In-Law-In-Waiting Is Unusually Fond of Bleach' and 'I Am Co-Habiting with a Nordy Prod' or 'I Wish I Was Skinnier but I Like Batter Burgers Too Much, Unfortunately'.

So where were we? Well, since we last convened I had two baby girls at pretty much the same time. I then spent the guts of a year looking after them, helped in no small part by my Nordy Prod, while following several sets of conflicting parenting advice in books recommended by Amazon.

'Róisín,' Amazon would say (in that passive aggressive bullying way it has), 'you seem like just the kind of person who needs to be told how to be a parent and is afraid to rely on their own instincts. You'll be needing this book, and this, and maybe this one and definitely that one,' and so on. The upshot is that we had to have more bookshelves built and I could now give a seminar on a parenting style I like to call Attachment Contented Baby Whispering Nurture Shock.

Now I am back at work. The other kind of work. The kind that doesn't involve a Masters in poo or the verbatim retelling of the story of Daisy and Pip and their epic game of hide and seek 57 times a day.

In one of my books I learn that at this stage it's perfectly normal to be consumed by guilt – with a capital G. Twice the guilt for twins, obviously. I am supposed to be sneaking off to the toilet every half hour to retouch my mascara and repair the damage done by a tsunami of tears.

There should be a framed photograph of them on my desk. Their faces (vulnerable, abandoned, impossibly cute) should catch my eye when I am on the phone and my voice should falter. This

Seán Fitzpatrick from the Star of the Sea school, Sandymount, in Dublin, at the Natural History Museum which reopened after refurbishment. Photograph: Brenda Fitzsimons.

should make the person at the other end of the phone ask, 'Hello, are you still there?' and, struggling to regain my composure, I should say, 'Yes, yes of course!' in a bright-yet-heartsick voice because, though I feel like the Wicked Witch of the North (Strand), I am a professional and I must go on.

The truth? I am delighted to be back at work. While I am sure the novelty is going to wear off soon (it might have even worn off by the time you read this), for now I can't tell you how much I am enjoying the simple pleasures of being a Parent Who Works Outside the Home (PWWOTH). Take cycling to the office, for example. Never has nearly being knocked over by a bus or taxi been so much fun. I even got my skirt caught in the spokes of the wheel, which gave me a little jolt of nostalgia for the freewheeling person I was before I

learned to cook a fortnight's worth of food for two people in half an hour with one hand, while administering Motilium suppositories with the other.

People come up to my desk as though approaching the recently bereaved and ask, 'Are you okay?' At first, I am confused. Then I remember that leaving them is supposed to be tearing me apart inside and, just like that, the guilt arrives, nestling like a piece of gristle somewhere below my breastbone. Oh great. So now I am feeling guilty about not feeling guilty. 'Welcome to parenthood,' says my friend (who knows about these things).

Thankfully, it turns out the guilt about not feeling guilty is only guilt with a small g and it melts away at the first unspilled, fully consumed cup of coffee enjoyed by the new PWWOTH. It also feels better to know I am not alone. One colleague confessed that coming back to work was like winning the lottery, if only for the joy of being free to talk rubbish to people by the photocopier. Soon, I am talking rubbish by the photocopier and understanding exactly what she means. I have a conversation with someone in the lift about the weather and I enjoy it so much it scares me.

I love my children – in case you are the kind of person who thinks my enjoying being back at work means I don't. I love them in a way I could never do justice to here. But my first day back at work felt like getting reacquainted with a person I recognised and hadn't seen for ages, someone I thought had disappeared. It feels like an achievement that I get into work without sick on my

shoulder and tights that I have colour-coordinated with my outfit. Another bonus is that my productivity appears to have increased, having spent a year engaged in extreme multitasking.

One experienced mother who, with two 20-something daughters is only now retreating from the frontline of parenthood, texts me in the spirit of working-outside-the-home sisterhood. 'How was the first week back?' she asks. 'I really enjoyed it,' I reply. 'NEVER say that out loud!' she texts back immediately. Sorry sisterhood – but I really did.

This weekend Róisín will be taking Fiona McCann out for dinner to say thanks for keeping the seat warm for her. She will also continue to resist writing her first tweet because she is afraid that, like her relationship with a certain brand of potato-based snack, once she starts she won't stop – and anyway, where do people find the time? Apologies to the 221 people following her on Twitter. The guilt.

THURSDAY, 8 APRIL 2010

End of an Era and of Type-Written Riddles from Zimbabwe

Lorna Kernan

Derek Crozier pictured on the occasion of his 90th birthday.

Derek Crozier was always charming to work with, a gentle man with a clipped voice who began his sentences with the old-fashioned, 'Now my dear . . .' He must be the longest lasting contributor to *The Irish Times*, having supplied his Crosaire crosswords for just over 67 years. He must also have been the most senior, at age 92.

This is the end of a unique era: one of tapping out words on a manual typewriter, with carbon paper copies and hard copy arriving at various intervals from Zimbabwe in brown envelopes

Envelopes in which Derek Crozier's Crosaire crosswords arrived in **The Irish Times'** *Dublin offices from his home in Zimbabwe. Photograph: Bryan O'Brien.*

marked by hand with 'surface mail' and 'printed matter', reminiscent of an earlier time.

His cryptic puzzles were a microcosm of his marriage to Marjorie – she the avid crossword solver who, until her death, filled in grids with words, he the reluctant cruciverbalist who took her words and moulded them with clever clues.

The story began in December 1941, when Derek's goddaughter gave him a present of a book of crosswords. Even though he didn't do crosswords, he decided after a few days that he would 'have a go', only to discover that Marjorie had solved the lot.

'Right,' he said. 'Now I'll make you up one that you won't be able to solve.' And he did. Later on, he woke her in the middle of the night and suggested offering crosswords to *The Irish Times*. She told him not to be silly and to go back to sleep.

This was all the rag he needed: 'Right,' he said, 'I'll show her.'

At Christmas Eve drinks in 1942 with Jack White in the Pearl Bar in Fleet Street, he boldly approached the then editor of *The Irish Times*, Bertie Smyllie, and his deputy, Alec Newman, to offer his expertise and, after a few samples were approved, the weekly Saturday Crosaire began on 13 March, 1943. Wednesdays were added in 1950, Tuesdays in 1955 and the go-ahead for today's six-day formula came in 1982.

The crosswords took three to four hours to complete, with Crozier's workload set at one and a bit a day. Poignantly, it was on Good Friday last, while conjuring up his last one, that he became ill.

Those who were frustrated with his clues often contacted me, not in outrage but more in search of a reasoning behind his answers, or asking when we were running the Crosaire how-to guide again.

As far as the philosophy of the genre went, cruciverbalists were a mystery to Derek, who always admitted he never in fact did crosswords. He couldn't ever solve them. If he was presented with one of his own creations after a decent interval, he was floored and couldn't solve it either.

Living in Zimbabwe, correspondence with *The Irish Times* wasn't easy. Yet his familiar brown envelopes always seemed to arrive well in time, emblazoned with different postage stamps including Irish, English and South African. Some were marked 'by hand' and were delivered to *The Irish Times* offices in person.

Derek always found someone – friends, friends of friends, and friends of Crosaire itself – to take his envelopes and post them safely. Such was his fear of not getting them to the office in time for publication that he worked ahead, with military regularity, and has ensured there is a bag of Crosaire crosswords to publish for at least the next 12 months.

Derek was always surprised and delighted at how popular his crosswords were and how interested his fans were in him. He was worried when we began to supply answers to his crosswords by telephone and fax. I never did tell him that today the answers can be accessed by mobile phone.

He was amazed at the web and the Crosaire blogs propagating his fan-base across continents, where fans met to discuss Crosaire clues.

He declined to co-operate with a documentary-maker from Ireland who wanted to travel to Zimbabwe to interview him and document his life. He was primarily concerned that a journalist arriving with all the equipment to film and record him might be put in danger.

After all, who would have believed she was doing a story on an old crossword compiler? When a friend of mine was travelling to Zimbabwe last January, I asked Derek if there was anything I could send him. 'Yes, my dear . . . well, that's if

they still make them. A couple of erasers; the ones that would do ink. That would be lovely, my dear.'

Mourners Warned Against Protest as Toyosi Is Laid to Rest

Kathy Sheridan

'No amount of protest, no demonstration will bring back this boy's soul. Your good mind is what he needs – not fighting, not crying,' Imam Shehu Adeniji told mourners at

Toyosi Shitta-bey.

Mourners at the funeral of Toyosi Shitta-bey in Newcastle, Co. Dublin. Photograph: David Sleator.

the funeral of Toyosi Shitta-bey, the 15-year-old Nigerian-born student killed last Friday in Tyrrelstown, west Dublin.

Referring afterwards to the march planned for Dublin city tomorrow, he said: 'Demonstration is uncalled for. We do not approve of it. It is creating social unrest . . .' Their concern was about the 'intention of those who want to protest', added the assistant imam at the mosque in Dublin's Sheriff Street, Alhaj Saliu Adewunmi Adeniran. 'It can instigate problems with teenagers and we are worried about where it might lead.'

The funeral ceremonies, conducted according to Islamic rites, began with the ritual washing and embalming of the body at a Lucan funeral home, attended by Toyosi's father, Segun Shitta-bey, his two brothers, Sodiq (22) and Tunde (12), and close family members. Later teachers, community leaders, football club officials and many young school friends and soccer teammates from

Littlepace and Shelbourne clubs filed past his open coffin.

Two 16-year-olds emerged together, both obviously in shock: 'It looks nothing like him', said the Irish boy. 'I never saw a dead body before,' said his Nigerian friend. As they walked off in silence, Segun Shitta-bey too was leaving, to return home to be with his wife, Bola. According to Nigerian culture and custom, parents do not attend the burial of their child. Afterwards, the coffin, draped in the flag of Shelbourne soccer club, was driven by hearse through Lucan village and on to Newcastle, Co. Dublin, at the head of a long cortège with a garda escort.

On arrival, the 'Respect' flag of UEFA was placed on the coffin, and as time had not permitted prayers at a mosque, the imam and chief mourners, with the coffin to the side, away from the main body of mourners, held a short private service, after which the coffin was returned to the

The remains of Toyosi Shitta-bey are removed from his coffin and laid to rest according to Islamic tradition, following his funeral. Photograph: David Sleator.

graveside, where young friends from Littlepace soccer club formed a guard of honour.

Then the lid was opened and the shrouded body removed, amid loud wailing, weeping and calls to Allah. It was lowered gently into the grave to the waiting arms of two imams and thence onto wooden slabs, where 15-year-old Toyosi Shitta-bey was laid to rest on his right side, facing east.

Sodiq and Tunde were the first to throw soil onto their brother's body, followed by friends and teammates. There would be a 'big reward' from Almighty God for those who would 'help to put the sand back in place', said Imam Adeniji, while the crowd began a slow chant: 'There is no deity worthy of worship except Allah and holy prophet Muhammad, who is the messenger of Allah . . ,' repeating the lines over and over in trembling voices.

The imam then spoke in English, telling the mourners – many of them youths – this was 'just a big lesson for everybody so it can improve our lives. Say from now on, I will be law-abiding and follow the way of God, I will not be negative for now'.

'There is no one who will not die. Follow the way of Allah . . ,' he said, urging people to give every kind of moral and financial assistance to the Shitta-bey family.

Among the attendance were Mary White, Minister of State for Equality and Integration; the Nigerian ambassador, Dr Kemafo Nonyerem Chikwe; Joe Higgins MEP; Insp. Gerry Bergin, Supt Dave Dowling and Sgt Vincent Connolly, community policing officer and family liaison, all from Blanchardstown Garda Station; John Delaney, chief executive of the Football Association of Ireland, and the body's integration officer, Des Tomlinson; representatives of Shelbourne football club, Fran Renwick, John Phelan and Philip Devereux; Cllr Ruth Coppinger; Cllr Kieran Dennison; Seán Fitzmaurice, deputy principal of Hartstown Community School; Toyosi's year head, Eoin Brady; and Fr Dan Jo O'Mahony.

Death Leaves Gaping Hole in Polish Public Life

Derek Scally, in Warsaw

Two minutes of silence at noon yesterday marked the start of a black week of mourning for Poland. The death of Polish president Lech Kaczynski, his wife, Maria, and an array of important figures has left a gaping hole in Polish public life. When the mourning period ends, Poles will be anxious for answers – not just about what caused the weekend aircraft crash in Smolensk, but how the country can fill the void in government and move on.

The most pressing question posed by Kaczynski's death is where it leaves the national conservative Law and Justice (PiS) party he founded with his surviving twin brother, Jaroslaw. Political analysts are agreed that, three days after the tragedy, anything could happen in Poland's largest opposition party. Throw in the unpredictable former Polish prime minister, Jaroslaw Kaczynski, and an unpredictable outcome is almost guaranteed.

Jaroslaw Kaczynski was and remains the central strategist in PiS and, though Saturday's crash killed many key PiS figures, analysts agree it has not fatally wounded the party. 'The party is far from decimated but, from a personnel perspective, it is in a critical condition,' says Eugeniusz Smolar of the Centre for International Relations.

Analyst Krzysztof Bobinski of the Unia Polska think-tank agrees with that assessment. 'It all depends now on how Jaroslaw holds up,' he says. 'Considering the special relationship between twins he may just fall apart, particularly as his mother is seriously ill too. Or he may be reinvigorated and take on his brother's mantle to contest the presidential election.'

If Jaroslaw Kaczynski decides not to contest the election, due by 30 June, he could field an able

Jaroslaw Kaczynski kneels before the coffin of his twin brother, President Lech Kaczynski of Poland, at the military airport in Warsaw yesterday. Photograph: Alik Keplicz/AP Photo.

protégé such as Zbigniew Ziobro. Just 39, Ziobro served as Jaroslaw Kaczynski's feared justice minister and proved to the party's many enemies that its 'Law and Justice' name was not just a label.

The Smolensk disaster might even give PiS an edge in the upcoming election. After five years in the presidential palace, Lech Kaczynski stayed the distance on the political stage longer than Jaroslaw, whose fractious coalition lasted just two years. But polls showed Lech Kaczynski's star was on the wane too. His passing means the party is no longer forced to back his candidacy just to save face. 'PiS and its supporters now have their dead hero and any PiS candidate can run on that,' says Bobinski.

Ahead of the crash, polls suggested the man likely to be president in the autumn was Bronislaw Komorowski, the speaker of parliament. Now acting head of state, Komorowski has no idea what PiS candidate he will face in two months.

One thing is certain: a PiS victory on a Smolensk sympathy vote would be a serious setback for Warsaw's relations with Europe, carefully rebuilt by Donald Tusk's centre-right Civic Platform (PO) since 2007.

At home, a PiS presidential election win would guarantee more friction with Tusk's government of the kind that has paralysed Polish lawmaking and reform for three years.

The bitter irony of Kaczynski's death, on his way to honour the 22,000 Polish soldiers killed in the Russian forest of Katyn in 1940, has not been lost on Poles. But perhaps an even greater irony is if, as some analysts have suggested, Kaczynski's death gives a boost to relations between Poland and Russia, for decades two of Europe's frostiest neighbours.

Things were already improving of late. Poles were surprised and touched by recent Russian gestures in the lead-up to this week's 70th anniversary of the Katyn massacre. Some 20 years ago, Moscow first admitted responsibility for the 1940 atrocity. Ahead of this year's anniversary, the Russian authorities offered considerable assistance to Polish survivors and victims' families to travel to the Katyn site.

Last week, Russian prime minister Vladimir Putin honoured those who 'bravely met their death' there. Even if he stopped short of a full apology, it was a long way from the nationalist rhetoric of the Stalin era that Poles have had to put up with from Moscow in recent years.

Since the crash, the Kremlin has gone out of its way to do the right thing: images of Putin and Russian president Dmitry Medvedev praying in a chapel went down well, as did the extensive facilities erected on site for families travelling from Poland to identify their loved ones. 'The Poles really appreciate such gestures at a time like this,' says Henryk Suchar, an international affairs analyst specialising in Polish-Russian relations.

Kaczynski was perhaps the sternest critic of Moscow in the central European region, one who never missed an opportunity to support countries he viewed as victims of Russian aggression. He supported the Orange revolution in Ukraine and flew to Georgia in the middle of its war with

Isabelle Grant (6) from Wicklow at the launch of Buy My Dress, the country's largest one-day charity dress sale, which will be held in aid of Down Syndrome Centre. With her are (from left): Olwyn Enright TD, Holly White, Shona Ryan, Gillian Quinn and Irma Mali, all wearing designs from the Kellogg's Design a Little Red Dress Competition, which was won by Mona Atkinson from the National College of Art and Design in Dublin. Photograph: Dara Mac Dónaill.

Moscow in August 2008, even coming under fire from Russian troops when he travelled to the border with Georgia's breakaway regions. With his passing, Suchar says Russia has lost a man they loved to hate.

'Kaczynski was very anti-Russian in a clumsy way and gave Poland a very negative image in Russia,' he says. 'The irony of his death is that it could well result in improved relations. That would be the president's unforgettable contribution to Polish-Russian relations.'

The Smolensk crash, just 20 km from the Katyn site, has reawakened two Polish wartime traumas: the 1940 forest massacre that wiped out many leading army majors and generals; and the mysterious plane crash in 1943 of Wladyslaw Sikorski, Poland's exiled prime minister.

Former Solidarity leader and Polish president Lech Walesa suggested yesterday that this latest tragedy was comparable in scale to the 1940 massacre. 'Then, they shot our intelligentsia in the back of the head. Now we've lost a huge part of our nation's elite in a plane accident,' he said, adding: 'It's Katyn number two.' His remark has been pounced on with triumph by Kaczynski supporters, but has prompted much head-shaking in other quarters. Moscow has yet to comment.

Yesterday evening, Kaczynski returned to the presidential palace in a coffin, ending the first act in this Polish tragedy. It is too soon to say for sure whether it will heal the bitter divisions that characterise Poland's emotional style of politics. 'The politically correct thing to say would be that it would make Polish politics more calm and circumspect,' says Bobinski, 'but the likelihood is that it will just redouble Jaroslaw Kaczynski's paranoia towards his political opponents.'

Looking ahead, some urgent decisions have to be made in Warsaw even before the looming state funerals. The death of central bank governor Slawomir Skrzypek meant there was a most urgent position to fill to stabilise the zloty after weekend trading. Skrzypek's experienced deputy, Piotr Wiesiolek, has already stepped in; appointing a permanent replacement is a priority for the acting president.

Other personalities will be impossible to replace, such as 'Solidarity Godmother' Anna Walentynowicz. It was her firing that prompted the 1980 Gdansk shipyard strike and spread the Solidarity trade union activism that eventually toppled communism in Poland.

Warsaw political watchers are confident that, though Poland will struggle, it will eventually fill the gaps left by the Smolensk crash. 'We lost some really brilliant people who were important in building up Polish civic society in the last 20 years,' says Smolar, of the Centre for International Relations. 'I don't think it will have a huge effect on the country. Poland will recover and go on.'

TUESDAY, 13 APRIL 2010

Turning Back the Clock to Meet a Patient

Maurice Neligan

Out of the blue, Mr and Mrs David Doyle of Enniscorthy invited the HA and me to the wedding of their daughter Jeanne to Mr Aidan Kinane. A long time ago I operated upon Jeanne in Our Lady's Hospital for Sick Children in Crumlin. Following surgery and initial follow-up, I told her mother and grandmother that I would not need to see her again until her wedding day. Jeanne, who is now a teacher in Rockwell College, told me she was marrying a fine Tipperary man.

I want you Jeanne and your family to know that your invitation was very special to me and is deeply appreciated. I wish you and Aidan every happiness, in every way. To digress slightly I wish your charges in Rockwell and the college itself success in the future. I appreciate that you might have other things on your mind.

Barcelona striker Lionel Messi celebrates in front of his fans after scoring the second of his four goals against Arsenal, during last night's Champions League quarter-final, second leg tie at Camp Nou. Photograph: Albert Gea/Reuters.

Jeanne was referred to me for surgery by Prof. Conor Ward who held the chair of paediatrics at UCD and was a cardiologist of note on the world stage. Conor described, in the *Journal of the Irish Medical Association* in 1964, a hitherto unobserved familial cardiac rhythm disorder in children. The following year, a Dr C. Romano independently noted the same arrhythmia and published his findings in the *Lancet*. The complex is known as the Ward-Romano syndrome and is one of the causes of sudden death in childhood and adolescence. Now when noted, it can be treated. Conor was largely responsible for my appointment in Crumlin and became a great colleague and friend.

At the beginning of the unit in Crumlin, great strides were being made in this facet of heart sur-

gery. This was largely due to a greater understanding of the anatomy of congenital heart disease, much of this facilitated by the retention and study of postmortem hearts. This showed the complexities of anatomical variation and was absolutely necessary to allow the surgeons devise operations to remedy them. This led to problems down the line, not foreseen in those pioneering days. The operations were only one aspect of the treatment. The anaesthesiology and the intensive care had to be of very high standard and they progressed very rapidly with skilled and enthusiastic staff to a stage where today they are second to none.

It is deeply distressing to hear of theatre and intensive care closures and staff shortages in this wonderful unit delivering world-class treatment. It

James Joyce (right) with Sylvia Beach, first publisher of Ulysses.

Gardaí stand by as firefighters in Galway tackle a gorse fire close to Moycullen, near the Spiddal Road. Photograph: Joe O'Shaughnessy.

She was very close to many other Modernist writers, Hemingway and William Carlos Williams in particular, and later to Richard Wright, who came to Paris after the second World War. Later still, she was a keen supporter of the drug-fuelled fantasies of Henri Michaux, many of whose works she translated, winning prizes in the process. Nothing fazed her, as must already be evident.

Encouraging though all this is, there is something a little melancholy about the letters of the later years. In Joyce's wake, there were considerable difficulties. The bookshop did not reopen after the war (another shop of the same name remains a port of call in Paris). Beach was aided, not just by the sale of manuscripts, but also by generous gifts from many friends. She continued to live 'above the shop' in 12 rue de l'Odéon, where she died on 6 October, 1962.

Unfortunately, Beach is not well served by this collection of her fascinating letters. The collection is not complete – there are some 108 unpublished letters from Beach to Joyce that are now in the Zurich James Joyce Foundation and are being edited 'in-house' – but even apart from that there are other gaps in the volume.

Moreover, the notes and other apparatus are unreliable, with numerous errors and misreadings: Paul Léon did not die in Auschwitz; Lucia Joyce was not in Zurich when her mother died there; when Beach refers in 1958 to 'the first draft of a Portrait of the Artist' she does not mean the manuscript that was published as *Stephen Hero*. These are not particularly esoteric items and do nothing to encourage confidence in other aspects of the editing by Keri Walsh, assistant professor of literature at Claremont McKenna College in Claremont, California.

In June 1962, Sylvia Beach was the guest of honour at the opening of the James Joyce Tower in Sandycove as a Joyce museum. While in Dublin, she was interviewed by Telefís Éireann, as it then was. The piece was recently rebroadcast and a very charming interview it is. Some four months later, she was dead. These letters, imperfectly presented though they are, amply confirm the interview's evidence of a woman of indomitable spirit whose personality shines through in every word she wrote.

SATURDAY, 1 MAY 2010

Brightest Light on the Airwaves Is Extinguished Too Soon

Kathy Sheridan

'My talent is to imbue a project with much more significance and theatricality than it actually deserves. This gives a lot of incandescence to it that makes things that are not all that bright shine very brightly. I can bring that to the party.

'But, like it says in *Blade Runner*, the light that burns twice as brightly burns twice as fast. How brightly I have shone.' In light of his early death at 53, Gerry Ryan's own words as they appeared in his sharply self-aware, self-mocking autobiography in 2008, take on a starker hue.

What would the impish, irreverent, crass, supremely intelligent broadcaster have been thinking yesterday, as some of RTÉ's finest twittered about his sudden passing? As people who disdained his broadcasting were suddenly feeling a lurch of dismay that he was gone?

Would he perhaps be rather pleased about it all, that he would be the first iconic presenter to pass away, that he would not grow old as they would, shuffling towards an inglorious fade-out in a world where youth, vigour and motor mouth are paramount?

'I don't think so. I'm pretty sure he wouldn't be too happy about this,' said his long-time friend and producer, Siobhán Hough. 'And I don't say that necessarily because of the new relationship he was in, but because of his five children. He absolutely adored them. They were his life and his soul. He was completely devastated when his daughter Lottie went to New York last year. Now he's not going to see them married, or hold his grandchildren.'

He was also regaining his equilibrium after the break-up of his 26-year marriage in March 2008, said Hough. 'He was still very good friends with Morah. He was already making plans to go off to Disneyland with the kids in the summer. I think he was in a good space, so it's all the more tragic.' She believed too that he had found happiness with his new partner, Melanie Verwoerd. An interesting woman herself, she served as the South African ambassador to Ireland from 2001 to 2005, and her former father-in-law was Hendrik Verwoerd, the principal architect of apartheid.

Though Gerry Ryan's life was always the stuff of farce, mischief, scatological self-revelation and high drama, the way he handled his marriage break-up was 'one of the best things he ever did', said journalist and friend Kate Holmquist. 'Throughout it all, neither he nor Morah ever broke faith or broke cover.'

For listeners long used to the saucy innuendo about Morah, and such things as an intimate knowledge of Ryan's digestive tract and blocked sinuses, as well as the tabloid reports of the rich friends, the first-class flights, champagne and the lavish lifestyle, such discretion was a revelation.

For those who knew him well, it was simply further testament to his loyalty. It was also indicative of his consistency as a broadcaster. He took no time off work and unknowing listeners would have noticed no difference in his exuberant chatter.

Morah Ryan and her children, Lottie, Rex, Bonnie, Elliott and Babette, leave the family home in Clontarf, Dublin, to accompany Gerry Ryan's remains to the nearby Church of St John the Baptist. Speaking during the funeral Mass, Rex said his father was 'the definition of a cool Dad ... He was a man who was too big for this world. He shone more brightly than anyone I have come across.' Photograph: Dara Mac Dónaill.

Some eight months later, when newspapers were providing saturation coverage of his new relationship, he was equally discreet. 'I'm in a lot of the newspapers this morning,' he said. 'Modesty forbids me from commenting.' And he never did.

Perhaps the combination of a regular, middle-class dentist for a father, and a mother, Maureen Bourke, who was a member of the Dublin theatrical family and Dame Street costumers, fashioned this blend of drama and discretion.

Reared in Clontarf, he used to tell stories of how he was expelled by the Holy Faith nuns and claimed they tried an exorcism on him. By the time he arrived in Trinity, after a dreary year as a solicitor's apprentice, he was already wearing costume-style clothes, frock coats and fancy shirts.

'He was a naughty, naughty, wild, wild boy among that whole generation of students,' said Holmquist.

He began his broadcasting career in pirate radio, then presented evening pop shows on RTÉ before moving on to the more prestigious late-night slots. Reprimanded at an early stage for talking too much, he attributed his career in Donnybrook to a shortage of 'people who can talk'.

Then in 1987 came the 'Lambo' incident that could have wrecked anyone else's career. Out on an SAS-style survival course with a bunch of volunteers for *The Late Late Show*, he claimed to have clubbed a lamb to death with a rock in a sock and eaten it. It turned out to be a hoax; he had lied outrageously to the public, but it was the making of him.

People signing the book of condolences in memory of the late broadcaster Gerry Ryan, at the RTÉ radio centre in Donnybrook, Dublin. Photograph: Eric Luke.

'When you think about it, he was way ahead of his time. He was doing the *I'm a Celebrity Get Me Out of Here* stuff 20 years before anyone else,' said Holmquist. Yesterday, Siobhán Hough laughed at the memory of his chutzpah. 'His own headed notepaper and envelopes were printed with a lamb on it. No, Gerry was never penitent. Far from it. That notepaper lamb sums up his sense of mischief.'

Despite the nay-sayers who reeled at his coarse, hammy, bombastic radio persona and his delight in appealing to his audience's crassest instincts, he was a consummate broadcaster. Chris Evans, the equally brilliant British talk radio host who recently took over Terry Wogan's morning show, credits Ryan with putting him on the road to recovery after he 'lost the plot' and wound up in Killarney.

It was when he heard Gerry Ryan on 2FM that he suddenly missed the special bond between a good broadcaster and his audience, he said. 'If I was looking to escape the magic of radio, I had chosen entirely the wrong country to do it in,' he wrote in his autobiography.

Anyone who has ever been interviewed by him – as this writer was on many occasions, often on legally sensitive topics – will attest to his ability to listen, to pick up on a fresh line of thought rather than stick to the script, to let his interviewee speak, to allow a silence develop, while asking the questions Darren and Sharon out there would want to ask, given the chance. He would have read the brief and could be trusted not to land anyone in the High Court amid flying libel writs.

Yet Ryan's repeated attempts to make it into television never quite worked, despite the succession of vehicles conjured up by RTÉ; they included *Secrets, Gerry Ryan Tonight, Gerry Ryan's Hitlist, Ryan Confidential* and *Operation Transformation.*

While some of these shows were relatively successful, Ryan never managed to crack it as he did on radio. Siobhán Hough suggests that 'television had just one idea of what he was. He was always being formatted into silly programmes. They had an idea of this mad, zany persona but they hadn't the budget to support it. The one place he found his niche was on *Ryan Confidential.* And the other one he loved was *Operation Transformation,* partly because it involved our listeners. He knew he hadn't the sleek image for a health programme but he didn't care.'

MONDAY, 10 MAY 2010

Potential Partners Size Up Room for Manoeuvre

Mark Hennessy

So far much is unclear about the efforts to form a government in the United Kingdom, bar one essential point – Conservative leader David Cameron wants an administration that will last. Facing into some of the toughest economic times for years, Cameron will tonight brief newly elected Conservative backbenchers in the House of Commons, though a deal with the Liberal Democrats is unlikely by then.

During an intensive weekend of talks, Cameron and Liberal Democrat leader Nick Clegg have attempted to gauge their room for manoeuvre with each other and with their own parties. Cameron, it seems, may have more freedom than he first thought. The Conservatives deeply resent demands for electoral reform, particularly the grassroots; but MPs are now divided about the idea of a formal coalition with the third-largest party.

Last night, Cameron went to the House of Commons and made himself available for meetings with his backbenchers, both to sense the winds among his own and to counter accusations that he has run his leadership too tightly up to now. Given that he is the man most likely to become prime minister, some in his own ranks will have to stifle their real feelings lest they damage their own hopes for preferment subsequently.

Clegg, meanwhile, is not going to get anything like the level of electoral reform he sought during the campaign from Cameron, if a deal is to be done. Indeed, there is no guarantee that Cameron will go much beyond his offer on Friday of a parliamentary inquiry. Clegg's ability to stand to the colours on this issue may weaken today if the financial markets, which are already in frenzy over the euro, react badly to the perceived instability in the UK.

The Liberal Democrats have a number of options in front of them.

Firstly, they could join a full coalition, receiving a number of cabinet posts and a commitment to a full-term parliament. In turn, they will have to be bound by collective responsibility. The first two years of any such government would be brutal. Savage spending cuts will occur, while the differences between the parties on the European Union, taxation and defence would poison the environment.

If drastic government action worked, the danger for the Liberal Democrats is that the Conservatives would be the ones to get the credit in the longer-term from voters – if the cuts worked, and that is a big if. The Liberal Democrats could limit their exposure by agreeing to the confidence and supply arrangements spoken about by Cameron on Friday, where they get a few minor posts in return for co-operation on a limited number of policy areas.

This would be enough for Cameron to introduce a Queen's Speech on 25 May and a subsequent budget, but the Liberal Democrats, who

Conor Pope being put through his paces at boot camp in Co. Mayo. Photograph: Ciaran Duignan/Abaca.

public finances – a subject Sutherland did not mention when he was urging fiscal responsibility on the Greeks on Sunday.

The illusion that Sutherland wishes to maintain is that there is a 'we' that includes ordinary citizens and high-flyers of global finance in a shared pain. There is no such 'we'. There is just us and them.

SATURDAY, 15 MAY 2010

Blood, Sweat and Tears in Mayo

Conor Pope

To say I was alarmed as I arrived at the boot camp, just outside Westport, would be an understatement up there with 'Nama's probably going to cost us a few quid' or '*Finnegans Wake* isn't the easiest read

in the world'. I wasn't alarmed, I was terrified. Thanks to an unfortunate twitter post and a demon texting habit, I'd shared my plans with far too many people. And they'd all reacted with a mixture of hilarity and horror. 'You're doing what? Appalling! It's going to be hell. Bring painkillers. Bail.'

A day into the three-day adventure, bailing is definitely on the table. My limbs, having apparently aged 60 years in 24 hours, are on fire, and even thinking about climbing the stairs to bed is making me very, very sad. As I hobble up to my room I curse myself for not doing just a bit of research beforehand. If I'd spent 10 seconds on the Fitness West website I'd have learned that the whole plan was to take me out of my comfort zone. That's a zone I like and am very comfortable with, thanks very much.

The phenomenon of paying money so people can shout at you and make you do push-ups and sit-ups has taken off in recent years, as twenty- and thirty-somethings with more money than sense look for alternatives to the monotony of the gym and the loneliness of the long-distance run.

The Fitness West course is a new kid on the boot-camp block. It was set up four months ago by a pharmacist and a printer who met while competing in triathalons, and they are marketing it as a combination of fitness course and away-from-it-all weekend break.

The setting is stunning. The sea is a few metres from the back of the house and Croagh Patrick looms large out front. The living space is communal and the food is cooked by a chef who, incidentally, is also a psychotherapist.

The first morning starts with a three-kilometre jog along the seafront to a nearby pier. There isn't a sinner on the road and the only sound to be heard is the water lapping gently against the shore, and my less-gentle breathing. At the pier we do some stretches, then jog back to the house, where a breakfast of porridge, smoothies and fresh fruit awaits.

So far so easy. Then the kettle balls come out. There's a reason Russian soldiers are as hard as nails and it's because of these metal balls. They weigh anything between four and 24 kilos and were invented to toughen up all the tsars' men more than 200 years ago. They're in vogue in the most upmarket gyms after receiving the endorsement of some of the world's beautiful people. In truth there's little that's beautiful about the kettle-ball routines. We swing them between our legs using only our hips to get them moving, we swing them over our heads (or try to) and we do ridiculously painful lunges, over and over.

After the kettle balls comes the three-minute routine. Three minutes? How hard can that be, I think. We skip for a minute, then star jump for a further minute. There was a third exercise but I've completely forgotten what it was, because by the time its turn came I was so chronically deprived of oxygen that my mind had gone blank. I'm pretty sure it involved some class of jumping, though.

'That's a real lung buster, isn't it?' says the instructor with a broad smile. I'd respond, but I'm too busy wondering whether I should throw up before or after I collapse.

There is a momentary respite as we do some postural-realignment stretches. After that it's off up the Reek. With such a famously challenging climb as Croagh Patrick on their doorstep, the Fitness West boys would be foolish not to exploit it, and before I can say 'Ah, no, I'm all set – I've climbed it before,' I'm bundled into a van and taken to the base.

It's a hard climb no matter how fit you think you are. The first stretch of rocky hill is bad enough, but it is the near vertical ascent up loose, pointy rocks at the finish – known locally as the Cone – that's the real killer. I'd like to say I climbed it like a mountain goat, but unless that mountain goat was old and infirm, with a gammy leg, I'd be lying.

Back at the house, dinner is wolfed down in near silence. The stairs are climbed slowly and painfully, and not at all silently. There's nothing to do in the house once the trainers leave at 8 p.m., so the choices are to chat with your fellow guests or go to bed.

Morning two and the gentle jog to the pier is replaced by some less-gentle hill running. You sprint up a steep hill near the house. You feel your lungs burning and your eyes popping out, then you jog back down the hill. And do it again. And again. And all before breakfast.

After that it's on to the obstacle course. This is tough. The group is split into four pairs. While one pair do bear crawls along logs, jump over and slide under hurdles, lift tyres and do press-ups, the others perform a combination of star jumps, weights, burpies – nowhere near as relaxing as the name suggests – and other incredibly exhausting leaps and bounds. 'That's a real lung buster, isn't it?' the instructor says again. And again I'd like to respond, but I can't breathe. There is just time for lunch before a 40 km cycle on and down some

Some 150 volunteers from the Irish Blood Transfusion Service form the shape of a drop of blood, on Sandymount Strand in Dublin, to highlight the need for people to donate blood. Photograph: Yvette Monaghan/Studio77.

reliance on anti-cyclonic weather systems, Windymedia is Ireland's only left-wing low-pressure group.

TINTO

Radical union of teachers who think they are miners.

Ógra Gerry Féin

Radical youth wing of Gerry Féin, Ireland's largest British political party. Will not attend demonstrations as such, but may post a picture of two members holding up a home-made banner on its website afterwards.

Bus Drivers for Palestine

Radical public transport workers demanding a withdrawal of Israel to its 1967 frontiers, followed by a phased restoration of full Palestinian sovereignty, to be introduced in parallel with heated steering wheels on all vehicles in the Ringsend Depot as per UN Resolution 6593/A/21-D.

Unwaged Action

Radical community activists who make a full-time job out of being unemployed, without noticing the paradox in this position or much liking anyone who points it out.

SCOOBYTU

Radical union of public sector workers, who would have gotten away with it too if it hadn't been for those meddling kids.

WEDNESDAY, 19 MAY 2010

Portrait of a Serial Writer

Arminta Wallace

I rish crime fiction has been a long time in the cooking. But like a good casserole whose lid has finally been lifted, it contains all kinds of mouth-watering goodies. We have Brian

Cartoon by Martyn Turner.

A red banner covers the body of a protester killed during the military operation to evict anti-government protesters from their Bangkok encampment. Photograph: Fayaz Kabli/Reuters.

criticised for failing to build political support to revise a military-written constitution that overtook a 1997 charter seen as Thailand's most democratic constitution.

Talk of civil war is most likely premature, chiefly because the Thai army has the guns and the Red Shirts have very little beyond handmade rocket launchers and some grenade launchers. However, there are question marks over the loyalty of factions within the army and the police. Moreover, should events escalate further, then the allegiance of these factions will become clearer.

Attention also turns to King Bhumibol Adulyadej, who is 82 and has stepped in to end previous deadly crises during his 63 years on the throne. However, he has been in hospital for months now and has not commented publicly in a

significant way on this latest upheaval. The king's health is an extremely sensitive topic in Thailand because of concerns about his succession. His son, Crown Prince Vajiralongkorn, does not yet have the stature or moral authority of his father.

Online revelations accusing him of at-times odd behaviour, especially related to his dog, means that he has still to gain in the stature fitting to his office in the eyes of many Thais.

The king, the world's longest-serving monarch, is revered by everyone in Thailand, high and low, yellow and red. In recent years the royal palace has come in for unprecedented, although ever discreet and usually mild, criticism because of allegations that the king's advisers have been too busy playing politics, including playing a part in inspiring the coup that ousted Thaksin's government.

Megan Devin (13) from Hartstown, Co. Dublin, embraces her father, Cpl Brian Devin, at Dublin airport, on his return from serving with the United Nations/European Union mission in Chad. He returned home along with the other members of the 102nd Infantry Battalion. Photograph: Eric Luke.

Seán Dunphy (right), uncle of John O'Brien, waits with relatives near Helvic Head, Co. Waterford, as the search continues for the two men who went missing while fishing. Their bodies were found subsequently. Photograph: Patrick Browne.

That administration was blighted by corruption and cronyism, but it was still a democratically elected one.

What most people agree on is that the political system needs reform, especially rules that tend to favour the elite over rural masses.

If pushed aside by his powerful backers, Abhisit would likely be replaced by a coalition partner reckoned to be acceptable to the public in a caretaker role. That would do little to resolve the problem, potentially inciting more protests and strengthening the case for immediate polls the protesters' allies would likely win.

Abhisit needs to win support, but also needs to address the problems that are tearing the country apart. When that happens, the rest of the world can hope that Thailand's smile will be back soon.

FRIDAY, 28 MAY 2010

Sloppy Seconds

Donald Clarke

The second *Sex and the City* film is, of course, atrocious. Vulgar, reactionary, lazy, puerile, racist, smutty, sluggish: it seems intent on exhausting the viewer's lexicon of pejorative adjectives. Still, you couldn't say that it doesn't acknowledge the great traditions of the TV spin-off. As *Are You Being Served?* demonstrated in 1977, the best strategy for such a big-screen project is to send the cast on holiday. Hold on to your handbags. The girls are off to Abu Dhabi.

A hot air balloon taking part in the Birr International Hot Air Balloon Festival in Birr Castle Demesne, in Co. Offaly. Photograph: Seán Curtin/Press 22.

Come to think of it, the franchise increasingly resembles that popular situation comedy. The copious puns in the first film fairly made the blood curdle, but, in comparison with those on display here, they played like the work of Ben Johnson.

'I've only been on holiday 10 minutes and already I've got a date,' Kim Cattrall, back as the lascivious Samantha, says while tucking into some succulent middle-eastern fruit. Here comes the Australian rugby team. Will Samantha make a joke about balls? Just try and stop her.

More poignantly, the four principal characters – sexy Samantha, anal Charlotte, ambitious Miranda, neurotic Carrie – are beginning to suggest the frustrated Mrs Slocombe. I make no comments on their appearance, but, like Molly Sugden's grumpy widow, they all seem increasingly embittered at the cards life has dealt them.

Carrie, played by an uninterested Sarah Jessica Parker, is snapping unreasonably at her patient husband. Cattrall is going through a comedy version of the menopause. Charlotte (Kristin Davis) fears her Irish nanny (more anon) might seduce the father of her children. Miranda (Cynthia Nixon) hates her job.

You knew it would happen. The socially conservative TV series, despite its decadent turns, may have been primarily concerned with propelling its subjects towards the bourgeois, settled existence, but it always seemed likely that the single years would remain the happiest period of the cabal's trivial lives. Who thought *Sex and the City* 2 would be so bleeding miserable? At any rate, the gang's solution to their torpor is to make for Abu Dhabi.

Here, after a reasonably harmless opening, featuring a weird turn by a poorly embalmed Liza

Elle, Sydney and Lulu from Dogs in Distress, an animal rescue organisation, weigh up the competition at the auditions for the Irish canine cast of **Chitty Chitty Bang Bang**, *at Dublin's Grand Canal Theatre. Photograph: Andres Poveda/CPR.*

Minnelli, this absurdly long film – two-and-a-half deadly hours – starts to turn properly dubious. The tourist corner of the Emirate is, you see, everything the team really wants New York to be. As in the American city, the opportunities for obscene consumption are endless.

Unlike New York, however, Abu Dhabi allows complete isolation from the yellowed eyes of the undeserving poor. It is, on this evidence, an awful, awful paradise. The shamelessness of the enterprise appears to suggest that the (largely male) film-makers are impervious to criticism. Listen carefully, however, and you will detect a degree of defensiveness. When the four musketeers launch into a version of *I Am Woman*, they appear to be suggesting that any disapproval of their characters constitutes disapproval of the entire gender.

'American men pretend they like strong women, but they don't,' Miranda says. This may well be true, but the unsubtle subsidiary implication – that the negative reviews of *SATC* are a reaction against powerful female role models – is, among other outrages, deeply offensive to the many female writers who see the franchise as a betrayal of feminism's most significant advances.

Any pretence that the creators have even a cursory understanding of gender politics vanishes when Carrie and company encounter a party of Emirate women in traditional dress. They remove their abayas and everyone concerned comes to a happy realisation. Why, look at what the Arab ladies are wearing underneath.

This just goes to show that all women – whether in Hackney, the Bronx, Glasnevin or

185

Sydney – are essentially the same creatures with the same interests. Valentino? Yves Saint Laurent? Sisters everywhere walk around in shoes that cost the same as BMWs and dresses that are more expensive than cabin cruisers.

Depending on your personal philosophy (and bank account), you will either nod in warm agreement or search desperately for something to contain the vomit rising through your oesophagus.

Is that enough to put you off? Oh, yes the Irish nanny. Readers should be aware that the first film's undercurrent of ambient racism has now swelled to take in our own dear country. Every time Alice Eve's begorrah peasant rolls into view, the soundtrack surges with jolly tin whistles. You have been warned.

Why Israel Does the Things it Does

Denis Staunton, in Tel Aviv

As dusk closed in on a Thursday evening, just days before Israel's attack on ships carrying aid to Gaza, Tel Aviv's popular Gordon Beach emptied out and fell almost silent. The only sounds were of waves breaking on the shore and the gentle pock, pock of a few stray ball games. The crowds had gone home to prepare for the weekend, but they'd be out again in a few hours, strolling along the broad, tree-lined Rothschild Boulevard and crowding into the city's smart bars and restaurants.

If the people of Tel Aviv looked cheerful as they took in the balmy summer evening, they had much to smile about. Israel has weathered the global economic crisis more comfortably than any other country, and the economy is expected to grow by almost 4 per cent this year, powered by the highest density of high-tech start-ups in the world.

Interest rates are low and house prices are rising, but the Bank of Israel has stepped in to prevent overheating, discouraging mortgages of more than 60 per cent of a home's value. Israel's healthcare system is the envy of the world, with full-service clinics in every neighbourhood and world-class research hospitals, all free of charge.

The country's acceptance last month into the Organisation for Economic Co-operation and Development boosted national confidence, and the threat of a terrorist attack has receded so far for most Israelis that when the government staged a national security drill last week half of the population ignored it.

If, however, the suicide bombings that brought fear into the streets of Israel's cities during the first half of the last decade are an increasingly distant memory, a new anxiety is haunting Israelis. 'Many people are very concerned that Israel is becoming a kind of pariah in Europe. Many Israelis have despaired of Europe,' says Alexander Yakobson, who teaches history at Jerusalem's Hebrew University.

That anxiety can only have intensified this week as Israel's attack on the flotilla of ships carrying humanitarian aid, which left nine activists dead, provoked outrage around the world. The attack may have done irreparable damage to relations with Turkey, long Israel's closest military and diplomatic ally in the Muslim world, whose citizens accounted for most of the dead.

Even in the US, where support for Israel is overwhelming in both parties and within the administration, the naval commando raid has prompted second thoughts about the policy of blockading Gaza. For many Europeans the bloodbath at sea simply reinforced a view of Israel as a rogue state willing to take any measure, however disproportionate or legally dubious, in the name of security.

In numerous conversations with Israelis last week, even before this week's commando raid, almost everyone complained that Europeans apply

An Israeli flag flutters in the wind, as a naval vessel (not seen) escorts the **Mavi Marmara,** *a Gaza-bound ship which was raided by Israeli marines, to the Ashdod port. Ten pro-Palestinian activists were killed in the incident. Photograph: Amir Cohen/Reuters.*

harsher standards to Israel than to any other country. Why, they asked, do Irish campaigners call for a boycott of Israeli goods but remain content to trade with Arab dictatorships and with China, which has an execrable human rights record?

The 86-year-old president, Shimon Peres, told me Irish critics should consider that, surrounded by hostile neighbours and threatened with annihilation by a regime in Iran determined to develop nuclear weapons, Israel has a smaller margin for error than other countries.

'Ireland is a wonderful country. I don't know what is your permission to make mistakes. We don't have permission to make one mistake. If we should lose once, we should be annihilated,' he said. 'Wars are not a pleasant thing and I am not an advocate of wars. I do not want to justify wars. I want to justify only the right to defend our lives. NATO and Europe attacked Kosovo, you killed 600 innocent people, you destroyed the Chinese embassy.

'I never saw that everybody suggested an investigation. There were events in Chechnya, in Afghanistan, in Iraq. Nobody ever dared to suggest an investigation. Why was Israel picked out?'

During the early 1990s Peres started the secret talks with Yasser Arafat's Palestine Liberation Organisation (PLO) that led to the signing of the Oslo Accords in 1993. The accords provided for the creation of a Palestinian Authority and envisaged a gradual transfer of control from Israel of Gaza and most of the West Bank, with issues such as borders, the status of Jerusalem and the right of return of Palestinian refugees to be agreed within a few years.

Weary of violence, and impatient with the Jewish settlers who built on Palestinian land, most Israelis backed the Oslo process, and hundreds of thousands took part in peace rallies. As he was leaving one such rally Yitzhak Rabin, the prime minister who signed the Oslo Accords, was shot dead by Yigal Amir, a right-wing radical, on 4 November, 1995.

Next to the formal memorial at the spot where Rabin died is a section of wall covered in graffiti. The messages, now protected by glass, are calls for peace and reconciliation with the Palestinians.

Many Israelis stayed with the peace movement after Rabin's death, but Arafat's rejection of a peace deal brokered by Bill Clinton in 2000 and the violence that accompanied the Second Intifada later that year hardened attitudes in Israel. Alexander Yakobson, a former member of the left-wing Meretz party, who has become more hawkish in recent years, was further disillusioned by the failure of Israel's withdrawal from southern Lebanon in 2000 and from Gaza in 2005 to bring peace.

'Land for peace must mean if you give up land, you must not end up with less peace,' he says. 'There is no country in the world where people will accept that.' The threat of a nuclear-armed Iran under president Mahmoud Ahmadinejad, who has cast doubt on the Holocaust and called for Israel 'to vanish from the pages of time', has heightened Israelis' sense of being under threat.

Yakobson acknowledges that many Israelis have become insensitive to the injustice and humiliation suffered by Palestinians in Gaza and the West Bank, comparing Israeli attitudes to those seen in the US after 9/11. 'Conflict coarsens people,' he says. 'Guantánamo didn't just fall from the sky. It came from people being frightened.'

Behind the police station in Sderot, a town of about 20,000 people in southern Israel, less than a mile from Gaza, stands the Qassam gallery. Laid out on racks like vintage wines are dozens of twisted, rusting pieces of metal, some of the thousands of Qassam rockets that have rained down on the town from Gaza since Israel left the Strip five years ago.

Mostly improvised out of sewerage pipes filled with fertiliser and sugar, each crude missile has a marking to identify the group that fired it – red and green for Hamas, yellow for the al-Aqsa Martyrs' Brigades and red for Islamic Jihad. The bus shelters around Sderot are made of reinforced concrete, doubling as bomb shelters when the siren sounds, offering a 15-second warning of a rocket attack.

Like many of her neighbours, Shula Sasson has built a bomb shelter at home, a tiny reinforced closet where she and her family have spent whole nights as the rockets fell. A pile of thin mattresses stands by the window of her tile-floored living room, where her husband lies sleeping on the sofa in the middle of the afternoon. Wearing a sleeveless floral-patterned housecoat, fidgeting nervously, Sasson recalls that when her son was eight years old he saw a rocket rip his best friend's left foot off.

'Since then he's been completely traumatised. He hasn't been able to sleep by himself,' she says. 'To forgive is very hard. My children have been very damaged.'

Sasson says she regrets the loss of civilian lives, particularly children, during Operation Cast Lead, the Israeli bombardment of Gaza in late 2008 and early 2009 that left more than 1,400 Palestinians dead. She insists, however, that Israel was right to attack. 'We shouldn't have wasted time since the first rocket. Israel shouldn't have waited eight years to go in,' she says. 'The world calls us Nazis because of what happened with civilians being killed but they don't know what we've gone through.'

Few Israelis know what the Palestinians go through every day, under siege in Gaza and imprisoned within a system of enclaves on the West Bank. The Israeli settlements are gone from Gaza, but they have expanded rapidly on the West Bank and now house between 350,000 and 500,000 people.

Ian Millichip, chairman of the Herpetological Society of Ireland, with one of his red-eyed tree frogs. The society aims to promote awareness and understanding of reptiles and amphibians. Photograph: Fran Veale.

Earlier this year I visited Jeflik, a Palestinian village in the Jordan Valley, part of the West Bank that is under direct Israeli administration, where local farmers have watched the settlers grab more of their land each year. The settlers enjoy a separate infrastructure supplying water and electricity, and many roads are off-limits for Palestinians.

Medico International, a German NGO, was helping the villagers to build a modest kindergarten and to create a playground from waste materials such as old tyres and cans. Throughout the West Bank, Palestinians spend hours each day queuing at checkpoints on their way to and from work, and entire villages are walled in, with a single gate opened by Israeli soldiers for 15 minutes, three times a day.

Few Israelis visit the West Bank and fewer still enter Gaza, but even within Israel the mainstream Jewish community knows little about the Arab-Israelis who make up a fifth of the population. 'You can watch TV from the morning until the evening and not know that there are Arabs living in this country,' says Amal Elsana Alh'Jooj, an Arab Bedouin who works as a community organiser with Arab and Jewish Israelis in the Negev desert.

Schools in Israel are segregated on the basis of language, with Jews educated through Hebrew and Arabs through Arabic. Alh'Jooj and her colleagues in the Negev Institute for Strategies of Peace and Development have teamed up with the city of Be'er Sheva to support one of the few schools in Israel where Arab and Jewish children learn together.

The walls of the classroom are lined with Hebrew and Arabic letters, along with the Jewish Star of David, the Muslim crescent and the Christian cross. Each class has two teachers – one speaking Arabic and the other Hebrew – and the children are evenly divided between Arabs and Jews, all of them slipping easily between the two languages. 'You can't tell which are which, can you?' a teacher whispered to me. 'Neither can they.'

The institute works with Palestinian partners to bring communities on both sides of the conflict together to work on common projects, often focusing on social and economic development. 'We have to build a base of interaction between people on this side of the fence and that side of the fence, on this side of the conflict and on that side of the conflict. That's what builds mutual trust, that's what builds mutual confidence, that's what builds mutual understanding, that's what creates new realities that would not have existed if you hadn't worked together,' says Yehuda Paz, the group's New York-born founding chairman.

'If the so-called peace brings no change in people's lives, brings no change in the reality of their existence, brings no change in the hope they have for their children, then the peace rings very shallow. And when it rings shallow, the roots of hatred are very strong indeed and hatred flourishes.'

Despite the current impasse in the peace process, with few in the region holding out hope for the indirect talks between Israelis and

Designer John Rocha (centre) and Pierre de Villemejane (right), chief executive of brand owners WWRD, watch master glass blower Thomas O'Reilly at work during the opening of the new Waterford Crystal manufacturing facility and visitor centre in Waterford. Photograph: David Sleator.

Palestinians brokered by the US envoy George Mitchell, Paz is resolutely optimistic about the future. He believes Israelis could be persuaded to embrace a peace strategy that could achieve reconciliation not only with the Palestinians but with neighbouring Arab countries.

'One has to be able to project an alternative vision of what life in this part of the world could be like. Not a situation in which survival depends only on physical strength and military strength, but to envision a situation in which Israel could be a part of a whole different kind of framework for the Middle Eastern region,' he says. 'The other thing, of course, is to point out . . . that until you settle the basic issue of peace in the Middle East, all the apparent achievement rests on fragile foundations.

'As effective as it is and as impressive as it is when you get the kudos for your financial system and your Bank of Israel, unless you build the foundation of peace in the Middle East and establish a situation in which we in Israel become an accepted part of the Middle East, in which there is a just solution and the Palestinian people have a just solution, and there is a two-state solution, until you do that, then all the glitter is built on sand.'

FRIDAY, 11 JUNE 2010

Rogue Sheriff Investigated for Civil Rights Violations and Abuse of Power

Lara Marlowe, in Phoenix, Arizona

What kind of law enforcement officer boasts of using 'the world's only female chain gang' to bury dead indigents? Of housing convicts in furnace temperatures next to the city dump? Of feeding his prisoners 20-cent meals and forcing them to write home on postcards bearing his picture?

Joe Arpaio is the rogue sheriff of Maricopa County, the largest in Arizona, encompassing the state capital, Phoenix.

He has been elected five times since 1993. Two weeks ago he decided not to stand for governor because he is involved in a dispute with his own board of supervisors, two of whom he has had arrested. He did not want to give the board the satisfaction of replacing him.

Arpaio says the federal government is investigating him 'for alleged civil rights violations, abuse of power, all that. Do you think I'm worried? Why would you be worried if you did nothing wrong?'

Meanwhile, the sheriff remains the most prominent figure in Arizona's crusade to rid itself of undocumented Mexicans. If he had entered the gubernatorial race, he might well have won. Candidates from all over the country seek Arpaio's endorsement. The right-wing Tea Party love him and his local ally, J.D. Hayworth, could defeat Senator John McCain next November.

The Sheriff thinks SB1070, the immigration law that is turning Arizona into a pariah, is great, but it won't change much for him, he says, ensconced in his fortress-like 19th-floor office in downtown Phoenix.

In certain circumstances, a legal exception known as 287g enables local law enforcement to act in place of federal agents. Late last year, the Obama administration yanked Arpaio's 287g authorisation.

'Under the 287g programme, we arrested and charged 318,000 people, starting in April 2007,' Arpaio says. 'Out of that, we detected 35,000 were here illegally, which means they have to stay in jail.' Arpaio spews statistics: 'We average 8,000 to 10,000 prisoners on a given day. About 30 per cent of them are Hispanic; 19 per cent of the people in jail are here illegally. If they weren't here, we wouldn't have those crimes. Fifty-five illegals in jail have been charged with murder . . .'

The Obama administration's assault on Arpaio's authority 'doesn't make any difference', he says, 'because I'm still doing the same thing'. Two state laws, one on human smuggling, the other on employer sanctions, enable him to get round the loss of 287g.

'Under the human smuggling law, we just arrested 61 people in the last 24 hours, coming into this county,' Arpaio says. 'We charged them with smuggling and co-conspiracy. We're the only ones doing that. We've arrested more than 2,000 people in the last two or three years [in addition to the above-mentioned 318,000].

'It's a class-four felony, which means they can't get out on bond. We arrest the people in the vehicle that have paid the smuggler and we charge them with the same crime.'

On 28 May, the Obama administration asked the Supreme Court to void Arizona's two-year-old law on employer sanctions, on the grounds it infringes federal prerogatives. Law SB1070 may fall on the same grounds. So the feds don't want Arpaio to do it? 'Well, Sheriff Arpaio is doing it anyway,' he says.

The sanctions law has given Arpaio the pretext to raid 35 workplaces. He arrested 18 illegals in two recent raids on McDonald's and more at the Burlington coat factory last week. 'It had nothing

Sheriff Joe Arpaio, of Maricopa County in Arizona, with a pair of his pink underwear that male prisoners in his charge are obliged to wear. He sells this version to finance his 'posse'. Photograph: Lara Marlowe.

John Kelly, brother of Michael Kelly, and Jean Hegarty, a sister of Kevin McElhinney, both of whom were killed on Bloody Sunday, tear up a copy of the Widgery Report, at the Guildhall in Derry, following the publication of the Bloody Sunday Inquiry Report which exonerated them. Photograph: Dara Mac Dónaill.

and were not guilty of any offence and that the killing was unjustifiable,' he said, adding that he believed the book was now closed on Bloody Sunday.

When Mr Cameron's statement ended and the families finally emerged from the Guildhall, the scenes were reminiscent of innocent prisoners released from jail. The families threw victorious fists in the air, they pointed and shouted and smiled at the crowd, clutching the report as if they would never let it go.

There was a minute's silence to remember all those who died during the Troubles, as giant black-and-white banners featuring all 14 who died were held aloft behind their relatives. They spoke one by one, reiterating the innocence, as found by Lord Saville, of their loved ones.

The Widgery report was torn to pieces by one relative, Jean Hegarty – the infamous publication

turning to blue confetti that swirled in the air. Widgery was now old news.

Lord Saville had told the world what the people of Derry have known for 38 years: the victims of Bloody Sunday were innocent, all innocent.

WEDNESDAY, 16 JUNE 2010

Exoneration of Victims Delivers almost all the Demands of Families

Dick Grogan

The judge has danced a delicate dance between the possible and the likely, employing plenty of 'either' and 'or', and seems to have left his audience dazzled by his footwork, for the moment at least.

Three senior Protestant church leaders — Rev. Paul Kingston (left), President of the Methodist Church in Ireland, the Rt Rev. Dr Ken Good (centre), Bishop of Derry and Raphoe and Rev. Dr Norman Hamilton (right), Moderator of the Presbyterian Church in Ireland — presenting Jean Hegarty with a copy of the **Hands Across the Divide** *statue, on the city's Foyle Bridge, as a gesture of goodwill following publication of Lord Saville's Bloody Sunday Report. Photograph: Dara Mac Dónaill.*

But his report, however exuberantly received in Derry yesterday, may prove to have similar characteristics to those frequently attributed to a Chinese meal — satisfying at the time of eating but leading to renewed hunger pangs a short time later.

It may seem churlish to cavil at aspects of a report that — on the strength of its 60-page summary — appears to have delivered almost all of the primary demands of the families of Bloody Sunday victims. Those basic demands were, of course, for the unequivocal exoneration of their loved ones from any hint or suspicion of blame or guilt — and for the outright repudiation of the Widgery report.

Lord Saville has delivered the first of these in reasonably plain words; but he has addressed the second demand only by inference.

Perhaps no more could be expected of him. Certainly, if his report had been issued in place of Widgery's version at the time, Bloody Sunday might have become a painful but dissolving memory, instead of festering and fuelling more bloody armed conflict for 30 years in the North.

Yet his careful pirouette around the issues of higher-level responsibility for the disastrous military operation on Bloody Sunday could leave one considering the remark of George Bernard Shaw that: 'Truth-telling is not compatible with the defence of the realm.' To go any further must await an examination of the full 5,000-page report – the devil is always in the detail.

Is it enough to say – as he appears to in his summary conclusions – that the civil and military authorities could not have foreseen what was likely to happen when an aggressive frontline combat unit was unleashed into the Bogside? One's reflex answer is: No, it is not enough.

Yet again we are left wanting more supportive or corroborating evidence when Saville says he accepts Gen. Sir Robert Ford's denial that the army plan on Bloody Sunday was to cause a confrontation with the IRA.

Saville's summary conclusions state: 'We are sure that there was no such plan.' 'Sure' is not, of course, 'certain' – but it is close enough, and the justification for it must be winkled out of the full report if it is in there somewhere.

Gen. Ford was, as Saville points out, responsible for deciding that 'in the likely event of rioting' the parachute regiment units should be employed as an arrest force. We know, however, from the documents adduced to the inquiry, that the arrest operation involving the paras was discussed and cleared at the highest political level in London and Stormont. We must trawl the full report for more on this, but, as a first reaction, did nobody really think of possible terrible consequences if this trigger-happy regiment breached firing discipline?

Other findings of the inquiry run baldly and directly counter to the whitewash perpetrated by Lord Widgery 38 years ago. Saville specifically exonerates the organisers of the civil rights march from any responsibility for the deaths and injuries on Bloody Sunday; Widgery in his primary conclusion implied that they were hugely to blame.

Saville, most significantly, finds that the soldiers fired first in the Bogside that day; Widgery had said the opposite, asserting: 'There is no reason to suppose that the soldiers would have opened fire if they had not been fired upon first.'

Widgery declared that there was no general breakdown in discipline; Saville says there was 'a serious and widespread loss of fire discipline' among the soldiers of the support company.

Widgery had lauded the soldiers for their 'steadiness' and declared that, in his opinion, the accounts they gave of their firing were in general truthful. Saville now as good as accuses some of them of falsifying their accounts.

Without even mentioning Widgery, this present-day law lord has effectively buried most of his predecessor's report.

Most but not all, one should hasten to add. Both Widgery and Saville exonerate Gen. Ford and both seem to clear Brig. MacLellan who – they concur – gave the order for the arrest operation.

As many observers had predicted over the years, the 'fall guy' turned out to be the commanding officer of 1Para, Col. Derek Wilford, who is bluntly accused of not complying with his orders. Was it really all as simple as this: the fault of one colonel and a handful of 'loose cannon' squaddies? If so, could we not have determined this years ago and at much less cost and effort?

(Dick Grogan was in Derry in 1972 on Bloody Sunday and reported for The Irish Times.*)*

FRIDAY, 18 JUNE 2010

In Defence of the Delectable Delights of Dalkey

John Waters

It's a bit of a nuisance having an address for which you are constantly expected to apologise, though of course this happens in all societies. In the financial quarter of Soweto, I have no doubt that there are stock-jobbers who seek to conceal from their fellows the fact that they come to work every morning from a shantytown on the remote posterior of the city. In Ireland, naturally, it's the other way around.

For much of the past two decades – perhaps the reason why I have not yet written the Great Irish Novel – I have been creatively stretched to offer plausible explanations for the fact that I live in Dalkey.

When the subject comes up in certain politically correct quarters, my 'confession' tends to elicit much the same responses as when I mention that I drive a BMW, which I usually do in the next breath, although this is an untruth calculated belatedly to attach a booster of irony to the culturally and sociologically damning revelation I have just delivered.

Conscious of the belligerent stares this announcement invariably provokes, I tend to add that I live in a two-bedroomed cottage, that I bought it during the first Gulf War when the market was briefly depressed and that I got it cheap because the vendor had to sell rather urgently to close a deal on a property he was acquiring in Longford. (The mention of Longford – or sometimes I say Blanchardstown – tends to ground and normalise the discussion significantly by connecting Dalkey with more pedestrian forms of Irish reality.)

The most effective 'excuse', I have found, is to explain that just before I bought my house I gave up drinking alcohol. (This, unlike the bits about Longford and the BMW, is true.)

If the cultural resentment factor is running particularly high, I tend to launch into a complex mathematical calculation in which I factor in the 1990 mortgage interest rate and price of the pint, ending up by demonstrating that the monthly difference in outgoings between living in a fashionable and ideologically uncompromising semi-d in Stoneybatter, while pissing half your income up against the tiles in Kehoe's, was back then about the same as living in Dalkey and swearing off the, as it were, batter.

This justification tends to shut people up without dissipating their resentment, generally attracting silent glares which declare that, as well as being an enemy of the working class, I am also someone who can't enjoy a jar like a decent Celt.

When speaking to well-adjusted people, I am proud to say I live in Dalkey. It is a stunning place, so it is not surprising that wet-brained fellow-journalists are so jealous. Dalkey is the kind of place that if you went there on holidays you would be writing home about. But it is also, contrary to popular prejudice, a microcosm of small-town Ireland, the country that actually still exists beyond the crude brushstrokes affected by an increasingly cliché-ridden and out-of-touch media.

All of which is by way of elaborate introduction to a rather blatant and unapologetic plug for the first Dalkey Book Fair, which takes place this weekend. This event is a response by locals to the challenges posed by the economic downturn – as severely felt in Dalkey as elsewhere – and the additional disadvantage of having a local authority that seems determined to bankrupt the local business sector with its draconian and vindictive anti-parking regime.

A decade ago, a senior official in Dún Laoghaire-Rathdown County Council proposed that Dalkey Quarry, across the road from our house, be converted into a halting site for Travellers – replete, naturally, with a scrap-breaking facility. When asked why, he responded somewhat enigmatically: 'Nobody lives up there but rich rock stars and writers.'

In typical local authority stopped-clock fashion, he was partly right: Dalkey is stuffed with scribblers and the book fair has been organised by some of these, including the economist and author David McWilliams and Ireland's pre-eminent historical biographer, Tim Pat Coogan. The line-up may provide raw material for a Christy Moore classic.

Conor McPherson, Bruce Arnold, John Connolly, Declan Lynch, Eamon Dunphy, Declan Hughes, Ross O'Carroll Kelly, Des Cahill, Maeve Binchy and Joseph O'Connor have mysteriously managed to combine living in Dalkey with the

Eimear Tangney and Simone McCarthy cool down at Torc Waterfall, Killarney, Co. Kerry. Photograph: Valerie O'Sullivan.

writing of Great Irish Novels. Robert Fisk, who offsets his ownership of a feck-off pile on Vico Road by evincing an intense love for Palestinians, will be in public conversation with Vincent Browne, who will be journeying to Dalkey for the occasion from his flat in Ballymun.

Answering Comrade McWilliams's call to support my local community, on Sunday afternoon I will be reading, at Idle Wild café on Patrick Street, from *Beyond Consolation*, my recently published book about non-stupid reason, God and absolute hope, more or less in that order.

Because these are such unsuitable themes for an *Irish Times* columnist, we have been doing our best to conceal the existence of this book and especially its insistence on its own factuality. Now it's all bound to come out. As if it wasn't bad enough owning up to living in a stop-traffically beautiful place.

TUESDAY, 22 JUNE 2010

Giant Step from Giant's Causeway

Philip Reid, in Pebble Beach, California

Call it fate, call it a rite of passage, but the journey taken by Graeme McDowell from the rugged seaside terrain of Portrush, close by the Giant's Causeway on the Antrim coast, could only

Graeme McDowell savours the moment after holing the winning putt to claim the 110th US Open Championship, at Pebble Beach. Photograph: Hans Deryk/Reuters.

find a landmark its equal on this crop of turf on the Monterey peninsula hanging into the Pacific. A spectacular setting for an extraordinary odyssey.

As the sun dipped into a becalmed ocean on Sunday night, the roar of acclaim that greeted McDowell from those crammed in the grandstands and on the hillocks around the 18th green were eerily like those of old. Seismic roars that had once hailed Jack Nicklaus and Tom Watson and Tom Kite and Tiger Woods were now reserved for a 30-year-old Ulsterman who alone had conquered the toughest examination in major golf, a player who held the US Open trophy in his hands as if it were too precious to let go.

McDowell, the 110th US Open champion, clutched the trophy and, adopted by the crowd as one of their own, gave them the clichés about filling the cup with Guinness and how he would never let it down. Just as he had done on

the course, G-Mac – as he is known – wooed them with his charm and intelligent banter. Yet, behind the twinkle in the eye, there was recognition that he, more than anyone, knew this was his destiny.

Close by, his father Kenny, who had introduced him to the sport as a seven-year-old, stood at the back of the green, sunglasses on to hide the tears as much as to block out the low sun, shaking his head.

Shortly after McDowell had rolled in the short par putt on the 72nd hole, his 284th stroke of a championship that had left carnage and chaos for other contenders, the father had run on to the green to embrace his son. 'Happy Father's Day,' whispered McDowell. 'You're some kid,' replied the dad. Some kid, indeed.

In a final round in which the unfortunate Dustin Johnson, who had carried a three-stroke cushion into the final day, suffered a meltdown so cruel you wanted to look away, and in which some of the greatest names – Ernie Els, Phil Mickelson and Tiger Woods – could not step up to the plate, McDowell stayed cool and collected. So much so, his finishing 74 gave him a one-shot win over Gregory Havret of France.

By winning the US Open on the back of his victory in the Wales Open in his previous start, McDowell joined greatness. Only two others, Ben Hogan and Woods, had won the major in their next start after a regular tour win. 'Two of my heroes,' remarked McDowell, when informed of the stat.

McDowell, as he does, hung tough to win. Johnson, despite having won the last two AT&T National Pro-Ams on the regular stop-off here each spring, was in unfamiliar territory in the majors. We didn't have long to wait for the meltdown, which was extraordinary by any standards as he ran up a triple bogey on the second, and followed that by hooking his tee-shot into the trees on the third, which led to a lost ball and a double bogey.

Graeme McDowell hugs his caddie, Ken Comboy, after victory: 'He really is my rock; he has been for four years. I attribute a big part of this win to the help he has given me over the last four years.' Photograph: Hans Deryk/Reuters.

In contrast, McDowell, with his experienced caddie Kenny Comboy keeping him on the level, played par golf before a birdie on the short fifth jumped him clear of those threatening in the matches ahead, most notably Ernie Els at the time, but also Havret, ranked 391st in the world going into the tournament but who played wonderfully well when thrown into the heat of battle.

Disaster, though, befell all of the big guns in turn. Woods, strutting the course with menace at one point, hit a three-wood over the cliffs on the sixth. Els would also flight a tee-shot over the edge of the sheer drop on the 10th. And Mickelson struggled in vain to find the inspiration or shots to follow up on his US Masters win in April.

Instead, as they came down the home stretch, Havret was the chief pursuer. But, critically, McDowell literally had him in his sights as the Frenchman was in the match ahead, along with Woods. When Havret bogeyed from a greenside bunker on the 17th, it gave McDowell a two-stroke cushion. But McDowell also found sand there and bogeyed the hole.

Still, McDowell walked to the 18th tee with a one-shot cushion. Then, from just in front of the cypress trees on the final fairway, he could see that Havret failed to birdie the 18th. It led to a change of tactics from the Irishman, who abandoned any inclination to go for the green with his two-iron and instead hit a five-iron lay-up. Then, from 99 yards, he hit a wedge to 25 feet. Two putts later, McDowell was US Open champion.

'To withstand some tough holes the way Graeme did and to come out on top, he played great golf,' observed Mickelson. 'I thought Graeme was playing very well headed in (to the tournament). He's played very solid on a large stage a number of times. So, from a player's point of view, this wasn't a surprise, no.' A surprise? No. But, in terms of taking a first major, McDowell's timing and choice of venue to take his place in history was perfect.

Graeme McDowell's brother Gary at his brother's local club, Rathmore in Portrush, with members of the club celebrating Graeme's victory in the US Open. Photograph: Arthur Allison.

WEDNESDAY, 23 JUNE 2010

Dark Plots Being Hatched against Petty Egg Regulations

Sarah Carey

The egg inspector hit town. Damn and blast this malodorous figure whose profession ranks among society's bottom feeders. Like private clampers who prey on harried parkers and music rights detectives harassing hairdressers with a radio in the salon, the inspectors sent out to rid the world of contraband eggs leave a trail of negative energy in their wake.

These are days of simple pleasures and there is none more humble or exquisite than a farm egg. Scrambled, fried, soft- or hard-boiled, in an omelette or a cake – our house ploughs through two dozen a week. We are obsessed with both technique and sourcing. What's the point in debating the merits of poaching over boiling if the egg is the product of a miserable creature from a battery farm? We crave real eggs from real hens that wander about in the open all day.

I have dreamed of going into production myself and sighed over the hen-houses on chic-hens.ie – gorgeous painted affairs on stilts. Alas, the shortage of funds in the capital account and the long-term return on investment means I hesitate to order the penthouse for pullets.

Nor am I willing to risk a home-made effort knowing that Mr Fox's skill in breaking and entering is far superior to my ability to construct a

Pauline Boland, Betty Boland and Esme Mulcahy from Leopardstown and Shankill, Co. Dublin, admiring the Devine Nurseries Silver Medal winning stand at Bloom 2010, in the Phoenix Park. Photograph: Alan Betson.

fortress that will keep him out. So like an emotional cripple I avoid disappointment by not getting involved.

I buy official eggs regularly, but enjoy the delicacy of true eggs through less formal supply chains. My uncle gives us a half a dozen a week in exchange for garden produce. But that leaves a shortage that has to be filled through the black market.

The system is an environmental dream in sustainability. Local farmers drop their surplus eggs into village shops. Just a few dozen come in a week so discerning consumers have to be quick to get them. Then we drop the boxes back for reuse. Obviously it's easier in summer to maintain a good supply because the hens lay better and the foxes aren't as determined.

Unfortunately the Egg Inspector is determined. Despite angry exchanges, within an hour of his arrival in the village last week the counter-tops were cleared of real eggs.

His power is drawn from EC 1039/2005, an amendment to Regulation 1907/1990 which lays down the law for egg producers. This requires the registration of producers who are subject to surveillance to ensure compliance with the usual plethora of rules relating to hygiene, date-stamping, grading and record-keeping. Like all regulations it costs a fortune to comply with and another fortune to enforce.

Fortunately, the Fourth Law of Legislation states there shall be no EC regulation without a corresponding derogation. The lawmakers recognised that low-income holdings for whom egg production is a mere sideline have great social and economic importance. They agreed that these 'table eggs' should be available for sale and that member states could exempt producers with less than 50 hens from the regulations.

They recognised that an egg from a hen that's been scratching around a farmyard is a perfectly fine product deserving of liberation from incomprehensible rules.

Unfortunately, Big Egg was hardly going to let common sense prevail and secured a key qualification to the exemption. The exemption applies only where the farmer sells his eggs directly from the farm, a local public market or door-to-door.

Once the eggs are sold through a third party, the hen must stamp her egg in accordance with the regulations.

Thus the Egg Inspector triumphantly pounced on the few boxes displayed on the shelf in our local shops.

What's annoying is that the rules have nothing to do with the quality of the product. This is all about the commercial issue of market access. He who controls the channel dominates the market. If the battery egg and the farm egg sit on the same shelf then they must obey the same regulations – a level laying field if you will.

The fact that duck eggs are excluded from the regulations entirely is telling. There are no major producers so where there's no money, there's no law. You can sell a duck egg wherever you want.

I'm not entirely without sympathy for the position of the commercial producers. The demand that their competitors obey the same rules has some merit. Globalisation has led Irish beef farmers to complain that they must comply with endless rules and yet compete with Brazilian beef produced free from rules and regulations.

But there is a principle and there is pettiness. A few dozen eggs a week during the summer months hardly represent a threat to the margins of major egg producers. Yet the Government sees fit to pay officials to travel the country stamping out unstamped eggs. How about a little light-touch regulation for poultry?

Needless to say the clampdown has simply forced the trade underground – or rather under the counter. Yesterday as I went about my foraging I asked for some 'eggs' while significantly raising my eyebrows. I got a significant nod in response and the precious package was surreptitiously placed in my bag.

I'm sure if Michael McDowell was in power he'd be gravely warning about middle-class recreational users of illegal substances supporting criminality. But criminalising the egg-loving community is surely unwise. It drives us into the black economy where who knows what illegally sourced products are traded. From good eggs to anarchy – won't someone stop the madness?

WEDNESDAY, 30 JUNE 2010

Sure, No Harm in a Short Walk on the Wild Side

Tom Humphries, in Johannesburg

The hotel is new and unfrayed, built for the World Cup on the edge of a suburb which is transforming slowly from poor to black middle class. The staff are lovely. We have our fun.

There are power cuts and for a day the water has been off. Last night the alarm went off by accident a couple of times and a stern, tape-recorded voice told us in those clipped Sith Ifrican tones to evacuate the hotel. On arriving in the lobby each time we were greeted with smiling faces asking innocently if it was the alarm which had got us up. We went back to bed sure that they just wanted a bit of company or mischief.

Each new staff member you encounter asks where you come from. 'Ireland', you say. 'U2', they reply. Yesterday at lunchtime, alarmingly and distressingly, Jedward were being piped through the radio as we talked at reception. 'Ireland', I said, pointing at the speakers and forgetting to be embarrassed. Grave nods. Things are hard in Johannesburg but the people are capable of compassion.

World Cup fever is hard to find in such a large and fractured city. Where it exists, in the middle class white areas, notably Sandton, it has the ersatz feel of a summer festival arranged by the council. The whiteys are passingly interested, but Sandton is

where what tourist money is spent in Johannesburg will be spent. So the effort is made.

Elsewhere the South African flag and knots of people gathered in front of televisions are the sole evidence of the competition. It's not Italia '90, not that great abandonment of the world and its responsibilities which we Irish experienced. Life is still a little too hardscrabble for that, and the sight of Bafana Bafana getting bounced so early and so briskly from the competition killed the romance.

The Irish Times is the only journalist in residence at the hotel and, as such, with his dangling accreditation and his access to matches, he is a thing of wonder. The nearest media hotel is three-quarters of a mile away. Less even. That's where the media shuttle goes from. When *The Irish Times* sets off for the media shuttle he is even more of a thing of wonder.

Three-quarters of a mile. Less, probably. It's tantalising. Too short a journey to be summoning a taxi for, let alone a dedicated driver. So *The Irish Times* yomps off by foot to catch the shuttle to work and they watch him disappear, shaking their heads.

Getting to the media shuttle is like completing a level of *Grand Theft Auto*. Up the hill and past the 24-hour garage and then across three lanes of the off-ramp from the motorway. Make it there alive and it's a final glance back and a heroic wave as the intrepid journalist disappears into the dark, fetid underpass of the motorway itself, nodding and waving at the surprised inhabitants.

Fortunately surprise paralyses whoever is dawdling there at any given moment. *The Irish Times* has a big bag on his back. The bag contains a laptop, a little camera, an iPod, a tape recorder, one of the posh pens *The Irish Times* likes to use when imagining himself to be a scribe and not a mere hack. And a mobile phone. Ho ho, says *The Irish Times* to himself. Who in this the murder capital of the world would want to harm me!

And so on back out into the light and across the three lanes of the on-ramp traffic, down a hill

South Africa's midfielder Lance Davids (front) and midfielder Steven Pienaar train in Johannesburg, ahead of the start of the World Cup in South Africa. Photograph: Alexander Joe/AFP/Getty Images.

and across some waste ground and around the security fencing of the media hotel wherein a variety of foreign hacks are lounging in wait for the shuttle.

They look up at the great sweating dishevelled beast of burden that comes among them from his residence which seems to be the motorway underpass. They keep their distance so there is no chance to tell them that there is actually another hotel over the other side of the motorway.

At night *The Irish Times*, manful and courageous and down with the street — though he doesn't like walking the waste ground and the underpass (it's the company laptop he fears for) — waits for the same Buddha-like shuttle driver. On the first night of shuttling *The Irish Times* set off with a theatrically defeated gait toward the middle of nowhere instead of into the media hotel.

Buddha asked *The Irish Times* what he thought he was doing. 'Just walking to my hotel,' said *The*

Irish Times in tones of immense sadness. 'Jizzes Chreest git bick in the biss min,' Buddha commanded.

Now we shotgun the bus through the underpass and Buddha pops *The Irish Times* out at the 24-hour garage.

The Irish Times loves the garage. It has a battalion of staff who spend these World Cup days playing keepy-uppy on the forecourt. Like a lot of places, there is no TV available and the lads are discouraged from ambling across to the hotel to have a look at what is going on.

In the afternoons and evenings the World Cup comes to them in fragmented bulletins wafting from car radios. Cars pull in and each man has his own pump to tend. The drivers seldom leave the cars and the attendants fill the tanks with their ears cocked to what is happening on the radio.

They have a wonderful way of moving, which involves a lot of energy and arm movement but basically is a very slow but stylish walk to each car. It makes the sad, defeated trudge of *The Irish Times* look like something from a much earlier stage of evolution.

They fill the tanks, move with the money, bring back the change if necessary, and then they go back to the endless keepy-uppy, heading and juggling an old ball about with an alacrity that is as casual as it is astonishing.

They chat away about the scores and the teams, with only the names of famous footballers and sometimes clubs discernible from their quiet tones and frequent laughter.

Passing them a couple of times a day we share little shards of conversation and nods of greeting and farewell. It doesn't look well paid at all, but it looks like a relaxed, chilled life playing keepy-uppy in the winter sun and laughing and joking with your friends.

During the power cuts the ATM on the forecourt ceased to work and a few times *The Irish Times* has trudged across in search of cash only to find the machine still deceased. On seeing *The Irish Times* approach one or other of the guys would shake his head. 'Still dead man.'

So the conversation grew a little longer every time.

Yesterday, for the first time, one asked where *The Irish Times* was from. Ireland, we said. And waited for mention of Bono and the chaps. There was a murmur of excitement. Grinning. 'Roy Kinn!' they said. 'Roy Kinn!'

And there on the forecourt we stood and talked about Roy Kinn and Saipan, and even though this World Cup was unfolding all around in Soccer City and Ellis Park and on the big screens of Sandton, the competition seemed as it did in childhood, like a fable with passages that everybody will always remember.

The ATM was working today. *The Irish Times* gave the lads a big thumbs-up. 'Very good Roy Kinn,' they grinned. 'Roy happy!'

New Chair Is a Poet in his Prime

Gerry Smyth

The Ireland Chair of Poetry was established in 1998 to mark the award to Seamus Heaney of the Nobel Prize for Literature three years earlier. The chair (or professorship) was defined in quite explicit terms by the Nobel Laureate himself when he declared that 'the post is intended to manifest the value of poetry within our cultural and intellectual life'.

As a standard-bearer for those values, the appointment of Harry Clifton as Ireland's new Professor of Poetry makes for a brilliant choice and one that will be welcomed by his readers, his peers and those of an older generation whose example he followed in his vocation as a poet. He is much admired and critically acclaimed, and his dedication to that vocation has been exemplary.

There is no doubt that his most recent, and virtuosic, collection, *Secular Eden: Paris Notebooks 1994–2004*, places him in the front rank of contemporary Irish poetry. However, his reputation is built on an even larger body of work published over almost four decades.

The status and recognition that comes with the chair has been admirably earned. From the start, since his first precociously adroit poems appeared in the 1970s, his work has shown real substance and assured technique; while the poet himself has always been a quiet and modest presence, keeping his attention on the functions of the imagination and his mind open to the experiences that mattered.

Even in his introductory, apprentice poems it was clear that Clifton was a poet who had set his artistic goals. Those poems achieved a level of accomplishment and formal music that was rare among poets still in the first flush.

Brian O'Driscoll and his wife, Amy Huberman, kiss after their wedding in St Joseph's Church, Aughavas, Co. Leitrim. Photograph: Brenda Fitzsimons.

When Michael Hartnett reviewed Clifton's inaugural collection, *The Walls of Carthage*, in this newspaper in 1978, he declared that he had in his hands the work of a poet who was 'here to stay'. While Hartnett discerned certain influences, he also remarked that 'the strongest voice of all is that of Harry Clifton'.

His subsequent books unfolded into a strong assembly of themes: issues of identity, the bonds of history, the nature of creativity, the intersections where lives and cultures meet, the uneasiness of the world he dwells in – a world in which, as he has suggested in one of his poems, there are powers 'no borders can contain'.

Many of the poems took their impetus from Clifton's travels and sojourns – up to a few years ago, his life was one of exile and outward journeys – Nigeria, Cambodia, South America, Italy, and 10 years in France that triggered the artistic payload in *Paris Notebooks* which sets him apart in the contemporary canon.

As exemplified in many of his titles – *The Desert Route, Crossing the Apennines, Berlin Suite, Field Hospital, Thailand, 1982* – these places became part of the transnational backdrop that added a cosmopolitan, even exotic, flavour to his poetry.

From the Dublin of his coming-of-age to St Augustine's Carthage and the boulevards of Paris, he has always been a poet on the move, observing and absorbing, and questioning – equally at home in the 'country of flux' and the 'country of still waters' (The Country of Still Waters).

Pointing to his abiding cultural curiosity, the American poet C.K. Williams observed in Clifton a poet whose work embraced 'so much geography, landscape, cityscape, re-peopled precincts of the imagination, so much human drama and comedy'. There may be high seriousness in the material he chooses as his themes, but the language never lacks surprise.

Clifton once described poetry as an 'ambivalent realm' but perhaps more tellingly on another occasion as an 'inwardly directed activity'; that said, he has always looked closely at the world and that looking has produced poetry that is allusive, evocative, inventive, interrogative and always richly suggestive in its imagery and observations.

Clifton is now a poet in his prime and his lectures as Ireland Professor of Poetry can be anticipated for the contribution they will make to the public understanding of poetry as an essential art and also, indeed, to its value in our cultural and intellectual life.

The Chair of Poetry title is bestowed for three years and the holder is attached for part of a year to each of three universities – Trinity College Dublin, University College Dublin and Queen's University Belfast – to teach and conduct workshops as well as give public lectures and readings.

Clifton will be the fifth poet to occupy the position, and the fascinating diversity of outlook of his predecessors is amply illustrated in *The Poet's Chair: The First Nine Years*, an overview collection of the lectures delivered by John Montague, Nuala Ní Dhomhaill and Paul Durcan. These were augmented by Belfast poet Michael Longley, who added further prestige to the position over the past three years.

FRIDAY, 2 JULY 2010

Soldier Was Among our Nation's Greatest

John Waters

There was a moment last Saturday afternoon in Newbridge, Co. Kildare, just after the completion of the military honours, when the crowd gathered around the last resting place of Dermot Earley did not know whether to remain or disperse. In that moment of hesitation, a male voice was raised in final salute: 'Up the Rossies!'

Although the immediate reflex was to laugh, it was in truth a devastating moment, perhaps the

Lt Gen. Dermot Earley. Photograph: Maxwells.

most achingly sorrowful of Roscommon's saddest week for a long time. Instantly, the gathering was transported by that verbal reveille from the uncertain sunshine of Co. Kildare in the high summer of 2010 to the dancing light of some indeterminate 1970s summer afternoon, and a different crowd, perhaps emerging euphoric from an encounter at which the all but superhuman powers of Earley had been on display, to a world indescribably enhanced on that account.

Or perhaps back to a Roscommon streetscape on some half-remembered summer's evening, and the shouted accounts of triumph or heroic failure carried breathlessly from mouth to mouth, and the intense pleasure of being part of that family of which Earley was such an adored elder brother.

That cry spoke of football as metaphor, as agent of communal cohesion, as the drama of the

tribal march towards an unknown destination. It conveyed defiance, nostalgia, hope, love, supplication, but also the merest hint of fear for a future without the chieftain about to be interred.

It is striking how deeply Earley's death has resonated, and not just on account of his relatively youthful and unfathomable striking-down. It is difficult to think of a comparable sporting figure, who had not achieved the primary honour, but who withal, as has emerged here, could scarcely have been more revered had he a display-case of All-Ireland medals at his back.

I met Earley only once, last year, just before the onset of his illness. Since his death, his handshake has become one of those clichés in which the media tends to excel, but I have no conscious memory of any vice. I remember a deeply impressive man who for an extended moment connected with me as surely as anyone I have ever met.

I remember his ease and confidence, a manifest capacity for affection, an exceptional sense of authority without aggression, as though he was so aware of his own strength that he matched it with a deliberate gentleness. He possessed in abundance the classical qualities of manliness: strength, energy, fearlessness, honour and physical grace, but carried them with a humility that was instantly distinguishable from false modesty.

In a time when leadership of almost every kind is disintegrating around us, Earley bore witness as Army chief of staff that the qualities of a sublime sportsmanship could be available to the public realm. By his pedigree and record, he provided reassurance, even as the State seems increasingly to turn into a nuisance or a monster, that the higher offices in the land are still amenable to the highest values of humanity.

Earley was a shining light of an Ireland that if you stayed in Dublin and relied on the media for your sense of things you might imagine had disappeared. But it is still here, in the countryside and smaller towns, an Ireland where people are easy about being unfashionable, where values relate to

few of the adults around her want to hear it. She has inherited the instinctive sense of justice her father has always lived by. He has given them an unusual level of freedom and, above all, allows them think for themselves. When he does bow 'to the inevitable' and buys them air guns, he cautions them, saying that they can 'shoot all the bluejays you want, if you can hit 'em, but remember it's a sin to kill a mockingbird'.

But Scout is not a paragon: having had to play as an equal with boys, she believes that most playground disputes can be settled by a punch in the face. Her narrative is comic, precocious and honest. It is this blunt honesty that frequently places her at odds with adults such as her aunt, who find the truth an uncomfortable proposition.

Lee brings a wealth of talents to the story: humour, characterisation, an instinctive feel for story and an insider's grasp of a small town's social dynamics. Above all, Lee, who was born in 1926 in Munroeville, Alabama, and grew up next door to Capote, is aware of the rhythms of southern speech as natural to her as breathing.

Scout is true to that voice. She could have seemed too intelligent, had Lee not skilfully balanced vivid memory with the perception of hindsight, and in doing so conveys a sense of childhood remembered. It is a sympathetic, sensitive narrative, never sentimental and not even particularly nostalgic. Atticus, Miss Maudie, the sheriff Mr Tate and Judge Taylor are all strongly drawn without appearing saintly.

Through Scout's reportage and her presentation of various incidents, the community emerges. To read Lee's novel and listen to Scout's voice is to walk the streets of Maycomb, to join the crowd packing into the hot courthouse for the trial that is the heart of the story.

The Finch children experience anger and eventually fear when targeted by local resentment as it becomes known that Atticus is to defend Tom Robinson, a black man charged with raping a white woman named Mayella Ewell. Scout says it

came to her that Ewell 'must have been the loneliest person in the world. She was even lonelier than Boo Radley, who had not been out of the house in twenty-five years'. It is obvious that Ewell was not raped by Robinson. Her father, known locally as a vicious thug, is the culprit. He has a history of beating his daughter, and he later sets out to settle his score with Atticus by stalking Jem and Scout, a pursuit that culminates in an attack.

Lee makes no attempt to conceal the polemical intent. In the trial, which proves so distressing to the sensitive Dill, Atticus (played so well by Gregory Peck in the 1962 movie version) articulates the driving force of the narrative as he concludes his defence of Tom Robinson by stressing to the jury in his calm, reasonable way: 'You know the truth, and the truth is this: some Negroes lie, some Negroes are immoral, some Negro men are not to be trusted around women – black and white. But this is a truth that applies to the human race and to no particular race of men.' Lee had no intention of writing a fairy tale, and the abiding stroke of genius is that Atticus does not win the case, while Tom is shot dead trying to escape.

Scout ponders her teacher's avowed hatred of Hitler and his treatment of the Jews, considering that she had heard the same lady, Miss Gates, making racist remarks on her way out of the courthouse after Tom Robinson's trial. Scout mentions to Jem that she had overheard the teacher. 'She was goin' down the steps in front of us, you musta not seen her – she was talkin' with Miss Stephanie Crawford. I heard her say it's time somebody taught 'em a lesson, they were gettin' way above themselves, an' the next thing they think they can do is marry us. Jem, how can you hate Hitler so bad an' then turn around and be ugly about folks right at home?'

After many years living in New York, Harper Lee returned to Munroeville, where she still lives. She stands apart from major stylists such as Flannery O'Connor, Carson McCullers and Eudora Welty. Lee is famous for her only book, a Pulitzer-winning novel that pre-empted Toni Morrison's achievement, 28 years later, with another Pulitzer winner, *Beloved*. It was Lee who accompanied Truman Capote to Kansas while he was researching the crime that inspired *In Cold Blood* (1966).

Independence Day dawns tomorrow. It's worth remembering that several years before the civil-rights movement was to consolidate its protest, Harper Lee exposed the rhetoric of righteousness and the concept of independence in practice through the eyes of a child.

TUESDAY, 6 JULY 2010

I Really Shouldn't Have Screamed

Shane Hegarty

Thirteen years ago. In the history of Irish comedy, I am a footnote in an appendix of a punchline to a joke nobody would tell. For a few months in 1997, I did some stand-up around Dublin. The core of my set was a riff on rave dances. I wasn't exactly Bill Hicks.

But that year, I qualified for the Edinburgh Festival Fringe's newcomer competition. It turned into one of the most enjoyable weeks of my life. And after it, I gave up comedy. There were two reasons.

Firstly, there was my experience at the competition So You Think You're Funny. I did and I wasn't. Not by an Edinburgh audience's standards anyway. My confidence hadn't been helped by how, and half an hour before the show, I discovered that the MC – Irish comedian Michael Smiley – didn't just perform a similar routine to mine, he owned it.

Smiley was responsible for a 'big fish, little fish, cardboard box' line that even now is comedy shorthand for rave dancing. So I bounded into the spotlight with shop-worn material and greeted a crowd that seemed only angered by having been lured into the venue for a two-for-one deal.

My set was eight minutes long, but I immediately realised that this was not going to be a night of glory and accepted the fact with stoicism as deep as the silence that greeted every punchline.

When it was over, I dragged myself out of there, leaving behind only the chalk outline of my comedy career. Peter Kay won the competition that year, allowing me some comfort in later years, but it was another future comedy star who provided my second motivation for getting out of clown town.

The very first act I went to see in Edinburgh that week was Johnny Vegas, at a time when his cocktail of heartache and lager was fresh, and when it featured the rather ingenious addition of a potter's wheel. He was a hit at that year's Fringe and, for me, a revelation. I'd never seen live comedy of that standard; and knew I could never hope to be that good. By the end of Vegas's show I had decided comedy would do just fine without me.

I didn't want to spend my life gurning for undignified publicity shots and writing weak jokes about my personal failures for the amusement of dwindling crowds. So, I took up journalism instead. Clearly, no parallels can be drawn.

Two weeks ago.

In the intervening years, I have made the mistake of occasionally mentioning that I did comedy way back when. When I say I 'mentioned', I mean 'went on about it a bit'. An eight-minute set in Edinburgh, played out to the damp mix of bored Scots and my cold sweat has since grown to be closer to a month-long sell-out run.

I may also have inadvertently given the impression that my absence from comedy constitutes one of the great losses to modern popular culture, that I am the Harper Lee of Irish comedy, a story that grizzled, veteran comedians growl to newcomers. 'You think Tiernan is good? You should have seen Hegarty. They say that, after one gig, his rave dance riff put 43 members of the audience in hospital with respiratory problems. . .'

For one night only . . . Shane Hegarty, comedian. Photograph: Bryan O'Brien.

Today, I will be called out on it. The Features Editor decides that because I did some stand-up in the months before I landed in journalism, this was the path through life I could have taken, the fork in my personal road, and that it would be hilarious to get me back on a stage once more.

'You could have been a comedian,' he grins. The subtext is clearly 'instead of becoming the office joke'. Through twitter, I am offered a slot by Des Bishop. He and his brother Aidan run the International Comedy Club four nights a week. It is the centre of the Irish comedy universe, with a regular open mic spot (although there is no actual microphone) for anyone willing to step into it: seven minutes, sandwiched between the 'real' comedians. It's a great venue with a good crowd.

It's the only place to do it. I couldn't be more nervous if someone ordered me to do an hour of interpretive mime to the inmates at Mountjoy Prison. After that, when people hear about my impending slot at the International, they respond in one of two ways: either recalling friends who tried stand-up and died so horribly that they're still disinfecting the venue; or colleagues who tell me, in softened voices, that I am 'so brave', as if I was donating a kidney rather than my dignity. Meanwhile, I work on my material.

My first mistake is to watch a few comedians on YouTube, mostly Stewart Lee, an English comedian who sets high standards not just for himself but for other comics too. He has a particular routine about the laziness of observational comedy ('What's the deal with women taking so long to get ready? What's that all about, eh?' etc). It is powerful and wicked, and I decide that he is right. I must push myself to write material that is strong, challenging, intelligent. But I can't think of anything. So I withdraw that challenge and come up instead

Jonathan Gunning, one of 250 street entertainers, amusing the crowds that turned out yesterday for the Macnas Parade at the Galway Arts Festival. Photograph: Joe O'Shaughnessy.

with a short sketch about a sore eye and a few jokes about the weather . . . what's all that about, eh? Eh?

Last Thursday.

On the day of the gig, the Bishop brothers are in New York. I call them for advice. It turns out that Des and I were in the same heat of So You Think You're Funny in 1997. It jogs a memory of how good he was that night but somehow didn't get through to Edinburgh. He seems to have got over it and he has some very useful advice, most notably this: 'Half an hour before the show, you'll have an idea that you think is hilarious. Do. Not. Do. That. Joke.'

'Don't try and talk to the audience,' advises Aidan, 'because you won't have the experience to deal with it. If you have something strong, use it at the start so that you establish yourself with the crowd. Confidence has a lot to do with it; it'll give you the upper hand, so try and have fun and don't

think about it. And don't go over seven minutes. Seriously.'

I arrive at the International to find a cloud of friends hovering at the door. I immediately regret telling anybody — anybody being everybody — that I was doing this. I regret reminding them repeatedly. And I deeply regret giving the impression that a seven-minute open-mic slot during a two-hour comedy show in a small room was as seismic as a Saturday night at the Apollo.

Tommy Nicholson is also on the bill. We both did So You Think You're Funny in Edinburgh in 1997, and I've seen him perform several times since — supporting Des Bishop in Vicar Street, entertaining a festival crowd at the Electric Picnic — he's an Irish comedy stalwart.

He performs before me; his act honed so that the character is fully formed and his comedy memory rich enough that he can run with whatever the audience throws at him. There are three other acts – Damian Clark, Rory O'Hanlon and excellent musical pairing Totally Wired. Added to that is compere Colum McDonnell, who clobbers the audience with routines about buses and self-service supermarket check-outs.

The other acts wait their turn on the stairs outside the door. I stay and watch the show. Rookie error. I realise that each of them has a joke every four seconds; knows where to start, how to sustain the laughs and how to end it on a big cheer. I have material about the weather and a sore eye.

As my slot draws closer, the jokes are shuffling into line in my mind, ready to plummet to their deaths from my dry mouth. McDonnell announces me.

I do my routine and learn the following:

1) Screaming too loudly, too early, does not put an audience at ease

2) Jokes about my gimpy eye are not as funny as you might imagine

3) There is a spot on the International's stage where the light shines so sharply in your eyes that you can't see the audience. It's a good place to stand

4) I forgot one of my jokes! Can I go back and pick it up? Too late!

5) I really shouldn't have screamed

6) Wrapping up a set with a meek 'thanks for that', as if someone has just handed you a monthly pensions report, is anti-climactic for everyone concerned

7) Remember Johnny Vegas

Afterwards, my friends are supportive, the other comedians are unwaveringly kind. I guess it wasn't a complete humiliation – I hope it wasn't – but I feel somewhat chastened all the same. 'It must have been a great buzz,' a few people say. It wasn't. It was weather-themed social torture.

Last Friday.

I report back to the office. The resignation note remains in my desk drawer. But I have worked out a plan for the future. Should a similar situation ever arise again, I will tell the Features Editor that I could have become a photographer for a bikini magazine.

You've been a fantastic crowd. Good night!

Benchmarking Chopin, the Man and his Music

Karlin Lillington

There is a park bench in Poland that plays Chopin. Actually, there are 15, as I discovered. They are part of a little Chopin tour for those who come to Warsaw and wish to know more about this very famous son of the city. Most people probably just accidentally stumble upon one or two during a city ramble.

The other 14 black stone multimedia Chopin benches throughout the city are at various locations associated with the composer. They are one of the city's special gestures this year to honour Frédéric Chopin's 200th birthday. What a wonderful, inspirational use of technology they are.

The bench I saw sits at the edge of a leafy little park next to an old church of the Visitation Nuns, which managed to survive the Luftwaffe's carpet-bombing during the second World War – one of a tiny number of original buildings in Warsaw's city centre.

Inside the church is an organ which the young Polish composer is said to have played during church services – or to be precise, Chopin was employed to play the church's organ for services. The existing organ probably has bits and pieces that have been there since when Chopin played. He was a student at the nearby Warsaw Lyceum.

He wrote to a friend in 1825: 'I have become the school organist. Thus my wife, as well as all my children, must respect me for two reasons. Ha, Good Sir, what a man am I! The first person in the

Kilkenny Arts Festival being launched with a choir conducted by Fergus Sheil, singing through the entire Festival programme at Dublin Corporation Fruit Markets. Photograph: Dara Mac Dónaill.

whole school after the Revd parish priest! I play once a week, on Sundays, at the Visitandines' on the organ, and the others sing.'

I went to look at the church – lovely and cool in the midsummer heat. An elderly nun was arranging flowers on the altar. I wondered whether the schoolgirls who attended the services back then found their young organist as dashing and tempestuous as his later reputation would have him.

I learned much of all this from the bench. Engraved in the surface were some basic details about the particular location and its Chopin connection. There was also a little diagram of the tour that lets you see at which bench you currently sit.

That's just the analogue side. The benches are especially interesting for their digital features. Press a button on the surface and you get to hear about half a minute of a Chopin piece – coming from the bench, which is lovely, if initially slightly disconcerting, as you try to figure out where the sound is actually coming from. You don't really expect the source to be a bench.

Embedded inside each bench is a small MP3 player and speakers (apparently, the batteries are replaced roughly every month by bench caretakers). Each bench plays a different snippet of music. It is lovely to hear a dreamy piece of piano playing in such an unexpected way.

Also set into the surface are a pair of large, two-dimensional barcodes. If you want more Chopin information, you can scan either barcode (if you have downloaded a barcode reader programme to your phone or your handset has one installed, as many now do). This takes you to a website with more detail about Chopin, music downloads and other information.

Twin brothers Noel and Cian Thomas from Moycullen, Co. Galway, with orphaned hedgehogs.

The benches are an intriguing way to do more than just offer static information to passers-by. They enable a visitor to get a quick bit of contextual detail then and there but also to retrieve a wealth of additional content then or later. How perfect to be able to actually hear the music in a relevant outdoor setting and remember why the man is celebrated in the first place.

When, in so many instances, technology is used more as a high-tech toy or an indifferent add-on purveyor of additional information in a museum or gallery which no one really wants, I found this simple enhancement of a living, outdoor space to be utterly charming.

All the more so for being – as I am sure it is for most people – an entirely serendipitous discovery while in an unfamiliar city.

Only time will tell how robust such an outdoor use of MP3 players will prove to be, or whether these barcodes – extremely popular in Japan – will catch on here to the degree that makes this kind of use more widespread. But these little stone benches certainly suggest technology can be put to much more intriguing, thoughtful and creative uses on the tourist and museum trail than is currently the case.

SATURDAY, 10 JULY 2010

If I Had Stayed Working in Dublin, I'd Probably Be Dead by Now

Rosita Boland

My instructions for reaching Michael Viney's house in the townland of Thallabawn, in Co. Mayo, are to cross the bridge at Louisburgh and drive south for eight miles exactly. That's it. That's it? I ask myself in Dublin, putting down the phone, looking at the map and writing the directions doubtfully into my diary. I already know I will get lost.

Some days later I am driving over the bridge at Louisburgh, my car buffeted by huge winds. I check the odometer. Continuing onwards is an act of faith. There are no signposts that say Thallabawn. There are several side roads, all unsigned, that drift off to both right and left. There are many houses scattered around. Sheep meditate against vivid ditches. In the distance, far below, is a ferociously beautiful yellow strand. There is nobody to ask directions from, so I keep going, very uncertainly.

Astonishingly, I do not get lost in this warren of hedgerows and boreens. I find the house. Or it finds me. Michael Viney and his dog, Meg the Second, who have heard my car, come out on the road to meet me.

In 1977 Michael and his wife, Ethna, both journalists, moved from Dublin with their small daughter, Michele, to their holiday house on an acre of land in this remote and lovely part of Mayo. Ever since then Michael has written and illustrated the Another Life column for this newspaper. In the early years it recounted the many challenges of adapting to their new life, in which they tried to be as 'self-reliant as was sensible'.

Then the focus of the column gradually changed to nature, particularly the features of landscape and ocean that surround what must be the most written-about acre in Ireland. Every column is accompanied by a small, precise drawing, latterly in colour, as well as answers to readers' queries, in Eye on Nature.

In 2010 many people still fantasise about doing what the Vineys did in 1977: giving up day jobs and moving from a busy urban life to an equally busy but simpler and less stressful rural one. What made them actually do it? 'I felt it would be a tremendous adventure to live more simply; to live here, in this beautiful place; to be in charge of our time and to do all these things we'd been putting off,' Viney, now 77, explains. 'So many people put off the future until their holidays, and we thought, no, there must be a way of living in a beautiful place *and* being self-sufficient.'

We are walking around the acre at the rear of the modest house. Viney has already apologised for the absence of geese, ducks, hens and goats, all of which once occupied part of the acre and whose husbandry often featured in the column. They may be gone but the acre itself and its polytunnel are marvels of hard-won bounty.

Squeezed in among the sycamores, roses and purple delphiniums are multiple vegetable patches. Peppers. Cauliflowers. Shallots. Red cabbage. Winter cabbage. Beetroot. Carrots. Broad beans. Courgettes. Parsnips. Brussels sprouts. Lettuces. Tomatoes. Cucumbers. Potatoes. Celeriac. Calabrese. Herbs. 'I garden in the clearings.'

Back in the house, every window ledge holds shells, sea urchins, glass buoys, driftwood, bird bones, skulls, goat horns; flotsam and jetsam from years of combing nearby Thallabawn Strand. In this place there is a sense that the outside is always coming inside, or simply reappearing again from where it has been hiding in the undergrowth: in his column last weekend Viney wrote about the revival of purple Cardinal de Richelieu roses he last saw in the acre 20 years ago.

A Bosnian Muslim woman sits next to a coffin of her relative at the Potocari Memorial Center in Potocari, 120 km northeast of Sarajevo, Bosnia and Herzegovina, on Sunday, 11 July 2010, the 15th anniversary of the worst crime of genocide in Europe since the Nazi era. Photograph: Marko Drobnjakovic/Associated Press.

deputy mayor of Donegal Pádraig Mac Lochlainn described as 'mind-numbing devastation' the tragedy that had again visited this, an incredibly tight-knit community.

'You've three parishes affected, Clonmany, Buncrana and Fahan, and there won't be anybody in the Inishowen Peninsula who won't know the victims – that's the extent of the devastation. Because of the spread of the families it would be nearly impossible not to know somebody.'

For the people of the area this latest crash brings back painful memories. Fr Eddie McGuiness, curate of Cockhill parish, said the following days would be hugely difficult for everyone, including local clergy.

'We have had multiple accidents in which more than a few people have died and it brings back memories for them. That's really one of the tragedies, that it's reinvoking the memories for all those people who lost their sons and daughters all in the same age group.'

His colleague, Fr John Walsh, the parish priest of Buncrana, spent much of Sunday night with the families who, he said, are naturally devastated by the sudden loss.

'It is a really cruel blow to this particular community,' he said, adding that the tragedy would also affect family members and girlfriends who have lost other people to road tragedies in the past. 'Young people must realise how fragile life is and be careful and cautious and play by the rules all the time,' he added.

Pat 'the Cope' Gallagher, MEP for the area, said the incident had cast 'a dark cloud' over the Inishowen Peninsula once again. 'My heart goes out to the families of all those involved and the wider community.'

THURSDAY, 15 JULY 2010

Simple Reflections, Desolate Tears at Funerals of Three Victims

Kathy Sheridan

As summer rain lashed Donegal's Inishowen Peninsula, Hugh Friel, 'a lovely, quiet, pleasant gentleman' who was 'easy pleased', was laid to rest in Urris cemetery, high in the misty Racthan Hills, overlooking the Atlantic Ocean. The funeral of the 66-year-old farmer and bingo enthusiast was the first of eight to be endured over three days by a small community, dazed and muted with grief.

Among the mourners in Urris were members of the McEleney, Doherty and Sweeney families, who will bury their own dead today and tomorrow. Others struggled with the logistics of getting to the funeral Mass of Mark McLaughlin (21) an hour later in Fahan.

His friend, P.J. McLaughlin (21), would be buried from the same church at 3 p.m., by the same priest, Fr Neil McGoldrick. Today many of the same mourners will try to make it to four more.

It is easy to spot the 'wake houses' in an area that maintains the tradition of waking the dead for two nights, before taking them directly from home

Young swallows nest in the safe sanctuary of the porch of St Joseph's Church, at Keelogues, Ballyvary, Co. Mayo. Photograph: Peter Waldron.

for the funeral Mass. Processions of pale, hollow-eyed young men pulling on new black ties. Hastily cobbled signs in deep countryside directing visitors to parking areas. The roads around Fahan, lined for miles with the cars of those paying their respects to the families of the McLaughlin boys.

At yesterday's three funerals, where mourners filled the churches well before the appointed hour, there were no lengthy eulogies or loud scenes of grieving. There were only short, simple reflections and prayers for the other grieving families and for the young driver, Shaun Kelly – fighting for his life in intensive care – and desolate tears coursing silently down young faces.

If there was a common theme, it was an implied attachment to road vehicles of some kind. 'Hughie always kept a lovely shiny car ... spick and span,' noted a neighbour of Hugh Friel. At Mark McLaughlin's Mass, Peggy Doherty recited a poem about his devotion to eight-wheeler trucks. It ended: 'You'd meet him coming anywhere and even day or night, his mobile phone to his ears, he'd wave and flash the lights. A lovely happy lad he was, but God had another plan. So proudly now we say farewell to our driving gentleman.'

The offertory gifts to mark P.J. McLaughlin's short, full life included a photograph of an old souped-up BMW and a star-shaped trophy naming him 'Driver of the Year 2010'. They also included a football shirt for a club poignantly represented in the guard of honour for his arrival at the church and his final journey to the nearby graveyard, from where the strains of *The Fields of Athenry* drifted back towards the church yard.

Hughie Friel's offertory gifts were a cloth cap and a bingo card, along with recollections of neighbourliness and a generation steeped in the tradition of the *meitheal*. In a reference to the circumstances of his death, Fr Fintan Diggin said: 'I'm sure he'd have used the phrase you hear so much these days – there but for the grace of God go I.'

FRIDAY, 16 JULY 2010

Air of Unreality as Inishowen Mourners Follow Funeral Trail

Kathy Sheridan

As mourners accompanied Paul Doherty on his last journey the few yards from St Mary's Church in Clonmany to his grave, an ambulance crew was tending to another young man who had collapsed, hitting his head off the pavement only a few yards away. In a community still numbed and muted, and by now, exhausted, it was hardly surprising.

A remarkable aspect of Inishowen's public grieving has been the absence – at least in public – of anguished sobs. There is only a deep, dazed silence.

Paul Doherty's was the first of four funerals on Donegal's Inishowen Peninsula yesterday, the seventh in two relentless days.

Images evoked of exuberant, vibrant young lads, full of fun and mischief, wild for *craic* and mad for cars, enjoying a few drinks in The High Stool in Clonmany and following country singer Mike Denver around the venues, contrast surreally with the ritual, the incense, the musical laments and the finality of the fresh-scented earth piled on to yet another grave.

With each funeral and each fresh wave of grief come the same young, pinched, wan faces above unnatural black suits and ties, the same musicians, the same football team, the same readings from the Book of Wisdom – 'Their going looked like a disaster, their leaving us like annihilation . . '

The limits of human endurance are daily stretched by people such as Felix and Sally Doherty, who were present at Ciarán Sweeney's funeral only hours after burying their own son, Paul, on what would have been his 20th birthday, in the same graveyard.

The constant thought for others' calvary is evident in the words of people like Éamon and Claire Sweeney, who used their reflection time to send out the message that they were holding no-one responsible in any way, for the loss of their 'beautiful son and brother'.

And there are the worn-out priests – some of whom were at the crash site on Sunday night – seeking to reassure their congregations and to beg them to change their behaviour.

Fr Fintan Diggin was at pains to assure the bereaved that the consensus of all those who had attended the scene was that the victims had died instantly and painlessly. Fr John Walsh begged his young listeners to remember they were not 'indestructible at the age of 22: You are very fragile. All of us are . . . When I was your age I too felt indestructible. But none of us is . . .

'So please, please live life on its terms, within its rules and boundaries; otherwise life will be cruel and merciless towards you and towards the family and friends who will have to bear you to the grave,' he said.

TUESDAY, 13 JULY 2010

Seven-Minute Verdict, Seven-Year-Plus Clean-Up

Simon Carswell

How the mighty have fallen. It took just seven minutes for the High Court to declare Seán FitzPatrick, the former multimillionaire chairman and chief executive of Anglo Irish Bank, bankrupt.

After some housekeeping and a little sparring between counsel for Anglo and Mr FitzPatrick over whether his proposed settlement or his bankruptcy offered the best outcome for creditors, the hearing was over in 12 minutes.

The legal bickering between counsels was academic. Mr Justice McGovern said he wasn't going to allow the bankruptcy court to be used to 'ventilate issues' between the sides. This could be done in 'another forum', the judge said.

Once in charge of Ireland's third-largest lender, worth €13 billion at its peak, Mr FitzPatrick must now disclose he is a bankrupt to borrow over €650. Mr FitzPatrick's financial roof began to fall in under the weight of his debts last December when his former employer, Anglo Irish Bank, sought repayment of loans – a year after he resigned as chairman over his hidden loans.

Talks followed and a 'standstill' deal was agreed, allowing him to sell his interest in a potentially valuable oilfield off Nigeria, which, at an estimated €14.7 million, he claims is his most valuable asset.

On 11 March, Anglo moved, issuing a lawsuit against him. Four days later, he secured High Court protection from his creditors to devise a settlement agreement. To secure a deal to allow him to repay some of his debts on an orderly basis over time – and avoid bankruptcy – he needed the support of 60 per cent of his creditors. Anglo held all the cards – it had €110 million of his overall debts of €147.9 million and 85 per cent of his unsecured debt of €70 million, giving it the power to block a deal.

By seeking protection under bankruptcy law, Mr FitzPatrick fast-tracked his bankruptcy. The court was told that Anglo was going to oppose any proposals he put forward. The bank disputed the assertion by Mr FitzPatrick that Anglo would be better-off under his proposed settlement.

Creditors were told they would receive more than twice what they would get on their unsecured liabilities under bankruptcy if they agreed to his settlement offer. 'It was clear from the outset that the scheme was never going to work,' said Anglo's lawyer Paul Gardiner S.C. Mark Sanfey S.C, for Mr FitzPatrick, said his client considered he should 'bow to the inevitable'. And that was that – Mr FitzPatrick was declared bankrupt.

Last Wednesday, he had a chance to put his plan to creditors. 'Clearly today is a particularly sad

Macnas performers Claire Howley and Lindsay Gavin Williams at a preview of the Galway Arts Festival.

day for me personally and also for members of my family,' he told creditors in his solicitor's office.

'There have been seismic happenings in the global economy over the past two years, 24 months, but I accept full responsibility for my own ruin, personal and professional, which has left me facing the real possibility of being made a bankrupt.' He expressed 'deep regret' for his creditors' losses. 'Throughout my business dealings, both personal and during my time in Anglo Irish Bank, I acted at all times in good faith and I always believed I was acting properly and prudently.

'I used my best judgment in my investment decisions and in taking on loan obligations,' he said. His main aim was to secure 'a fair and equal distribution of all of my unencumbered assets to all

my creditors', he said, and he would give full co-operation to 'whatever process is chosen'.

The control of his investments and property has now been handed to the official assignee, Christopher Lehane, a court-appointed official who handles the financial affairs of bankrupts.

The scale of Mr FitzPatrick's investments is vast and will take many years for the official assignee to untangle and sell off for the benefit of the creditors. Mr FitzPatrick's solicitor, William O'Grady, told creditors last week that his client's bankruptcy would last more than seven years.

The case is listed again for 26 July, by which time further details of Mr FitzPatrick's assets and liabilities will be provided, as he starts out on the long road to discharge himself as a bankrupt.

Ryan Tubridy enjoys a good laugh during his final morning show for RTÉ Radio One, broadcast from Bray Seafront in Co. Wicklow. The broadcaster moves to Radio Two to take over the vacant slot following the death of Gerry Ryan. Photograph: Joe Keogh.

THURSDAY, 15 JULY 2010

Bilocating Confucius Callely in the Wilderness for 20 Days and 20 Nights

Miriam Lord

I t's here, your super Seanad Summer Special for 2010! When the TDs are away, the Senators will play! Two whole days of action-packed thrills and spills from the upper house. No Dáil. Simply Seanad. That other crowd have gone. No publicity-mad deputies to steal the Senators' thunder. Now, at last, they can shine.

The Seanad is the centre of the Leinster House universe this week.

Hear them roar! But what's this? It can't be. Oh no, here comes Ivor Callely and he's going to ruin everything . . . Just when they thought they could snaffle a little bit of coverage for themselves in the absence of any business in the Dáil chamber, the saga of Ivor and his moveable expenses elbowed them off the stage.

Confucius Callely took his wise sayings to a select committee of the Seanad on Tuesday to argue why he was completely within his rights to claim allowances for living permanently in west Cork while even the dogs in the streets said he resided in the Dublin suburb of Clontarf.

As a result, his colleagues' golden opportunity to grab some media coverage for themselves in the absence of the Dáil was lost to the continuing Callely controversy.

Matters were due to come to a head last night, but in the meantime, while the business of the Seanad went ahead as normal, all eyes were on the committee investigating Ivor. The six members met in private twice during the day and indicated they would issue their findings before the house adjourned for the summer.

The man at the centre of the storm didn't seem too perturbed by all the fuss. He contributed during the Order of Business in the morning, addressing matters of international importance. He was also concerned at the length of the recess, given the 'challenges' currently facing the country.

However, Ivor was remaining chipper. This could be seen in his choice of statement tie – a gaudy geometric assortment of circles and squares. The morning before, when he faced into an afternoon of questioning by the committee, he sported a different tie of many happy colours.

Interestingly, he changed into a sombre grey

A passer-by berates the Burke family from Castlebar, Co. Mayo, protesting outside the Dáil against the Civil Partnership Bill, during its final passage through the Oireachtas. Photograph: Matt Kavanagh.

when the time came for him to be grilled by his peers. Confucius Callely has been the soul of serenity over the past couple of days. As he said during his committee ordeal: 'Today is history; tomorrow is a mystery.'

From whence did he pluck that little gem of wisdom? It recently figured large in the movie *Kung Fu Panda*. The quote continues: 'but today is a gift. That is why it is called the "present".' But there was to be no gift for Ivor.

Instead, the committee handed him a 20 sitting-day suspension and censured him for misrepresenting his normal place of residence for the purpose of claiming allowances.

It took the committee nearly 40 pages to say why they found reasonable cause to ground him, but that's the gist.

His peers are not amused, not least because they hoped to be away before teatime, but because they had to stay on until nine o'clock so the report could be officially presented to the Seanad.

It was Ivor who requested an hour-long adjournment before the report was laid before the house. So Senators had to cool their heels until then and, when the time arrived, Confucius Callely didn't show.

So many gems were overlooked because of bilocating Ivor's exploits. Yesterday, for example, while the dog-breeding legislation was chewed over yet again, the Seanad pondered the 'Definition of Bitch'. Nobody cared. The house was suspended for five minutes at lunchtime to allow the Minister for the Environment to send a text message to somebody. Again, hardly anyone outside the chamber noticed. Too busy on Ivor watch.

It appears the debate had run over time. As Minister Gormley waxed lyrical about groups of breeding bitches, he suddenly realised he had to be somewhere else. He became most agitated. 'It's coming up to half past one. I've further engagements,' he declared, all of a dither. 'I'm in a situation . . . I don't know how to go . . . I-I don't know what we're going to do. I-I-I really don't know.'

The acting cathaoirleach told him the debate was scheduled to run until two o'clock. John looked distraught. 'I'll just text someone.' Well. Talk about a rum do. You can't do those sort of things willy-nilly in Seanad Éireann. Paschal Mooney, who was in the chair, took command.

'Can I ask the acting leader to propose a suspension of the house for five minutes in order to facilitate everyone?' The house rose and John rushed away, clutching his mobile phone.

In the event, he wasn't detained too much longer and arrived in the canteen before two where he had lunch with his press adviser and other members of his staff. What could have been in that text he sent? 'Order me the soup and stuffed Portobello mushroom,' perhaps? But nobody was paying any attention to the Seanad.

On Tuesday, there was a fine turnout for the Order of Business. A great day for a bit of coverage, members might have assumed. Not a bit of it, thanks to Confucious Callely.

So nobody got to hear Mary White speaking out on behalf of older people and telling Senator Ronan Mullen that he should consider going out with older women. (Apparently, Ronan said, 'I don't go with older women,' at some stage during the debate on the Civil Partnership Bill last week. Yes, we're baffled too.)

She recommended a book to him by the man who coined the phrase 'ageism'. It had a great chapter on 'sex after 60', the redoubtable Sen. White told him. A brief silence settled over the chamber at this point. But did anyone care about the over-Sixties and their sex lives? No.

And then there was Sen. David Norris, who was very much concerned about the state of the 'magnificent' organ in the National Concert Hall. Heads swivelled to the press gallery. Notes were being furiously taken. But never used. Callely's fault.

He's in the wilderness now. Twenty days – the full half of a biblical banishment. Still, at least Ivor can enjoy the lovely wilderness of west Cork, and

Revellers, Seán Fleeton (centre) with his friends, bounce around on the inflatable beds before leaving the Oxegen Music Festival, at Punchestown Racecourse. Photograph: Brenda Fitzsimons.

the principal residence he doesn't actually own but has full residence rights – when he isn't in Clontarf, his other principal residence. Will he go quietly? Highly unlikely.

MONDAY, 2 AUGUST 2010

Cohen Serene Under Ben Bulben

Eileen Battersby

People of all ages gathered, carefully corralled, to walk along a path through the woods. They walked towards the light reflecting off the water in the shadow of a great house. They came to hear a poet sing his songs in a place still associated with another, earlier poet, long dead and revered.

Under the shadow of Ben Bulben's distinctive flat profile, made famous by Yeats, the faithful waited for Leonard Cohen, veteran Canadian singer songwriter, a poet who has pursued personal experience to its limits. His meditations on life and love, the spiritual and the sexual, the hunted and the haunted appeal to all ages for their strange beauty, the gentle melodies; their romance and their solitude. Bittersweet romance, subtle observation and humour run through the songs; there is also the jaunty courage of his odyssey as an artist, a lover, a man and a performer.

Many of the faces waiting for the music to begin seemed thoughtful as if remembering their younger selves, the people they had been when Cohen first began his career. For others, who had

Leonard Cohen performing at Lissadell House in Sligo. Photograph: James Connolly/PicSell8.

not even been born when Cohen was young, he is an icon, an influence. Girls in their 20s corrected their parents as to the titles of some of the songs. A father and son stood together, singing the opening lines of 'Famous Blue Raincoat' and left the mother poised to photograph them, on her own figuring out how the camera worked. An older woman, her own raincoat at the ready, looked around and sighed, 'The State should have bought this place.'

She was not alone, aside from the eulogies offered as to the enduring genius of Cohen, the most common topic of overheard conversation was that this magical part of Sligo should have been secured for the people of Ireland.

Leonard Cohen, serene and smiling, dark grey fedora firmly on his head, took the stage, along with his smartly suited band of musicians and singers. From the distance his figure seemed small against the flowing fabric backdrop of changing colours, but the huge TV screens provided close-up views of his wonderful face with its expression of benign irony. Here is a man who has seen most things and pondered them deeply. He knows about despair but he also sees the jokes. His repertoire includes many of the most distinctive songs written anywhere since the late 1960s.

Along with Bob Dylan and the great Paul Simon, Cohen inhabits a sacred place. His songs are poems; the lyrics live off the page. As a performer he is generous; his band is his family, his audience his friends, and 'friends' was the word he used to address the thousands who came to hear him.

Several of the gardaí on duty looked wistful, assuring us that they would be up at the concert if they weren't on duty. It was that kind of night; that kind of place, even the police seemed happy. It was obvious that the combined musical talent was overwhelming; Cohen showed them off like a proud parent, although the great Spanish guitarist, Javier Mas, is not all that much younger than Cohen, who was born in Montreal in 1934. We knew the songs, and the musicians did too, but when you're that good and the atmosphere is perfect, it is easy to improvise further.

The show, now on its way to Copenhagen, is terrific, no doubt about it, possessing an intriguingly European quality, yet at times, particularly with classics such as 'Suzanne', 'Famous Blue Raincoat', 'Sisters of Mercy' and 'So Long, Marianne', it would have been even more satisfying just to hear Cohen's tender, softly growling baritone. As a singer he is alert to every nuance; every word counts and with Cohen, every word is sung clear and emphatic. He is a lively, engaged performer but the wonder of his songs is best enjoyed in a more intimate setting because his songs are like poems and deserve pauses and space and time to absorb them fully.

Earlier on Saturday he had visited Drumcliff churchyard and paid his respects at the grave of Yeats, a poet whose work he had first read, as Cohen told his audience, 'at home in Montreal, about 50 years ago'. He smiled his wry, rueful smile.

In the visitors' book at Drumcliff church he wrote Leonard Cohen, Montreal, with a simple comment, 'Sublime'. Some four of five songs into the concert he looked into the crowd and spoke of how privileged he felt to be at 'this most historic setting'. His humility and calm demeanour gave new life to those most evocative lines. 'The light of evening, Lissadell,/Great windows open to the south,/Two girls in silk kimonos, both/Beautiful, one a gazelle.' (From 'In Memory of Eva Gore-

A horse-drawn carriage carries the coffin of former world snooker champion Alex Higgins through Belfast for his funeral in St Anne's Cathedral. Photograph: Cathal McNaughton/Reuters.

Booth and Con Markievicz'; *The Winding Stair and Other Poems, 1933*.)

Cohen began the concert saying that he did not know if he would pass this way again, but promised to give 'everything we have' on behalf of his band and himself and his backing singers, Hattie and Charley Webb, whose ethereal voices are ideal for Cohen's songs, and his collaborator, Sharon Robinson. They did and more.

Cohen at 75, singing his much-covered 'Hallelujah', on a drizzly Saturday evening in historic Lissadell outperformed the current version by opera singer Renée Fleming, such is his art and kindly humanity. The audience, growing in confidence, thundered its appreciation singing along with more and more songs. Each time Cohen skipped – and skip he does – off stage, the applause brought him back. His generosity as a performer is well known; he graced Lissadell. Yeats, a life-long presence for this singer of songs, would have approved.

MONDAY, 2 AUGUST 2010

Omey, Oh My, We Watched them Fly

Rosita Boland

The other Galway Races took place yesterday, on the strand at Omey Island, at Claddaghduff in Co. Galway. There were hats evident, but not ones featuring bright feathers, netting and extraordinary shapes: these hats were tweed caps, modelled by elderly Connemara men who would probably think Philip Treacy was the name of a horse. As for eye-catching footwear and high heels, well, many people didn't wear any shoes at all, but walked barefoot on the sand. It was Connemara's turn for the races yesterday, and an estimated 5,000 people turned up, the largest crowd in years.

Re-established as a tradition in 2001, the annual summer races at Omey, which take place between the high tides, have been steadily attracting greater numbers every year. Yesterday, the sun shone with rare generosity and Omey and Claddaghduff were looking impossibly postcard-beautiful: turquoise waters, butter-yellow strands, vast blue skies. Everywhere you looked on the walk across the strand there were ad-hoc picnics; some of them featuring bottles of wine and some of them featuring flasks of tea.

Among the thousands of people present was the newly crowned Festival Queen of the Sea, Gráinne O'Toole from Cleggan. She won her title last week, and was out at the races wearing her handmade sash and a gold and pearl tiara. 'It's the first time Cleggan had the Queen of the Sea competition since 1987,' she said, while small girls nearby stopped digging sand castles and looked on in awe at her glittering princess-like tiara.

Where did the tiara come from? 'It was donated by Rebecca Walsh from Cleggan – she'd worn it for her wedding,' O'Toole explained brightly. Even festival queens of the sea, it seems, are doing their bit of recession recycling.

While the adults dug into their pockets to place bets, the children just dug. I almost fell into an enormous moat constructed by six small, hard-working children. Forget binoculars. The must-have accessory of the day was a bucket and spade.

There were nine races on the card, except there was no card. Names of runners and riders were written up on whiteboards just before each race; the boards were propped up on the open-sided truck that also functioned as a commentary box, and as a stage for Irish dancing in-between the races.

Jockeys weighed in at the back of a horsebox. They signed in at the front of the horsebox. A man with a handbell, which looked like a school bell, signalled the completion of each lap. The winners enclosure was a little area on the beach, decorated with handwritten signs and a wooden tub of pink hydrangeas.

The only way to describe the first race of the day is that it was a one horse race. Three horses

Rides to the sea at Omey Races. Photograph: Joe O'Shaughnessy.

started – Jekyll and Hyde, Ghost and Poker Face – but two of them missed the first bend on the strand and went galloping out together towards the ocean, like Synge's *Riders to the Sea*. Meanwhile, Jekyll and Hyde went on to be the day's first winner.

'The bend on this far side might need to be looked at,' announced commentator Dingle Tom, otherwise known as Thomas O'Callaghan, from Dingle, Co. Kerry. Racing was temporarily halted while stewards put up additional fencing, to stop other horses doing a Synge on it. 'I love commentating at Omey,' O'Callaghan said simply, looking down with delight at the crowd. 'It's a nursery for young jockeys.'

The bookies were lined up in two rows at the back of the truck. Some of them were very fancy, with portable digital boards of the kind you see at airports giving information about flights, while others used flip charts or whiteboards to write up the names of the runners. Attracted by the name, I put a random, uneducated fiver on a horse in the second race with Colm McGinley's bookies from Letterkenny, Co. Donegal. The horse's name was the same as a colloquial expression in Co. Clare, Take it Handy, which was pretty much the mantra for the whole day yesterday.

There was also a horse in the same race that seemed to have two names; some bookies had him down as Smoking Gun, and others as Smokey Gun. I put another fiver on the horse known as Smoking Gun, but if Smokey Gun won, well, he was going to be my horse too.

Down at the edge of the temporary fencing, a steward scolded the crowd for leaning on the fence and dislodging the poles that had been driven into the sand. 'You're worse than the horses,' he said, shooing us back behind the fencing.

My horses looked beautiful as they walked up

THE IRISH TIMES BOOK OF THE YEAR

and down. I eyed them with expectant pride. They were going to earn me a modest, but important, fortune.

There were two false starts, but neither was made by my horses. After a second false start by the same horse, a small, energetic boy in a red T-shirt standing in front of me yelled encouragingly at the horse. 'Come on, ya plank!'

And then they were off. Only a stone could not have thrilled to the silken gallop, the slender legs fluently drumming a kind of music on the sand, the gorgeous contrasting surroundings of ocean, rock and field.

Each time the horses passed by, they re-ignited the excitement of the crowd in that particular place. I lost track of Take It Handy and the horse with two names. It all became a glorious blur of manes, tails and necks, with the ocean flashing constantly between their legs.

My horses did not win, or were even placed. They may have come last.

The winner was New Beginning. Never mind. I may have lost the race, but like everyone else on Omey Island yesterday, I won big on the experience of a very special west-of-Ireland day.

WEDNESDAY, 4 AUGUST 2010

Senator Ivor Callely

Editorial

Public confidence in the political system has taken a battering and the electorate is sick to death of the misbehaviour, ineptitude and complacency of some Oireachtas members. Higher standards of conduct are required and party leaders and the justice system have a duty to ensure that unethical behaviour is severely punished. A culture of nods and winks and cute-hoor politics should be consigned to the past.

The latest controversy concerning the Oireachtas has come, yet again, from Senator Ivor Callely, who was nominated to that position by former taoiseach Bertie Ahern. Following unjustified claims for more than €80,000 in Seanad travel expenses over a two-year period comes a report that he submitted invoices for equipment costing almost €3,000 from a company that had ceased trading. The Garda Síochána should be asked to investigate these matters.

Last month, Britain's most senior judges ruled that MPs and members of the House of Lords could not invoke parliamentary privilege to protect themselves from criminal charges that they had abused their expenses. As a result, six parliamentarians will be hauled before the courts for making false claims. Conceivably, they could end up in jail.

When Mr Callely's claim for travel expenses from his holiday home in West Cork was first discussed before the Senate, Senator Eugene Regan of Fine Gael proposed the matter should be referred to the Director of Public Prosecutions (DPP) and asked the pertinent question: Do the laws passed by the Oireachtas apply only to 'other people' or to everyone generally? We now know that, in Britain, they apply to everyone. Here, the jury is still out and the verdict remains uncertain. In a functioning democracy, this situation must be confronted.

In the absence of a response from Mr Callely to the latest allegations, Fianna Fáil had little option but to suspend his membership of the organisation. It did so 'without prejudice' yesterday, pending completion of an internal party investigation. But this is not enough.

The Seanad Committee on Members' Interests found Mr Callely had intentionally misrepresented his normal place of residence in order to maximise travel expenses. It suspended him without pay for 20 days and called on him to regularise his affairs. The findings were 'strenuously rejected' by Mr Callely.

The outcome did not suggest an appetite for radical reform. Involving the Garda and the DPP would help to reassure the public that the law applies to everyone.

Rose of Tralee hopefuls take to the water with photographer Domnick Walsh, off Fenit in Co. Kerry, as part of the launch of the 2010 festival. From left: Belfast Rose, Frances Rafferty; Cork Rose, Laura Mitchell; 2009 Rose of Tralee, Charmaine Kenny; Kerry Rose, Veronica Hunt; Tipperary Rose, Lynda Kelly; and Dublin Rose, Niamh Sherlock. The festival takes place from 20–24 August. Photograph: Eric Hanaton/Eye Focus.

futility when our lives are so short and our contributions so limited. It's more likely that houses influence us than the other way round.

But if that is the case, what was I now to make of this bad karma in the story of our house? I resolved to find out more about the history of the house – to set the record straight, as it were. It was built in the 1840s, but it wasn't until CIÉ sold the railway cottages to their occupants in the 1970s that they gained their first owner-occupiers. Thom's Directory tells me that Mrs Kelly, later listed as Bridget Kelly, lived here from 1936 at the latest until the 1980s, when the house was sold to a private buyer for the first time.

The Irish Times archives chart some of the main events to affect the estate over the years, in particular the decline of the railways. At one time, older neighbours tell me, CIÉ wanted to raze all the houses, while in the 1980s it planned to sell the works to a German company. Thankfully all its plans came to very little, and the area remained preserved in aspic for decades.

Not for much longer, though. The city, only three kilometres away, now surrounds the area and high-rise buildings are marching up from Heuston. Irish Rail wants to tunnel under the estate for an underground DART, and if the promised station materialises, development will inevitably follow.

The archives threw up little about Alexander Morrow. The newspaper article said he had only one known relative, a brother whose whereabouts was unknown, and his name failed to turn up in other records.

William Lyons, however, features in a number of historical records. Like everyone who lived in the estate at the end of the 19th century, he was employed in the railway works. The Great Southern and Western Railway controlled many aspects of people's lives in this area: the houses they rented; the Model School down the road they attended; and the refectories, church and cricket pitches, all laid on in the best paternalistic Victorian manner. Houses of varying size were allocated according to seniority, from the grand chief engineer's house in the works down to the more modest cottages around the estate. The join between work and home was seamless – people fenced their gardens with railway sleepers and used cinders from the foundry as underfloor insulation.

Lyons worked as a moulder and foreman, and with his wife Mary Ann he had 10 children, of whom six were living at the time of the 1911 census. Three were still at home. I wonder how many were born in the house; most likely all of them. Large families, of course, were nothing unusual. A recent contributor to a local website I run, inchicore.info, recalled growing up in a family of 17 in a three-bed house in the estate.

The census enumerators recorded a total of 156 people living on our road in 1911. I'd estimate this is about three times the present population. There were 126 Catholics, 22 members of the Church of Ireland – including William Lyons and his family – and eight Methodists. The names of some long-established railway families, such as Currivan, survive in the area to this day.

The death of Morrow doesn't seem to have been the only tragedy to befall the house at this time. Church of Ireland records available online show William and Mary Ann Lyons had a son, Charles, in 1895, and a daughter, Emily, in 1900, yet both names are absent from the 1911 census and even the 1901 census. The death notices of The Irish Times record the death of another son, John, in 1908, at the age of 15.

My amateur efforts at genealogy didn't manage to establish what happened to the Lyons family. Did they join the Protestant exodus from the newly independent Irish State in the 1920s, I

wondered, or were they hit by the subsequent decline of the railways? Most journalism is a sprint but historical research is a marathon event.

More time and expertise were called for, but one of its perils is serendipitous distraction. For now, Alexander Morrow and his troubled soul can rest easy, safe from these prying eyes.

FRIDAY, 13 AUGUST 2010

Met by Flashing Cameras and Obscenities from the Crowd

Conor Lally

Some members of the media had been camped out since Tuesday waiting for the moment, but, when it finally came, the exit from the prison gates of rapist Larry Murphy was over in a few seconds. His short walk to freedom from the main gate of Dublin's Arbour Hill Prison to a waiting taxi at 10.15 a.m. was illuminated by rapid-fire flash photography from within the 50-strong waiting media scrum.

Some members of the public, about 10, shouted obscenities as Murphy emerged from the prison that had held him since 2000. Wearing black sunglasses, a navy baseball cap and black hoodie top, the Wicklow carpenter said nothing as journalists shouted questions at him.

About 10 uniformed gardaí were on duty outside the prison and crowd control barriers had been placed on the road to keep it clear for the taxi that collected the father of two.

Carrying a large black sports bag containing his possessions from his 10½ years in jail, Murphy (45) was driven from the prison on Arbour Hill in the north inner city towards the Phoenix Park. He was followed through the morning traffic by two photographers on motorcycles as the Garda helicopter monitored the pursuit. Murphy was driven towards the city centre and on to Coolock on the north side of Dublin.

There he presented himself to gardaí at the local station. This was despite him being free to go where he pleased, with no obligation for another seven days to inform gardaí where he is living.

While it was first believed he had gone to the Garda station to complain about being followed, it subsequently emerged that the taxi he had used to leave the prison was being shadowed by undercover gardaí in unmarked Garda cars. This was part of a Garda plan to ensure members of the force monitored Murphy's taxi until he was able to escape from any pursuing media.

The plan was put in place because gardaí were fearful that if Murphy was followed to and pictured at a particular address, he might be attacked there by members of the public.

Murphy left Coolock in the taxi and was driven back into Dublin city centre, still being

Larry Murphy leaving Arbour Hill prison, in Dublin. Photograph: Alan Betson.

pursued by the photographers' motorbikes and shadowed by the undercover gardaí. He was driven towards Grafton Street, where he got out of the taxi and disappeared into the crowds on a pedestrianised street just before 1 p.m.

Garda sources last night said Murphy was tracked throughout yesterday and they were satisfied they knew where he was due to stay last night. Because he is a sex offender, he must inform gardaí within the next seven days where he is residing. Gardaí are not permitted to disclose this information but they will use it to monitor him closely. Murphy applied for a driving licence and passport while in jail and he can now travel anywhere in the EU.

Fine Gael's Charlie Flanagan TD says the standard entitlement of 25 per cent remission – time off for good behaviour – should be earned and should not be an automatic right, as it is now.

The Labour Women chairwoman Katherine Dunne has called for the electronic tagging of sex offenders. She has also called for stronger measures in relation to sex offenders being obliged to tell gardaí where they are living.

SATURDAY, 14 AUGUST 2010

'Everything Has Been Destroyed. Only God Knows what Will Happen to us Now'

Mary Fitzgerald, in Nowshera, Pakistan

The waters came silently like a thief under cover of darkness, and before Mukhtiar Akbar knew it the swirling currents were up to her neck. Long into the night, she and her family waded desperately through the floods, at times struggling to keep their heads above water, until they reached higher ground. Shivering from the cold, their hands

Mohammed Nawaz hangs on to a boat as he is rescued from flood waters by the Pakistani navy in Sukkur. Photograph: Paula Bronstein/Images.

wrinkled from hours immersed in water, Mukhtiar and her family huddled together as dawn broke, thankful that they had survived where so many others had perished.

More than a week after that night, Mukhtiar stands forlornly at the door of what remains of her house. Her stained, damp shalwar kameez is the only item of clothing she has left. The walls of her modest home tell their own story.

The water line left by the floods reaches almost to the ceiling. Just above it, on a shelf Mukhtiar reserved for her most treasured possessions, sits a delicately-patterned china tea set. Untouched by the foul-smelling sludge that has covered every-thing else in the room, it serves as a poignant reminder of life before the deluge. 'What little we had before is gone,' Mukhtiar says, as she swats away numerous flies. 'Everything has been

destroyed. Only God knows what will happen to us now.'

Mukhtiar, her family, and the neighbours that share this warren of narrow streets and alleyways in the northwestern town of Nowshera, now talk of their lives in terms of before and after. Before the torrential downpours that brought such devastation to Nowshera and massive swathes of Pakistan. Before the unprecedented floods which Islamist groups have declared a 'punishment' from God. Before the mammoth humanitarian and economic crisis that threatens to overwhelm Islamabad's already fragile government.

The UN has estimated at least one fifth of the country is under water, including huge tracts of Pakistan's agricultural heartland in central Punjab, but the scale of the destruction seems far greater. The figures collated so far offer only a bare sketch of this unfolding crisis, the magnitude of which hints at far-reaching social, economic and political repercussions.

More than 14 million people have been affected, of whom six million are children. The number of dead is tentatively estimated at more than 1,600.

Although the death toll so far is lower, the UN has noted that the total number of people whose lives have been turned upside down by Pakistan's worst flooding in memory outstrips the more than three million affected by the 2005 Kashmir earthquake, the five million affected by the Asian tsunami and the three million affected by the Haiti earthquake earlier this year.

But unlike those disasters, in which the enormity of damage was almost immediately apparent, this one has played out in slow motion over several weeks. After wreaking a path of destruction through the mountainous northwest province of Khyber-Pakhtunkhwa late last month, the deluge made its way south through bloated rivers, inundating vast areas in the densely populated provinces of Punjab and Sindh.

Amid warnings of further rainfall, there are fears that the worst is yet to come. Of particular concern is the threat to two of Pakistan's largest cities, Hyderabad and Karachi. Many in the humanitarian community fret that the world has not yet taken notice of the extent of the catastrophe. The UN has appealed for almost $460 million (€359 million) in emergency aid, but the total pledged so far stands at only $157.8 million (€123 million).

'The death toll has so far been relatively low compared to other major natural disasters but the numbers affected are extraordinarily high,' says John Holmes, the UN's under-secretary-general for humanitarian affairs. 'If we don't act fast enough, many more people could die of diseases and food shortages.'

To get to Nowshera from Islamabad, you must take the Grand Trunk Road, a route that dates back to the Mughal era and remains one of the most celebrated arteries in south Asia. A week ago,

parts of the road were submerged but now the waters have receded leaving it clear. On lower ground around Attock, where the River Kabul meets and intermingles with the mighty Indus, there is water as far as the eye can see. Knots of tree-tops here and there provide the only distraction in what looks like a series of joined-up lakes the colour of milky tea. Where once there were fields, farmsteads and cemeteries, now there is only shimmering water.

TV footage shows similar scenes across Pakistan's central and southern belt, the watery vista broken only by miserable archipelagos of isolated homes and makeshift tents erected on tiny patches of higher ground. Those who have not been evacuated wave frantically at the helicopters overhead, looking for food, water, and, above all, rescue.

Everyone expects the death toll to rise. 'Six thousand villages wiped off the face of the earth,' says Abdullah Hussain Haroon, Pakistan's ambassador to the UN. 'From 5,000 to 50,000 per village, we have no way of counting. We have nothing operational as to how many of those have died and how many are alive.

'It is horrendous . . . It is going to put us back so many years that we're not even starting on the infrastructure.'

In Nowshera, Mukhtiar's nephew Arif counts 20 to 30 people he knew personally who have died. Another man tells how three days after the waters had receded, he found the bodies of several friends who had not been able to escape. 'The floods came at night and many people were in bed,' he says. 'It happened so quickly, they drowned in their sleep.' Some talk of the countless others still missing, and wonder if their bodies lie buried under the thick silt surrounding the swollen river bank.

An elderly woman stands weeping as she surveys dozens of collapsed homes close to a mosque, where more than 180 women scrambled to safety at the height of the floods. For three days they were stranded on its roof top without food or water until army helicopters dropped aid packages from the sky.

Of the displaced, the lucky ones have set up home in empty schools. The not so fortunate are forced to endure Pakistan's searing August heat in fetid tents pitched along roadsides.

Nowshera's main market, once home to hundreds of shops and stalls, lies shuttered and deserted apart from a dozen or so vendors selling pitiful piles of mangoes, bananas and pears amid the churned-up mud. Much of the produce is beginning to rot, yet prices have more than doubled. 'The crops are all ruined and the roads are blocked; we had no other choice but to put prices up,' says Bahadar Ali. 'Most of us have lost our shops. This is all we have left.'

While the water may be slowly receding in towns like Nowshera, the anger and frustration of people is not. Dwindling food supplies have added to the sense of desperation felt by those who have lost loved ones, livelihoods and homes. 'I've seen people fighting like animals over small bags of food,' says one man from a nearby village, shaking his head. 'What will the next weeks and months bring if already people feel so desperate?'

Much rage is directed at Pakistani president Asif Zardari and his administration, which was already considered weak before the rains struck. Given the sheer scale of the floods, even the best-prepared government would have struggled to cope. Damage to roads, bridges and other infrastructure has severely hampered relief efforts, as has continuing rains.

But Zardari's behaviour has served only to fuel public fury. He chose to press ahead with an official visit to Britain and France last week, despite

A kestrel hovers after finding its prey (a rat) along Bull Wall, Dollymount Strand, Dublin. Photograph: Dara Mac Dónaill.

mounting evidence that Pakistan was experiencing the worst natural disaster in its history. Pakistanis were appalled to see TV reports of homes, crops and animals being washed away juxtaposed with footage of a grinning Zardari meeting British prime minister David Cameron or visiting his family's chateau in Normandy. Zardari's supporters insist his visit was necessary to secure international aid, but most Pakistanis disagree.

Fatima Bhutto, niece of Zardari's deceased wife Benazir, and a long-standing critic of the president, has described the floods as 'Zardari's Katrina' – a comparison with George W. Bush's much criticised management of the Hurricane Katrina aftermath.

The political fall-out is likely to be serious – many believe the crisis has dealt what may be a fatal blow to people's faith in the current civilian gov-

ernment while enhancing the standing of Pakistan's all-powerful military. The army has quietly taken the lead in relief efforts, using helicopters to evacuate people and dispense aid.

Also likely to benefit is the country's constellation of Islamist groups. As during the 2005 earthquake in Kashmir, these organisations and affiliated charities have lost little time in mobilising their extensive networks of volunteers to fill the vacuum left by government delays and ineptness.

The Falah-e-Insaniat Foundation, an alleged front for Lashkar-e-Taiba (LeT) – a banned militant outfit blamed for the 2008 Mumbai attacks – has been distributing food and aid supplies in several parts of the country. Another group, Jamaat ud Dawa, officially outlawed due to its links with LeT, has also been involved in relief work.

Kilkenny's Richie Power celebrates, after scoring the side's third goal, during his team's comprehensive 3-22 to 0-19 All-Ireland senior hurling championship semi-final victory over Cork at Croke Park. Photograph: Ryan Byrne/ Inpho.

Andrew Reel, aged five, from Kiltegan, Co. Wicklow, takes a rest with Snickers, his entry in the fancy dress competition at the 75th annual Tinahely Agricultural Show. Photograph: Eric Luke.

I saw one leaflet distributed by Jamaat ud Dawa which describes the floods as divine retribution, a message its activists are also disseminating by word of mouth in camps for the displaced. Analysts warn that Islamist groups may exploit growing public resentment to rebuild support, particularly in pockets of northwestern Pakistan where the military was forced to move against an emboldened homegrown Taliban last year. There are also fears that the militants – who have largely lain low since the army offensive – may take advantage of the post-flood chaos to stage a comeback. Last week, the Pakistani Taliban called on people to reject any aid provided by the US for flood relief. It also crowed over the impact of infrastructural damage on NATO supply routes into Afghanistan.

As the true scale of the flooding becomes apparent across Pakistan, aid workers have prioritised needs such as food, water and shelter, while medical personnel are focusing on preventing the spread of disease in chronically unsanitary conditions. Relief agencies, including Concern and Trócaire, are distributing emergency supplies. Many admit to struggling with the overwhelming nature of the crisis.

'Given the geographic scale of the situation, and the inaccessibility due to damaged roads and bridges in large areas, Concern's efforts are only a small part of the bigger needs of the population affected,' says Lucia Ennis, Concern's regional director. Her colleague, Mubashir Ahmed, agrees. 'The task before us is immense. We want to do more, we must do more, but we can do only as much as our resources allow.'

MONDAY, 23 AUGUST 2010

Civil War Wounds Healed by St Brian of Béal na mBláth

Carl O'Brien

Who'd have thought this was an incursion into enemy territory? As he stepped down from the podium, an adoring crowd surged forward, clapping and cheering at the first senior Fianna Fáil figure to deliver the keynote oration at Béal na mBláth.

Older women thrust their hands through the railings to shake his hand (or just tug at his trouser legs). 'You're looking smashing, Minister!' an elegant lady cooed. 'Well done, altogether.' Another woman tried to manhandle a photographer out of her way. 'We want to see the Minister! We want to see him!' she insisted.

One dyed-in-the-wool Fine Gaeler in his 80s jostled forward to get the Minister's autograph, dropping his crutches in the process. 'He's been cured!' shouted a woman alongside him, to roars of laughter.

As the Minister lingered in the sunshine to sign countless autographs and pose for innumerable family photographs, there was no mistaking the warm affection of the crowd. His speech had been marked by spontaneous and sustained ripples of applause, and a sense that this was a symbolic burying of old hatchets.

Brian Lenihan and Helen Collins, grand-niece of Michael Collins, embrace at Béal na mBláth, where the Finance Minister became the first Fianna Fáil politician to give the annual address in memory of the slain Civil War leader. Photograph: Eric Luke.

It was a world away from the dark mutterings in the weeks beforehand. Fine Gael senator Liam Twomey had warned that Lenihan – whose predecessors 'murdered' Collins – wasn't welcome. Young Fine Gaelers, too, said they would boycott the occasion in protest at the Minister's appearance. In the end, they seemed woefully out of touch with the spirit of the day. Helen Collins, Collins's grandniece, said: 'Michael belongs to all the people of Ireland and beyond.'

Among the hundreds waiting to get a word with the Minister afterwards was John-Joe Lyons, a Fine Gael voter in his 70s from Newcestown. He had brought with him two antique postcards – one of Collins, one of de Valera – to get signed by Brian Lenihan.

The event also drew Fianna Fáil supporters, many visiting Béal na mBláth for the first time. One of them was Tim Maher, a dairy farmer from Templemore, Co. Tipperary. 'I'm definitely Fianna Fáil. Why the reception? He's doing a good job in very hard times – at the end of day, he's doing a job no one else would do. People appreciate that.'

Also there to witness the event were many of Brian Lenihan's extended family, including his aunt Mary O'Rourke who was struck by the generosity of the welcome. 'We were going into the unknown, really. But it's been marvellous. Such a warm welcome. I couldn't but be partisan, but I was taken by all the people coming up to him. I think he's overwhelmed himself. He genuinely regarded it has a huge honour to be asked here.'

In a post-Civil War world where differences have been well and truly laid to rest, it may be inevitable the issue of a Fianna Fáil–Fine Gael merger will feature on the landscape. If it did rear its head yesterday, it did so discreetly.

For Tom O'Shea of Kilkenny, a staunch Fine Gaeler who's been coming to Béal na mBláth for decades, that's for another day. Yesterday was about laying old ghosts to rest. 'I used to bring my father here, who sent dispatches to Collins during the War of Independence. There used to be lots of old

IRA men here too. The divisions in those days were still quite raw . . . But I really welcome what's happened today. The talk of a boycott was uncalled for. It's 2010. It's time for us all to move on.'

THURSDAY, 2 SEPTEMBER 2010

Letting Anglo Go Would Trigger Lehman-Like Panic

Dan O'Brien

According to *The Banker* magazine, Anglo Irish Bank booked the biggest losses of any financial institution in the whole world last year. With yesterday's news of more massive multibillion-euro losses for the first half of 2010, it is likely to collect that dubious accolade for the second consecutive year.

If a behemoth bank in the world's largest economy – a Citibank or a Bank of America – had topped this list, it would be one thing. That a small bank in a small economy will top it for two successive years is almost beyond belief. The losses in the first six months amount to nearly €2,000 for every woman, man and child in the State. More pertinently, they amount to well over €4,000 for every person in gainful employment.

It is hard to know what to be more outraged about: that such a thing should have come to pass, or that the people responsible have not suffered the commonplace fate that usually befalls those whose businesses fail, often through no fault of their own.

Some consideration of how this situation has been arrived at is necessary, not least because many people (understandably) still believe that no taxpayers' money should be wasted on propping up the infernal institution. Consider four points.

Point 1: Banking is inherently a riskier business than most others. Banks take deposits, which must be repaid on demand, and make loans that cannot

Nine-week-old Florine de Groot rests on top of a leaf of the Victoria amazonica *at Rotterdam Blijdorp Zoo. Children could be photographed on top of the leaf on condition they did not weigh more than 15kg (33lb). The plant blossoms over two nights, producing flowers that are white on the first night and pinkish-red by the second night. Its leaves can have a diameter of up to 2.5 metres. Photograph: Jerry Lampen/Reuters.*

be called in at will. This mismatch means that banks can blow up easily.

Point 2: We know that economies do not function well with impaired banking systems and that governments everywhere step in to minimise the costs of banking crises, even if it means bailing out financial institutions.

Point 3: Given point 2, bankers understand that they enjoy an implicit guarantee from taxpayers. Faced with a 'heads I win, tails you lose' proposition, they take even bigger risks than they might otherwise take, making inherently fragile banking systems more fragile still.

Point 4: Given points 2 and 3, banking is subject to much more regulation than most other businesses. This regulation has failed and the largest bailout ever has taken place.

One central banker has described the evolution of finance in recent decades as a 'doom loop'- ever larger crises, leading to ever larger bailouts, leading to ever larger crises, and so on. Breaking that loop is perhaps the biggest public policy question facing rich countries today because the world will not be able to afford another banking crisis for decades to come.

It is not clear that the Irish State can afford the current crisis. So what would happen if the State were to withdraw its support for Anglo Irish Bank and let it collapse?

The answer is that nobody knows for sure. In September 2008, the US authorities allowed Lehman Brothers to collapse because it was relatively small and thought not to be systemically important. US regulators wanted to send a signal to

Wall Street that risk-taking meant just that. Letting Lehman collapse was done for the right reasons, but it proved very wrong.

Letting Anglo go is unquestionably the 'right' thing to do, but a collapse would cause collateral damage. Faith in the other banks would be undermined, perhaps gravely. The contagion effect is powerful in financial affairs.

The solvency of the Irish State could also be questioned even more than it has been hitherto. Those who lend money to the Government – so that it can continue to run massive budget deficits – already seek a very high premium to compensate for the elevated risk that they will not be repaid. Some people argue that if the State were to lessen its exposure to Anglo it would reassure lenders, and thus bring down the cost of financing ongoing budget deficits. This view is not illogical, but I believe it is wrong. In my judgment – and this is very much a matter of judgment – letting Anglo go would very probably trigger a Lehman-like panic.

It is worth noting that no European Union government has risked letting an institution with liabilities as large as Anglo's default since Lehman. European governments collectively have not risked letting Greece go, and have clubbed together to put a massive bailout package in place in order to rescue other countries, if that becomes necessary.

Governments have done all this because they understand that the international financial system as

Queen Elizabeth II and Pope Benedict XVI walk through the gardens at Holyrood Palace on the first day of his state visit to the UK. Photograph: John Linton/Getty Images.

it has existed in recent decades has failed. It is akin to a structurally unsound building that remains standing only because it is buttressed on all sides. A large-scale default – by a bank or a country – would be tantamount to triggering an earthquake. The entire edifice could come down.

Just as a default on Greece's government debt would have consequences far beyond that country's borders, default on Anglo's debts would ripple out across the world. They would have most effect in the rest of our currency union. The decision on the future of Anglo Irish Bank is thus not one taken exclusively in Dublin. The European Commission, the European Central Bank and other euro-zone governments all have a say.

The consensus is that it should be kept standing. This is in keeping with this take-no-risks, pay-any-price approach to containing the financial crisis in Europe in the post-Lehman era. The options now available to the Government to minimise the costs to taxpayers of Anglo Irish Bank are limited. The damage has been done. Everyone in this State – one way or another – will pay the price for years to come.

THURSDAY, 2 SEPTEMBER 2010

Rediscovering Metsu, the 'Other' Dutch Master

Aidan Dunne

From our point of view, the problem with Gabriel Metsu is that he isn't Johannes Vermeer. That wasn't always an issue. Go back to the 17th century, when they both lived, and to the 18th century, and the position was reversed. Unscrupulous dealers were even reputed to offer Vermeers for sale as Metsus. Anything with Metsu's name attached was sure to sell, but people shied away from Vermeer.

Nowadays, Vermeer's name is magic, made more magical by the fact that only a handful of his works, virtually all of them masterpieces, are known to exist.

Metsu, a close contemporary of Vermeer, lived only to the age of 37, but he was relatively prolific. The two artists were known to each other and cross-currents of influence are evident between them. Still, as National Gallery curator Adriaan E. Waiboer observes, several paintings by Metsu draw directly on aspects of Vermeer's style, as though made directly in response to works by Vermeer. Thanks to the Beit gift, there are superlative examples in our own National Gallery, the paired paintings of a man writing and a woman reading a letter.

The extraordinarily adept Metsu was something of an artistic chameleon who absorbed and reinvented the work of many of his contemporaries. To the extent, Waiboer writes, 'that his oeuvre reflects almost the entire scope of Dutch genre painting' of his time.

Waiboer has curated a major new exhibition, *Gabriel Metsu: Rediscovered Master of the Dutch Golden Age*, which opens on Saturday at the National Gallery of Ireland. The show features 40 of Metsu's works, including many of his finest paintings, many sourced from private collections, and the only two drawings reliably attributed to him, as well as a range of intriguing, related documentary material – such as the strikingly ornate drinking horn of Saint Sebastian's Guild of Amsterdam.

Metsu isn't Vermeer, and he frequently shifts style, but he also emerges as a gifted, compelling and extremely accessible artist in his own right.

Optically, there is a photographic quality to Vermeer's paintings – probably because he used a camera obscura – and a curious stillness and serenity. Metsu kept adding linear and expressive detail; in his later work to an almost microscopic level and, by comparison with Vermeer, who keeps his subjects at a certain distance, he is a chatty, voluble painter who wants to spin a yarn and tell a joke.

He's a storyteller. Even his simplest paintings are rich in anecdotal or narrative information. The

Aisling Jones (left) *and Emma Smith create a tableau vivant in front of two Gabriel Metsu paintings,* A Man Writing a Letter *and* A Woman Reading a Letter, *during the National Gallery of Ireland's preview of its new exhibition of 40 Metsu (1629–1667) paintings. Photograph: Bryan O'Brien.*

more you look, the more you see; a mischievous little dog you haven't previously noticed suddenly appears from the shadows, or your eyes light on an absolutely perfect, miniature still life in the corner of a composition, or you abruptly register the sceptical slant of a maid's eyebrow as her mistress is charmed by a flash suitor.

There's a wealth of observational detail in every image, illustrative of human nature, 17th century fashion, social customs and attitudes and culinary habits in the Netherlands. And, it should be said, the fantastic material wealth of the Dutch Republic, an unrivalled hub of trade and commerce. Metsu relishes in the exact description of rugs and carpets, furs and fabrics, pewter and glassware, flowers and foodstuffs, musical instruments and domestic interiors.

Born in Leiden in 1629, Metsu's father was a painter who died before Gabriel was born. His mother was a midwife. He was registered as an artist by the age of 14 or 15, and was active in Leiden, Utrecht and, from the first half of the 1650s, Amsterdam. There, he married Isabella de Wolff in 1658. It's worthy of note that while her father was, fairly conventionally, a potter, her mother was, unusually, a painter.

Metsu progressed through the pictorial modes of history painting, portraiture and still life but settled on and excelled at genre scenes from everyday life.

There is surprisingly little documentary evidence of his life and career, Waiboer notes, and he tended not to date his work, so much of what we know is inferred from indirect evidence, including that provided by the artist in his paintings.

Cardinal Keith O'Brien poses with the world's first papal visit plaid, next to piper Louise Millington, in Edinburgh. The St Ninian's Day tartan, designed by Scottish Tartans Museum director Matthew Newsome, was created to mark the September 2010 visit of Pope Benedict XVI to Scotland. Photograph: Reuters/David Moir.

hard-working Kilkenny forwards and driving his team back on the offensive.

Containing so much ebullience was too great a task for the champions but no one could accuse them of taking the shocking turn of events fatalistically. They grafted furiously and managed to retrieve the match after early setbacks but by the end they looked as if they were running on empty.

Tipperary's pace in attack created panic in the Kilkenny defence and by the end as the challengers outscored them 1-5 to 0-3 in the final quarter of an hour, the once formidable rearguard looked weary and ragged. Up front, though, the loss of Shefflin left the attack short of composure and tactical direction.

There was too much hitting and hoping, too much reliance on running frantically at Tipp and

although at various periods the steady supply of fouls and consequent frees kept the scoreboard moving there wasn't the assurance and cold-blooded calm in picking the right positions and optimising the options available.

The bench were slow to act on what was clearly a misfiring performance and given Michael Rice's stature as a centrefielder, he might have been switched to the middle earlier where Kilkenny were struggling and a couple of forwards could have been more quickly introduced given the success of Tipperary particularly in the forwards.

The persistent rain made conditions less than ideal and probably didn't help Shefflin's knee, although manager Brian Cody said afterwards that it has been just bad luck and that John Tennyson, the other cruciate sufferer, had lasted the 70 minutes.

But rolling the dice on such an injury even with the great apparent recovery always carried the risk of the knee going at an early stage – so it came to pass within 13 minutes. By then Shefflin had already looked a bit out of sorts and uncharacteristically missed an early free.

By the time he had to go Tipp were 1-3 to 0-1 ahead. The goal came from a long delivery by Shane McGrath – whose energy and commitment, hooking and blocking, at that stage typified the team's fierce application – into Corbett who plucked it from Noel Hickey and raised his first green flag.

T.J. Reid forced a smart save from Brendan Cummins – excellent in all he had to do, including a pointed free from his own 45 – and the match began to settle into its open, blow-for-blow patterns.

After an uneasy start, Richie Power found his free-taking rhythm and although Eoin Kelly was masterful at the other end and Maher, O'Brien and Ryan all stroked nice points, there was a feeling that the Kilkenny defence was tightening its grip after some hair-raising moments as when the perpetual motion of Noel McGrath carved through the heart of the defence in the 25th minute only to finish weakly.

The match was moved again into the marginal column in the 33rd minute when Eoin Larkin, who was forceful and dynamic without getting on the scoreboard, punched a hole in the Tipperary defence and sent in Power for a well-finished goal, a breakthrough that he garnished with two more frees to leave just one between the teams at half-time.

Kilkenny were right back in it and the match again teetered. Tipperary had to come again after letting the initiative slip and after conceding an equaliser to a Reid line-ball, they struck formidably.

In the 42nd minute Corbett completed a sweeping combination between Ryan and Noel McGrath to race in and to nail his second goal. Two minutes later Cummins dropped in a long

free and Noel McGrath pounced on the break to force the ball into the net for another seven-point lead, 3-11 to 1-10.

Still Kilkenny responded. At the back J.J. Delaney's exceptional season continued – at one stage in the first half he actually smuggled the ball out of Eoin Kelly's possession – as the team desperately sought a game-changing intervention. Instead it was the succession of Tipperary replacements – Séamus Callanan, Benny Dunne and Séamus Hennessy all scored – who made the late impacts with the *coup de grace* being delivered by Corbett in the third minute of injury-time, as he again stole in behind the full backs to drive in his third goal, the first player to achieve a hat-trick in a hurling final since Cork's Eddie O'Brien 40 years ago.

It's the county's 26th All-Ireland and the first they have won through the qualifier dispensation and marked a joyous landfall for a team that just three months ago looked shipwrecked after hitting the rocks in Páirc Uí Chaoimh.

TUESDAY, 7 SEPTEMBER 2010

Decoding of DNA May Unlock the Hidden Medical Histories of Irish Lives

Eoin Burke-Kennedy

The decoding of the first Irish genome represents a significant advance in the quest to understand the link between genetic variation and disease susceptibility on this island. This places the Irish genetic code in the public domain for the first time and permits it to be compared with mappings of the codes of other population groups.

This is important as it is only by comparing the genome with other sequences that scientists can hope to isolate a specific 'Irish genetic signature' and to understand the genetic basis of our susceptibility to certain diseases.

A principal reason for sequencing Irish DNA was that it was not represented in any of the large genomic studies under way, explained the Irish project's originator Prof. Brendan Loftus of University College Dublin's Conway Institute.

'Certain gene variants can become locked in a population due to factors like geography. Irish people's genes mirror the island's peripheral location in Europe, which makes it an interesting subgroup to sequence,' Prof. Loftus said.

'Some 13 per cent of the variation we uncovered has not been seen before. It's likely that some of that variation is specific to the individual and some is more diagnostic of him being Irish. We will only find out which is which over time.'

A Mayo-born graduate of Dublin City University, Prof. Loftus spent the 1990s working in the US under the well-known Craig Venter, collaborator on the first human genome sequencing project completed in 2003 at a cost of €2.7 billion.

In contrast with the original human genome project, the Irish project was carried out with the resources of a small lab over about 13 months and at a cost of €30,000. Prof. Loftus said the project illustrated how rapidly the accumulation of genomic information on a population level can be generated. But he acknowledged that while the capacity to generate the sequence data is proceeding at pace, the rate at which the data can be reliably interpreted has lagged behind.

One area where genetic sequencing is likely to play a major role is in patient response to

Prof. Brendan Loftus, with colleagues Dr Amanda Coogan and PhD student Pin Tong, holds up flow cells containing DNA code from the first Irish genome at the UCD Conway Institute. Prof. Loftus led the research team in its work for about 13 months at a cost of €30,000. Photograph: Frank Miller.

medication. 'The majority of blockbuster drugs, from aspirin to cancer medication, don't appear to work on significant sections of the population,' said Prof. Loftus. 'There is a big thrust in the medical community towards personalising medicine and nutrition because people respond in different ways to the same product.

'And one of the most likely reasons for this is their genetic background. The drug companies are interested to see who these people are and to find out if they will respond to variations of the existing drug compounds.'

Since the first human sequence was generated in the US in 2003, between 20 and 30 full human genome sequences have been published.

However, the rapid acceleration in DNA sequencing technology in recent years has seen a proliferation of projects, with more than 100 separate projects in progress. With the cost of sequencing dropping all the time, experts maintain it won't be long before people will be carrying around parts of their genome on a USB key.

US company 23andMe, established by Anne Wojcicki – wife of Google founder Sergey Brin – already offers to sequence portions of the genome using a sample of saliva, for as little as $350.

Dr Gerard Cagney, principal investigator in functional genomics at the Conway Institute, said representative species from all branches of the tree of life – bacteria, fungi and plants, along with animals ranging from worms to insects and from fish to monkeys – are now being sequenced daily.

'Nevertheless, the technical difficulty associated with sequencing a small virus like HIV, containing some 9,000 units of DNA, pales in significance next to the challenge of sequencing a human genome, composed of more than three billion units.

'The problem is compounded by the fact that the entire sequence is assembled from short individual sequence fragments – typically less than 200 units – so the final product is similar to piecing together a huge jigsaw puzzle and requires the work of computer scientists and statisticians,' Dr Cagney said.

'There are also large regions of repeated sequence in human genomes and their biological significance is still not fully understood.

'The sequencing process therefore relies partly on comparison with other known sequences and it is for this reason that reading an Irish genome is significant.

'It can be used to place Irish genes in the context of worldwide human genome diversity.'

WEDNESDAY, 15 SEPTEMBER 2010

Singing Taoiseach Hits Bum Note as Critics Lap up 'Garglegate' in Galway

Miriam Lord

It was the *Morning Ireland* after the night before. The Taoiseach sounded dog rough. Wheezy. Groggy. Muzzy. A bit slow. Around the breakfast tables of the nation, butter knives hovered above toast and tea-cups paused mid-air as people listened, then mused: 'God, but Biffo sounds like he had a right skinful last night.'

Whereupon all hell broke loose and the roof caved in on Brian Cowen and Fianna Fáil. So began an extraordinary day in Irish politics and media. Here's your simple guide to Garglegate:

Was The Taoiseach out way past his bedtime drinking pints?

Yes.

How do we know?

Because we were there.

Should he have left the pub before half three in the morning?

Yes.

Did he belt out a song for a cheering crowd and do a few funny impersonations?

Yes.

Was he any good?

Yes, actually. He was a hoot.

Did he look drunk?

No.

Did anyone whisper to him that it was time to go?

Not that we saw.

Has he only himself to blame?

Yes.

Is he utterly mortified now?

Yes.

Does that matter?

No. The genie is out of the bottle now.

By the end of an incredible day yesterday, a sore head was the least of Brian Cowen's problems. He was a humiliated man with a badly damaged reputation, a laughing stock in the international press and an embarrassment to his appalled colleagues who had to rally to his defence.

In the Ardilaun Hotel, party handlers and the Taoiseach's closest allies wandered about, stunned, whispering into their mobile phones.

The skies have opened over Fianna Fáil and the party is sinking. The Taoiseach took his demoralised troops to Galway in an effort to put some steel in their souls but in his accident-prone fashion, he managed to insert it between their shoulder blades instead.

The politicians should have been returning to their constituencies yesterday afternoon with a clearer outlook and a bit more pep in their step, but if they were fragile before they arrived, they were shattered when they left.

All because their boss sounded hungover during his interview on *Morning Ireland*. This led to a bizarre chain of events as the media went into overdrive and Fianna Fáil went into meltdown. Why such a frenzied reaction to this 13 minutes of airtime? Because in the media, it has often been

Pat Carey, Brian Cowen, Mary Coughlan and members of the Fianna Fáil parliamentary party prepare for the official photograph at their conference in Galway. Photograph: Eric Luke.

hinted that our sociable Taoiseach is overly fond of a drop, but nobody had ever said it or written it straight out.

When radio shows and the internet began buzzing and tweeting about Cowen's woeful performance, and one of those questioning his level of sobriety included an Opposition frontbench spokesman, the journalists had legitimate grounds to broach this sensitive issue.

Some have been waiting for this opportunity for a long time – Cowen gave it to them on a plate. Had the storm not erupted, Monday night's very pleasant and relaxed gathering in the bar of the Ardilaun would not have been reported in any great detail.

Think-ins are a blend of business and socialising. Some say the bonding element is every bit as important as the speeches and the workshops. There is usually a sing-song in the bar after dinner. The leader usually circulates. Pints are bought. Gossip swapped. Contacts cemented.

We're not talking Sodom and Gomorrah here (although we had a snigger yesterday morning when an attractive young female journalist told us how one Fianna Fáil backbencher, a noted letch, bought her six gin and tonics and then promised to introduce her to the Taoiseach).

In fact, only two major incidents come to mind in the history of the think-in drink-ins. Fianna Fáil's Peter Kelly once juggled a pitcher of water on his head while juggling his shoes and then sang a medley of Elvis numbers into his upturned tie. On another occasion, Enda Kenny said in an interview that he looked better in cycling shorts than Bertie Ahern – images that still give us nightmares.

On Monday, there was the usual dinner in the ballroom. This was followed by an address from former GAA president Joe McDonagh, who finished his contribution with a rousing rendition of 'The West's Awake'. After the meal, some deputies went into the city for a drink. Some retired for the night and more headed for the hotel bar, Cowen among them.

Senior Ministers – interestingly enough, the ones who would be spoken of as leadership contenders – schmoozed journalists at the small bar in the ballroom, but the lure of the sing-song was impossible to resist.

Two non-drinkers, Senator Donie Cassidy and MEP Brian Crowley, were directing the entertainment. Brian played the piano for a while. Donie was MC, beating people up to sing. He pleaded all night for a representative of the media to sing. It was by the grace of God that nobody took him up on it. Cowen sang just the one song, a passionate rendition of 'The Lakes of Pontchartrain'.

It was well after midnight and nudging 1 a.m. when the Taoiseach was prevailed upon again. This time, he did a very funny routine, mimicking Micheál Ó Muircheartaigh along with a famous Kilkenny hurler and a quintessential Dub. He brought the house down. Encouraged by the ovation and as the crowd called for more, he agreed to do an encore.

Wagging a finger at the journalists – also enjoying a drink and enjoying the show – he cautioned them not to get him into trouble by reporting his performance.

He then did an extremely funny impersonation of former Ryder Cup golfer Philip Walton who had a rather high-pitched voice, and his then team captain, the gruff Scotsman Bernard Gallacher. He swung an imaginary club as he spoke, then exhaled to give impression of a ball flying through the air. It was very good.

Then the Taoiseach joined some friends for a drink. From what we saw he was having a few slow pints. Various people sang. A man played the tin whistle. It was a bit like the afters of a country wedding. Cowen chatted for a while with Batt O'Keeffe.

We left as the time neared 3 a.m. At this stage, Cowen was talking to people in the lobby. He didn't have a drink with him. We hear he retired at about 3.30 a.m. It was a good night. Nobody went mad, at least from what we could see. Which

Wexford's Josie Dwyer and Caroline Murphy celebrate their 1-12 to 1-10 victory over Galway in the All-Ireland senior camogie final at Croke Park. Photograph: Cathal Noonan/Inpho.

brings us to what happened next. That awful interview – it wasn't what he said but the manner in which he said it.

Calls flooded into radio stations. Was Cowen still drunk? Hungover? Did he realise how bad he sounded? Suddenly, the atmosphere in the Ardilaun became highly charged. When the Taoiseach arrived, TV3's Ursula Halligan asked the question crackling over the airwaves: was he drunk or hungover during the interview?

The Taoiseach looked shocked, as his minders pushed Ms Halligan out of the way and steered him into the hall. He took grave offence at the question and, highly indignant, absolutely denied the charge.

A media frenzy ensued, although some of us were stranded in a strange place between sanctimony and complicity. As the morning wore on, reinforcements arrived down from Dublin newsagencies. Already, the Taoiseach's denial had made the *Wall Street Journal.*

The price of Irish bonds jumped, ratings agency Standard and Poors pronounced. An air of hysteria took hold. Two senior Ministers were trotted out to rubbish the allegations. Inside the hall, they were talking about Nama and the €30 billion Anglo bailout. Outside, Micheál Martin was insisting 'clearly, that the issue seems to be he was a little hoarse'.

Then Noel Dempsey (both Ministers were nearly driven through the backdrop by the advancing media) declared: 'I think Brian was a little bit nasal' before saying: 'I often have a frog in my throat in the morning.'

Dermot Ahern said on radio that it was widely known 'the Taoiseach suffers from congestion'.

'I understand he has a cold,' said Seán Haughey. Tony Killeen blamed the clattering of cutlery in the background for putting Cowen off his stride.

Seán O'Rourke, meanwhile, on the lunchtime news, was getting stuck into Simon Coveney. 'Do you stand over your tweet?'

'A man is being knocked back because he is hoarse in the morning and congested,' said Mary Hanafin.

On and on it went. Until finally, with the hacks on the brink of exhaustion and the handlers on the verge of a nervous breakdown, the Taoiseach came out. He apologised for being hoarse. He attacked Fine Gael for playing dirty politics. His grim-faced Minister colleagues flanking him.

Then, the question that made his fellow politicians wince. 'Taoiseach, are you worried about your drinking; do you ever think you drink too much?' There was a low hum of disapproval from the TDs and Senators. 'Shame!' said one. But Cowen silenced them with a wave of his hand. He was happy to take the question. And he answered – 'everything in moderation, including moderation'.

That moment evoked another electric scene involving a Fianna Fáil leader – when Bertie Ahern, new leader, was asked about his marital status. His supporters loudly booed, but Ahern silenced them and took the question. They cheered his answer and cheered him from the room. Cowen was cheered too but not half as sincerely. A little hoarse and a storm in a stirrup cup? Or the beginning of the end? Time will tell.

Mícheál Ó Muircheartaigh poses with the Sam Maguire trophy outside Croke Park, shortly after announcing that the 2010 All-Ireland final would be his last as a commentator. Photograph: Cyril Byrne.

FRIDAY, 17 SEPTEMBER 2010

Ó Muircheartaigh Goes Off-Mic a Legend of Eloquent Commentary

Frank McNally

It's not true what the cynics say: some people really are indispensable. So it was with the late Mícheál O'Hehir, whose retirement as a television commentator left a gap that has never been filled for the generations to whom he was the voice of summer. And so it will be with his spiritual heir, radio commentator Mícheál Ó Muircheartaigh, who will broadcast his last All-Ireland Final this Sunday.

The announcement that he was quitting must have come as a shock to many people, as must the news that he was 80 years old. Not that he should have been any other age, in particular. But that's the point. He seemed to have become ageless, at least on the airwaves: where more than half a century of covering GAA matches had left both his eloquence and energy levels undimmed.

In fact, a criticism levelled at him – even until recently – was that he made every game, however awful, sound like a classic. But he was, after all, an entertainer.

The mere fact of his commentary gave each game he covered an extra dimension. Thus, for his hardcore fans, the reality of actually attending the event was not enough: ideally you listened to it on earphones as well. His voice was – and is – unique in both State languages. In fact, one of Ó Muircheartaigh's many charms has always been the ease with which he moved from one into the other. An antidote to the cúpla focail school of official bilingualism, he often seemed to slip into Irish unselfconsciously, before remembering himself after a while and reverting to English.

Maybe it was this that made him so adept at interweaving different plot lines in a hurling or football match. If a dog or streaker appeared on the pitch, he could pick up that theme and run with it, while missing none of the main drama either. And he had a playwright's genius for cross-cutting the central storyline with subplots, as in one famous example: 'Pat Fox out to the 40 and grabs the sliothar – I bought a dog from his father last week. Fox turns and sprints for goal – the dog ran a great race last Tuesday in Limerick. Fox to the 21, fires a shot. It goes to the left and wide . . . And the dog lost as well.'

Speaking of dogs, one of my favourite Ó Muircheartaigh interviews is one he did with a fellow greyhound owner, Britain's Prince Edward. This would be a challenge for any Irish broadcaster: balance due respect for a dignitary with awareness that listeners' ears would be finely tuned for any hint of obsequiousness. But as usual, he got it right: opening with the unorthodox but impeccable address: 'Tell me, Prince . . .' and taking it from there.

He could set the scene for a big match like no one else. Two weeks ago, he trumped the hype about the Kilkenny-Tipperary showdown by reminding listeners of the first recorded hurling match, played in 1272 BC, between the Tuatha dé Danann and the Firbolg. His billing might often be a hard act to follow but at least in his commentaries the teams usually succeeded.

It is yet another tribute to Ó Muircheartaigh's professionalism that, proud Kerryman as he is, his impartiality in calling even their games has always been beyond question.

He was and remains the GAA everyman. As a Monaghan supporter, I still fondly recall the 1985 All-Ireland semi-final against Kerry when Eamon McEneaney had a last-minute free, nearly 50 m out and near the sideline, to earn a replay. Ó Muircheartaigh wished the ball over the bar – 'Monaghan deserve it,' he said – and we never doubted his sincerity.

Sad as his loss will be, he is at least choosing the time of departure: unlike Mícheál O'Hehir, whose retirement was forced by ill-health. Like sports stars almost half a century his junior, Ó Muircheartaigh is quitting at the top of his game.

Voice of a Legend Ó Muircheartaigh in his Own Special Words

'If the streaker doesn't mind, it will be going over his direction now. He sees that, he sees the danger.

He's moving out the field now towards open territory on the far side of the field, and the ball goes out over the line, Hogan Stand side of the field. The stewards are moving in on him now from all sides …

He's now gone past the centre of the field. Níl fhios agam cad as a thánaig sé. B'fhéidir piobaire sídh slí Gleann Molúra é. He's dodging his way now, trying to get away from the maor.

He has made a good run. He's on the 50-yard line now on the other side of the field, he's brought to the ground … tá an streaker ag imeacht an páirc.'

'He grabs the sliothar, he's on the 50! He's on the 40! He's on the 30! He's on the ground.'

'Seán Óg Ó hAilpín … his father's from Fermanagh, his mother's from Fiji. Neither a hurling stronghold.'

'Charlie gets it on the 50-yard line … over the shoulder, in towards the goal by Charlie Carter and over the bar. Charlie Carter, who was more interested in the dressing room an hour ago about how my greyhound performed at Shelbourne Park last night than the impending hurling final.

He's doing better at the hurling today than the greyhound did at the hurdles last night. Didn't jump them well, the puckout coming now from Stephen Byrne …'

'We have (listening) three TCD students who are studying Chinese Mandarin in Taipei in Taiwan. Could you say in Chinese 'ni hao ma?' That means 'conas atá tú?' in Chinese.'

'Teddy looks at the ball, the ball looks at Teddy.'

'Stephen Byrne with the puckout for Offaly. Stephen, one of 12. All but one are here today,

The one that's missing is Mary; she's at home minding the house.'

'And the ball is dropping i lár na bpáirce …'

'The stopwatch has stopped. It's up to God and the referee now. The referee is Pat Horan. God is God.'

'And we're listening to Sunday Sport on Radio One. And through the internet and everything it's going all over the world and maybe beyond.'

SUNDAY, 19 SEPTEMBER 2010

Resilient Rebels Do just Enough to End their Agonising Wait

Seán Moran, at Croke Park

Cork 0-16 Down 0-15

In the end it was the experience of a more recent tradition that proved decisive. Cork, extensively tutored in the various methods of losing All-Ireland matches, applied the lessons and in yesterday's All-Ireland football final they finished one golden point ahead of Down's total, so winning a seventh title, their first since 1990, and inflicting on their opponents an unprecedented September defeat.

Although Cork recovered from a five-point deficit on 30 minutes to reel back the match slowly and incrementally, they never cut loose as looked likely going into the last 10 minutes and Danny Hughes's point that reduced the winning margin to one in injury-time could have gone anywhere, as his fisted connection from Martin Clarke's line ball flew at the goal.

Instead Cork played out the final minute on the attack and when David Coldrick whistled the end of proceedings that one point felt too small to define as vast a gulf as existed between the elation of the winners and what they would have been feeling had they lost a third final in four years.

Cork's Donncha O'Connor celebrates at the final whistle, after their 0-16 to 0-15 victory over Down in the All-Ireland senior football final at Croke Park. Photograph: Lorraine O'Sullivan/Inpho.

Teams that have accumulated as much crushing disappointment as Cork have done over the years don't always cruise to success when their moment arrives and so it proved yesterday in a gripping match that kept Croke Park in a state of high tension until the end.

But the winners deserved their success, just about. They smashed Down's ball-winning capacity at centrefield and placed the previously magnificent pairing of Martin Clarke and Benny Coulter under arrest, conceding only a point from play from both of them combined.

Michael Shields was excellent all afternoon on Coulter and greatly restricted the Down captain, whereas Noel O'Leary gave a committed and, crucially, disciplined display just shadowing Clarke and preventing him from enjoying the amount of space he had exploited in the quarter-final and semi-final.

Cork's forwards showed enough gumption to get the scoreboard moving in the second half after a disastrous first half hour during which they managed just two points, neither from play.

Eventually manager Conor Counihan got his best team on to the field. As usual, Nicholas Murphy came into the match, this time immediately after the break, and not much later, captain Graham Canty, who had been withdrawn before the start, made his belated entrance. In both cases injury was the reason for the delay but both players had a significant impact.

Cork's strength-in-depth at centrefield was reflected in the manner in which five different players were used. After half an hour on the field, Murphy was injured and replaced by Derek Kavanagh and within minutes he required a blood replacement, Fintan Goold.

Yet, in amongst all of that experience, it was 20-year old Aidan Walsh who shone most brightly. His fielding ability, relentless work rate and much improved use of the ball made him a key operative throughout the afternoon, preventing Down from creating a platform for attack and helping to generate a generous supply for his own forwards.

Down were forced to live on scraps but they were up for the task, by the 27th minute building up a five-point lead, 0-7 to 0-2, which could have been greater but for an uncharacteristic wide from a 45 by Clarke and a number of other inaccuracies, which ultimately proved very expensive for the Ulster team.

For most of the first half, however, Down looked on course for a surprise win. They survived a torrid opening minute when Cork might have had two goals, Alan O'Connor galloping through within 10 seconds and steering wide his point attempt and 50 seconds later Ciarán Sheehan forcing a great save from Brendan McVeigh and just as he looked certain to palm home the looping rebound, Dan McCartan scrambled back to block the ball on the line.

Gradually Down recovered from the shock and Cork appeared to deflate at the point of these early jabs of misfortune. A wet and slippery pitch disadvantaged both sides, with players losing their footing, but mercifully no disasters ensuing as a result. Down's defence were well in control for most of the first half.

Both Kevin McKernan and Conor Garvey turned over possession with clever and precise tackling and Dan Gordon made Donncha O'Connor's life miserable until, in the great personal comeback of the day, the Ballydesmond full forward found redemption with a display of point-scoring that ultimately galvanised his team.

With Martin Clarke and Coulter not as prolific, although Clarke was still effective in possession

Cork's Paul Kerrigan and Down's Kevin McKernan in action during the All-Ireland senior football final at Croke Park. Photograph: Cathal Noonan/Inpho.